COMPUTER GRAPHICS WITH MULTIMEDIA

BASIC AND FUNDAMENTAL CONCEPTS

COMPUTER GRAPHICS WITH MULTIMEDIA

BASIC AND FUNDAMENTAL CONCEPTS

Dharamdas Kumhar
Avanish Kumar

ARCLER PRESS

www.arclerpress.com

Computer Graphics with Multimedia: Basic and Fundamental Concepts

Dharamdas Kumhar and Avanish Kumar

Arcler Press
4164 Lakeshore Road
Burlington
ON L7L 1A4
Canada
Email: orders@arclereducation.com

ISBN: 978-1-77956-347-7 (Hardcover)

ABOUT THE AUTHORS

Dharamdas Kumhar is Assistant Professor, Department of Mathematical Sciences and Computer Application, Bundelkhand University, Jhansi, U.P.-India of computer application. He has 22 years of teaching experience in the field of computer application. He has received his Doctor of Philosophy in Computer Science from Bundelkhand University, Jhansi U.P and Master of Philosophy in Computer Science from Madurai Kamaraj University, Madurai T.N. He completed his Master of Computer Application from Institute of Computer Science, Vikram University, Ujjain. He has attended many International Conferences, Seminars, FDPs and Workshops. He has published various research papers in International Journals and International Conferences. His areas of research are computer communication network, machine learning, computer graphics and theory of computation.

Avanish Kumar is Professor of mathematics, as well as Former Chairman, CSTT, and Former Director, CHD, Ministry Education, Government of India. He has completed his M. Sc., from Meerut University (presently CCS University), Meerut in 1989, M. Phil., from University of Roorkee (presently IIT), Roorkee in 1992 and Ph. D. in Mathematics, from Gurukula Kangri, University, Haridwar in 1999. He has awarded his 'University Medal' for standing First in First Class by University of Roorkee, Awarded Prof R C Mehrotra Best Teacher Award and Gold Medal for 'Outstanding contribution to the university services' by Bundel khand University Jhansi and Awarded 'Bharat Vikas Award' by Institute of Self Reliance, Bhubaneswar. He has 23 years of teaching and research experience in the field of Real Analysis, Complex Analysis, Operations Research and Distributed Computing Systems. He is Vice President of VIJÑĀNA PARISHAD of INDIA, and Former Vice President of the OPERATIONAL RESEARCH SOCIETY OF INDIA. He has also a Copyright for "Questionnaire on CSTT/CHD" has filed with Department of Promotion of Industry and Internal Trade, Govt of India under class Literary/Dramatic; Current Status- Re-Scrutiny. He has a Patent on "Method for Optimization of Supply Chain Finance Management based on Big Data". He has more than 15 Ph D Student as guided and co guided. He has published more than 60 research papers in International Journals and more than 50 research papers in International Conferences. He has attended many International Conferences, Seminars, FDPs and Workshops.

Contents

Preface

In this world of fierce competition, it is absolutely necessary for technocrats to keep updated and upgraded with ever-changing technology. As a teacher, it is our responsibility to keep pace with these changing circumstances and contribute to both the society and our country. This scenario of ever-changing technology has inspired us to write this book and help others keep up with the pace. This book has been written keeping in mind the requirements of students pursuing MCA, BTech, and BCA.

Features of the Book

- The concepts are explained with relevant mathematical derivations.
- Unsolved examples and multiple choice questions are included at the end of the chapters for practice and self-assessment.
- Hundreds of solved problems in computer graphics with step-by-step explanations.
- C program experiments based on various algorithms.
- A concise and simplified explanation of the algorithmic aspects involved in image synthesis.
- Numerous solved examples in each chapter.

Computer graphics is a multi-disciplinary subject that is studied by both undergraduate and postgraduate students in the fields of mechanical engineering, computer science and information technology. The aim of this book is to help readers understand all of the major topics of the subject. It focuses on the mathematical concepts involved in computer graphics. This book is an attempt to organize computer graphics concepts, ideas and methods in a clear, concise, and easily understandable form. The basic approach adopted in the preparation of this book is simple and elementary. At each stage, detailed experiments are given along with suitable figures to explain the concepts to the reader. We are sure the text is user friendly, which will encourage the students to read the book and understand the concept effortlessly.

We welcome comments and suggestions from teachers and students for the improvement of the quality of the book.

Dharamdas Kumhar
Avanish Kumar

1

Introduction to Computer Graphics

Computer graphics involves the display, manipulation, and storage of pictures and experimental data in order to visualize them properly using a computer. It provides methods for producing images and animations, which are sequences of images. This field deals with both the hardware and software support for generating images. In this chapter, we have introduced the subject of computer graphics and provided a top-down approach to its development. We have emphasized that computer graphics is a multi-faceted discipline with numerous applications. We have covered the Introduction to Computer Graphics, the History of Computer Graphics, Applications of Computer Graphics, and The Need and Use of Computer Graphics in the Modern World. The chapter also describes the features and characteristics of computer graphics, as well as its applications in various fields.

1.1 INTRODUCTION OF COMPUTER GRAPHICS

The definition of computer graphics has been different things in different contexts. Pictures and scenes that are generated by computers are considered computer graphics. The tools used to create pictures, software, and hardware; input/output devices are considered computer graphics. Computer graphics are also known for the use of computers to create, store, manipulate, query, and present pictorial output.

"Computer graphics is simply the art or science of producing and manipulating images on a computer". In other words, it is the art of drawing circles, lines, rectangles, ellipses, and other mathematical figures with a computer with the help of specialized software and programs. Thus we can say that computer graphics makes it possible to express data in pictorial form. In defining the computer graphic we need Pixel and Aspect Ratio. Pixel (Picture Element) in computer graphics are pictures and films created using computers. Usually, the term refers to computer-generated image data created with the help of specialized graphical hardware and software. In computer graphics, objects are presented as a collection of discrete picture elements. In a digital image, a pixel (Picture element) is the smallest item of information (numerical data value) in an image. Arranged in a two-dimensional grid (Row and column) and are often represented as dots or squares or rectangles on the computer screen. It is the smallest unit of graphics that is displayed on the computer screen. The intensity of each pixel is variable.

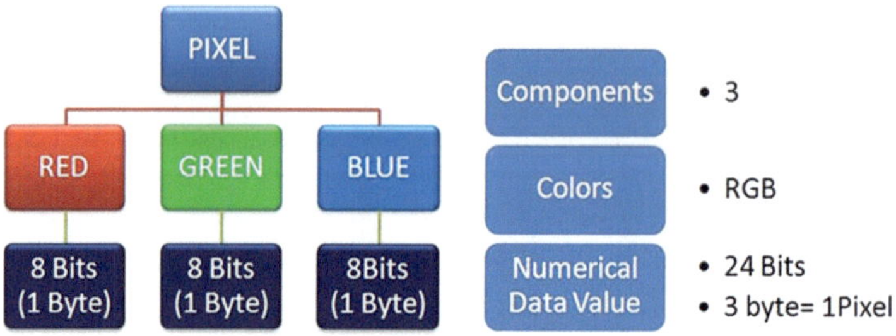

Figure 1.1: Pixel Intensity Value

One pixel has three components. RGB (Red, Green, Blue), each component has 8-bit values 3 × 8 that is one pixel = 3 byte. $2^8 = 2 \times 2 \times 2 \times 2 \times 2 \times 2 \times 2 \times 2 = 256$. The numerical value lies from 0 to 255. We can say that 256 shades of red, green, and blue are formed. Total shades are made 256 × 256 × 256 = 16.7 million. The composite of the 3 RGB values creates the final color for that pixel area, for example, how to make the yellow color is illustrate as follow.

Red	**+**	**Green**	**+**	**Blue**	
255	+	255	+	0	Yellow
0	+	0	+	0	Black
255	+	255	+	255	White
220	+	220	+	220	Light Grey
40	+	40	+	40	Dark Grey

A pixel mask is used to specify the inter-space spacing. The pixel mask is a string that contains 0 and 1 to specify the positions to plot along the line path, for example 1110000. Aspect Ratio gives the ratio of horizontal points to vertical points necessary to produce equal-length lines in both directions on the screen. The aspect ratio is generally used to determine the relative horizontal and vertical sizes of computer graphics. For example, if a computer graphic has an aspect ratio of 3:1, this means the width of the graphic is three times the height of the image. Table 1.1 shows the difference in aspect ratio.

Table 1.1: Aspect Ratio

Format name	*Format*	*Resolution in pixels*	*Aspect ratio*	*Other information*
Standard Definition	SD(480p)	640 × 480	4:3	Compact Disc (CD)
	SD(480p)	720 × 480	3:2	Digital Versatile Disc (DVD)
High Definition P-progressive	HD(720p)	1280 x 720	16:9	Office work, gaming
	Full-HD (1080p)	1920 x 1080	16:9	Watching DVDs and online videos
	Quad HD/2K (1440p)	2560 × 1440	16:9	Editing photos and videos with Smartphone's
Hi-Vision System (HV) / Ultra HD	Ultra HD /4K (2160p)	4096 × 2160	1.9:1	Used by Digital Cinemas Initiatives (DCI) YouTube now supports 4k videos
Super Hi-Vision System (SHV)	8K(4320p)	7680 × 4320	16:9	TV format in Japan from 2020 on Ultra HD (UHD)/4K: 2160p

Progressive scan video content displays both even and odd scan lines (the entire video frame) on the TV at the same time that is, interlaced video displays even and odd scan lines as separate fields. The even scan lines are drawn on the screen, then the odd scan lines are drawn on the screen.

1.2 TYPES OF COMPUTER GRAPHICS

There are two types of computer graphics Interactive Computer Graphics and Non- Interactive Computer Graphics.

1.2.1 Interactive Computer Graphics

It is the computer graphics in which the user can interact with the image on the computer screen. Here exist two-way communication between the user and the image. The image is totally under the control of the user. Example: Playing a computer game on the computer. Here user controls the image completely. According to the user's wish image makes the movements on the screen. Example: Computer Games (video game controller).

1.2.2 Non-Interactive Computer Graphics

It is also called Passive Computer Graphics. It is the computer graphics in which the user does not have any kind of control over the image. Image is merely the product of a static stored program and will work according to the instructions given in the program linearly. The image is totally under the control of program instructions not under the user. Example: screen savers.

Table 1.2: Differences between Interactive and Non-Interactive Computer Graphics

Interactive Computer Graphics	*Non-Interactive Computer Graphics*
User interaction is required	User interaction is not required
The user has full control over the content	The user only has control over some parts of the content
Programmed in a way that user can control graphic	Passive, totally controlled by the Program
Examples: Simulators (training pilots), Video games, User Interface	Examples: Videos, movies, images

1.3 ARCHITECTURE OF INTERACTIVE COMPUTER GRAPHICS

Working of interactive computer graphics is extremely simple. Figure 1.2 illustrates the framework of interactive computer graphics. It consists of two major components:

A. Software Level
- Application Model
- Application Program
- Graphics System

B. Hardware Level
- Interactive Devices
- Display Devices

At the hardware level, the computer accepts input from interactive devices and displays images on output devices.

At a software level, there are three components: the application program, the application model, and the graphics system. The application program is responsible for creating, storing, and retrieving pictures from the application model, which is the second component. The application model is the representation of the data or object that will be displayed on the screen, while a graphics system consists of a set of graphics commands that specify what should be displayed and how it should be displayed.

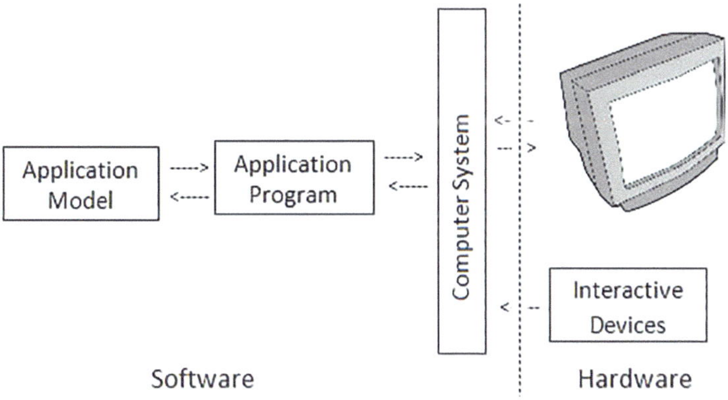

Figure 1.2: Architecture of Interactive Computer Graphics

1.4 COMPUTER GRAPHICS APPLICATIONS

Computer Graphics is used in numerous areas some of them are as follows:

Graphical User Interface (GUI)

A major component of the GUI interface is a window manager that allows a user to display multimedia window areas. Interface generally comes with a menu and icons for a fast selection of processing options. The icon is a graphics symbol designed to look like a processing option.

Computer Art

Computer art typically refers to any form of graphic art or digital imagery which is produced with the aid of a computer. Computer graphics are widely used in fine arts and commercial applications. Artists use a variety of applications like paint packages, mathematics packages, desktop publishing software, and animation program. These packages provide facilities for designing object shapes and specifying object motions. Examples: Cartoon drawing, paintings, product advertisements, logo design

- **Electronic painting**
  The picture painted electronically on a graphics tablet.
- **Morphing**
  A graphics method in which one object is transformed into another

Entertainment

Computer graphics allow us to create animated movies and games. It is used to create scenes that have special effects and animations. Computer graphics methods are now commonly used in making motion pictures, music videos, games, and television shows. Sometimes graphics pictures are displayed by themselves and sometimes combined with the actors and live scenes.

Presentations

In this application, reports are generated on slides or transparencies. It is normally used to summarize financial, statistical, mathematical, scientific, and economic data for research. Graphs & charts can be in 3-D formats to make the presentation.

Engineering Drawings (Auto CAD)

Computer Graphics gives us the flexibility to create 3D house models, house circuits and engineering drawings, etc. which is quite helpful for us. The use of computer graphics is in the design process of engineering and architecture systems. Computer-Aided Design (CAD) applications are designed to create buildings, automobiles, aircraft, spacecraft, textiles, and more models.

Education and Training

Train our students with simulators, through this they can learn about the machines without physically trying them. Computer-generated models of physical, financial, and economic systems are often used as educational aids. Various kinds of simulators program can be used to provide the training. For example, training of ship captains, aircraft pilots, heavy-equipment operators, and air traffic control personnel

Medical Imaging

MRIs, CAT scans, and other internal scans are possible because of computer graphics. Computer graphics can also be used to represent the various internal parts and processes of the human body.

Telemedicine

In this application physicians can consult with one another using video conferencing capabilities, where all can see the data and images, it brings together experts from many places to provide better care. Used in bio-medical instruments like cardiograms, CT-Scan reports, and X-ray.

1.5 DISPLAY/VIDEO ADAPTERS

A video adapter or display adapter is an integrated circuit card in a computer that provides a digital to analog converter, video RAM, and a video controller so that data can be sent to a computer's display. Figure 1.3 shows a display adapter

Figure 1.3: Display Adapters

1.5.1 Display Adapters Characterizes

There are the following characteristics of display adapters.

Image Resolution

Resolutions refer to the total number of pixels present on the display. It is often displayed as width by height, for example 1920 × 1080. That means the display's width contains 1920 pixels and the height has 1080 pixels, for a total of 20, 73,600 pixels. For example 640 × 480 and 1024 × 768.

PPI (Pixel Per Inch) how many individual pixels are displayed in one inch of a digital image is called Pixels per inch. Pixels per inch are measurements of the pixel density (resolution) of an electronic image device, such as a computer monitor or television display, or image digitizing device such as a camera or an image scanner.

Figure 1.4: Display Resolutions

Higher resolutions mean that there are more pixels per inch (PPI), resulting in more pixel information and creating a high-quality, crisp image. Images with lower resolutions have fewer pixels, and if those few pixels are too large (usually when an image is stretched), they can become visible like the image above.

On considering Fig. 1.4 and assume the screen diagonal size is 6.2 inches, then by using Pythagoras's theorem

So for the PPI = $\sqrt{(\text{width})^2 + (\text{height})^2}$

So here height is 2560 so, $2560^2 = 6,553,600$

Width is 1440 so, $1440^2 = 2,073,600$.

Now, $\sqrt{(6,553,600 + 2,073,600)} = 2937.20$.

So, PPI = 2937.20/6.2 (screen diagonal inch) = 473.74 PPI

Hence pixel per inch of this mobile is 473.74.

Example 1.1

If the resolution of an image is 1920 × 1080, what is the PPI (Pixel per inch) of an image. Assume the screen diagonal size is 5 inches.

Solution

We know that PPI = $\sqrt{(\text{width})^2 + (\text{height})^2}$

So here

Width is 1920 so, $1920^2 = 3,686,400$.

Height is 1080 so, $1080^2 = 1,166,400$

Now, $\sqrt{(3,686,400 + 1,166,400)} = \sqrt{4,852,800} = 2202.9071$.

So, PPI = 2202.9071/5 (screen diagonal inch) = 440.58 PPI

Hence pixel per inch of this image is 440.58.

Refresh Rate

It determines the speed of the display used to paint the dots on the screen. The original VGA displays run at 70Hz. A utility program is typically provided on the diskette to set the refresh rate on the display adapter for various resolutions.

Color Depth

It is determined by the no. of bits assigned to hold color value. For example:

- 1 bit = 2 Colors (Black and White)
- 4 bits = 16 Colors
- 8 bits = 256 Colors
- 16 bits = 32 thousand Colors
- 24 bits = 16 million Colors
- 32 bits = latest (true color)

The display adapter stores a value (4 to 32 bits) in memory for every dot on the screen. The amount of storage needed is determined by multiplying the no of dots (Resolution) by the memory required for each dot. For example, VGA having a resolution 640 × 480 with 4-bit color 256 KB memory is required.

Acceleration

It can draw lines and boxes, fill background color, scroll text, and manage the mouse pointer. With an accelerator, only the CPU has to send the video adapter a command to draw lines. With may include starting, ending point and width, and the color of a line. An accelerator card reduces the amount of data that must be transferred between the PC & display (video) adapter.

1.6 FLAT PANEL DISPLAYS

The term flat-panel display refers to a class of video devices that have a smaller volume, lighter in weight, and require less power compared to CRTs. A significant feature of it is that they are thinner than CRTs, which means they can be hung on walls or wear on our wrists. Emissive display and non-emissive display are two categories of flat panel displays.

1.6.1 Emissive Displays

Emissive display are the display that covert electrical energy into light. Examples are:

(a) Plasma panels.
(b) Thin-film electroluminescent display
(c) Light emitting diode (LED).

1.6.1.1 Plasma Panels

They are also called Gas Discharge Tubes; they are constructed by filling the region between two glass plates with a mixture of gases that usually includes neon. The essential components of the plasma-panel display are:

- **Cathode:** It consists of fine wires. It delivers negative voltage to gas cells. The voltage is released along with the negative axis.
- **Anode:** It also consists of line wires. It delivers positive voltage. The voltage is supplied along positive axis.
- **Fluorescent Cells**: It consists of small pockets of gas liquids when the voltage is applied to this liquid (neon gas) it emits light.
- **Glass Plates:** These plates act as capacitors. The voltage will be applied, the cell will glow continuously.

A series of vertical conducting ribbons are placed on one glass panel and a set of horizontal ribbons are built into the other glass panel. A firing voltage is applied to a pair of horizontal and vertical conductors, causing the gas at the intersection of the two pairs of conductors to break down into glowing plasma of electrons and ions. The picture definition is stored in the refresh buffer, and the firing voltages are applied to refresh the pixel positions (at the intersection conductor) 60 times per second.

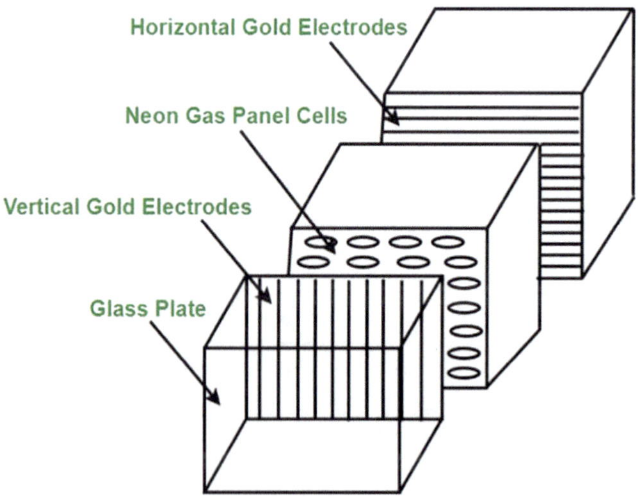

Figure 1.5: Plasma Panel Display

Advantages of Plasma Panel Display

- Refreshing is not required
- Produce a very steady image free of Flicker
- Less bulky than a CRT.

Disadvantages of Plasma Panel Display

- Poor resolution
- It requires complex addressing and wiring
- It is costlier than CRT.
- Plasma panel only applicable for monochromatic devices, but systems have been developed for displaying color and grayscale.

1.6.1.2 Thin-film Electroluminescent Display

The construction of Thin-film Electroluminescent Displays is similar to plasma panel, but the difference is that the region between the glass plates is filled with a phosphor such as Zinc sulphide doped with manganese, instead of gas. When high voltage is applied to a pair of electrodes, electrical energy is absorbed by manganese atoms then release the spot of light similar to plasma panel. It is more powerful than plasma panel and produce good color and gray scale.

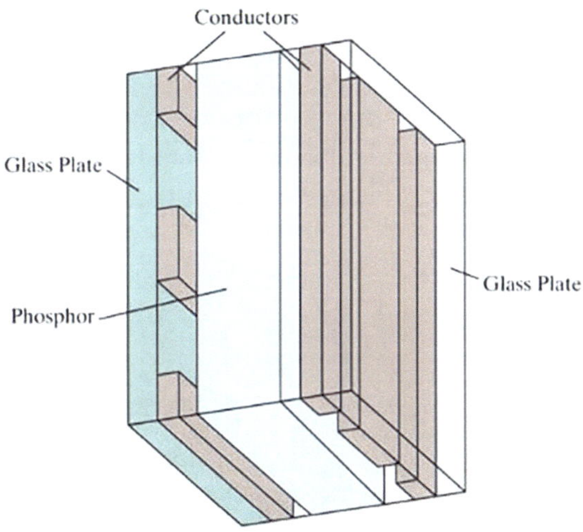

Figure 1.6: Thin-Film Electroluminescent Displays

Advantage of Thin-Film Electroluminescent Displays

- Low wattage and Long life.
- No external circuitry required.
- Can be manufactured into flat flexible panels, narrow strings, and other small shapes.
- Can be made in water proof computer systems which are more durable and lightweight than LCDs and Plasma screens.

- Not directional like LCDs when used as a computer monitor, looks good at all.
- EL can handle impressive temperature -60C to 95C LCDs can't do so.

Disadvantages of Thin-Film Electroluminescent Displays

- Not practical for general lighting of large areas due to low lumen output of phosphor so far.
- Reduced lumen output over time, although newer technologies are better than older phosphor on this point.
- Flexible flat EL sheets wear out as they get flexed, durability is being worked on.
- The lamps can use significant amount of voltage (60-600 volt).
- Typically EL needs converter when used with DC source such as on watches (to create higher frequency AC power, in this audible).

1.6.1.3 Light Emitting Diode (LED)

In an LED, a matrix of diodes is arranged to form the pixel positions in the display and picture definition is stored in refresh buffer. As in scan-line refreshing of a CRT, information is read from the refresh buffer and converted to the voltage levels that are applied to the diodes to produce the light pattern in the display. LED are very small in size and consume very little power.

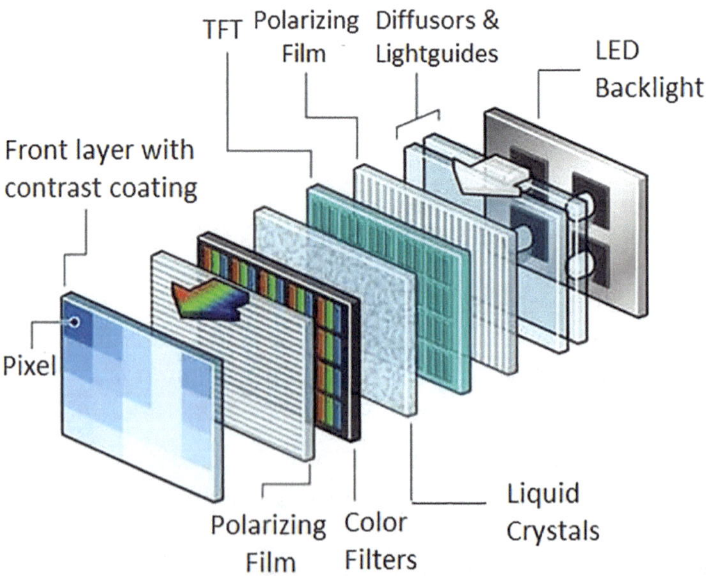

Figure 1.7: LED

Advantages of LED's

- The cost of LED's is less and they are tiny.
- By using the LED's the electricity is controlled.
- The intensity of the LED differs with the help of the microcontroller.
- The LED is available which emits light in the different colors like red, yellow, green and amber.

Disadvantages of LED

- The LED consumes more power as compared to LCD, and their cost is high. Also, it is not used for making the large display.

1.6.2 Non-Emissive Displays

They use optical effects to convert sunlight or light from some other source into graphics patterns. An example is Liquid Crystal Device (LCD).

1.6.2.1 Liquid Crystal Display (LCD)

LCD uses a liquid crystal to produce a visible image. Liquid-crystal is combination of two states of matter, the solid and the liquid. LCD commonly used in systems, such as in laptop computer screens, TVs, cell phones, and portable video games. LCD technologies allow the display to be much thinner as compared to CRT technology. LCD is made of several layers consisting of two polarized panel filters and electrodes. Light is projected through a lens onto a layer of liquid crystal. The liquid crystal display screen works on the principal of blocking light, rather than emitting light. Therefore LCDs require a backlight as they do not emit light themselves. Cathode ray tube draws more power compared to LCDs and is also heavier and bigger.

Working of LCD

We need to take two polarized glass pieces filters where as electric current is applied. The liquid crystal molecule tends to untwist. These Causes the angle of light which is passing thorough the molecules of the polarized glass and also causes charge in the angle of the hop polarizing filter. As a result little light is allowed to pass the polarized glass through a particular area of the LCD. Thus, that particular area will become dark as compared other. The electrons are made up of indium to oxide. The complete region of LCD has to be enclosed by common electrode and above it should be the liquid crystal matter.

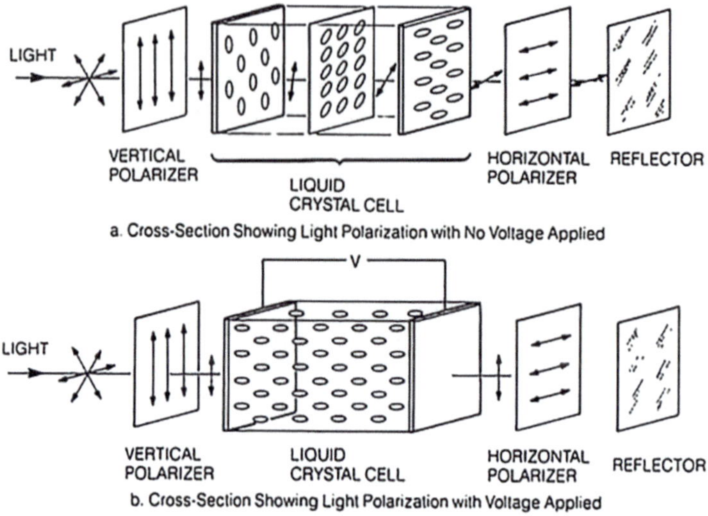

Figure 1.8: LCD

Advantages of an LCD's:

- LCD's consumes less amount of power compared to CRT and LED
- LCDs are of low cost
- Provides excellent contrast
- LCD's are thinner and lighter when compared to cathode ray tube and LED

Disadvantages of an LCD's:

- Require additional light sources
- Range of temperature is limited for operation
- Low reliability
- Speed is very low

1.7 MODES OF RESOLUTION

Many display adapters support several different modes of resolution these are Text Mode or Character Mode and Graphics Mode.

1.7.1 Text Mode

This video mode display screen is divided into rows and columns of boxes. Each box can contain one character.

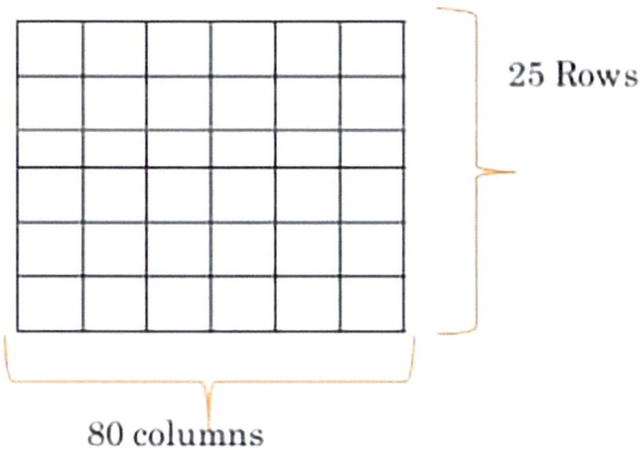

Figure 1.9: Text Mode Display Adapters

Including all Video Graphics Array (VGA) video standards PC, Supports a text mode that divides the screen into 25 rows and 80 Columns. Display Screen treated as an Array of blocks. Each can hold one ASCII Character.

1.7.2 Graphics Mode

This video mode display screen is divided into an array of pixels. Pixel is the smallest addressable element screen. Each pixel has a name or address so that we can uniquely identify that. Programs that run in graphics mode can display an unlimited variety of shapes and fonts, whereas programs running in text mode are severely limited. A program that runs entirely in graphics mode is called graphics-based programs.

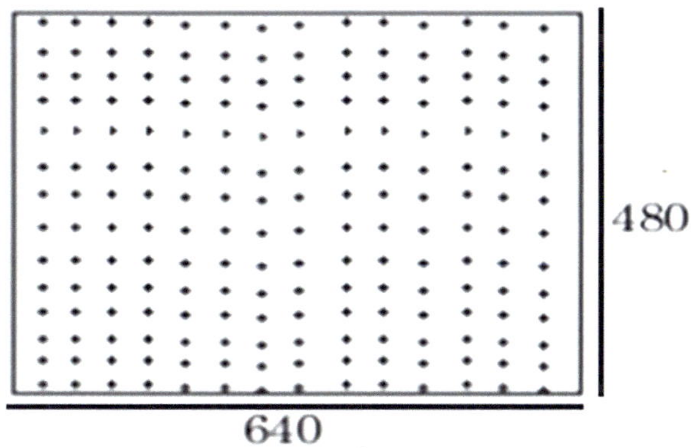

Figure 1.10: Graphics Mode Display Adapter

1.8 GRAPHICS MODE FUNCTION

If we want to start graphics programming then we need some files which are GRAPHICS.H and GRAPHICS.LIB. These files are provided as part of turbo C and C++. The graphics mode function required a graphics monitor and adapter card such as CGA (Color Graphics Adapter), EGA (Enhanced Graphics Adapter), VGA (Video Graphics Array), and BGI (Borland Graphics Interface). For Example /* sample example to draw line*/

```
#include<stdio.h>
#include<graphics.h>
void main()
{
int gd = DETECT, gm;
initgraph (&d ,&gm," C:/tc/bgi");
Line (200,200,100,100);
closegraph( );
restorecrtmode( );
}
```

1.8.1 Basic Graphics Mode Function

Basic graphics mode functions are two types.

Initgraph ( )

It is used to initialize graphic mode. In C program execution starts with main (), similarly Graphics environment starts with the initgraph ( ) function. It initializes the graphics system by loading a graphics driver from the disk and then putting the system into graphics mode.

Syntax

```
initgraph (int graphicsdriver, int graphicsmode, "path").
```

Where

Graphicsdriver: This is the argument that specifies the graphics driver to be used and it interfaces with the display adapter. Some available graphics drivers are CGA, EGA, and VGA.

Graphicsmode: Each graphic adapter can use several different possible graphics modes. The mode argument is used to select a particular mode.

Path: It specifies the path to the graphics driver. Graphics drivers are files with BGI file extensions. The path name is a string therefore it must be surrounded by quotes.

DETECT: It is a macro that automatically selects the driver.

For example

```
int gd = DETECT, gm;
initgraph (&gd ,&gm," C:/tc/bgi");
```

closegroup( )

It is used to close graphics mode. The closegraph function restores the previous display mode.

Syntax

closegraph ( );

1.8.2 Shapes Graphics Mode Function

Computer graphics has many inbuilt commands, which can be used either to draw a shape and/or for filling a colour in any bounded shape.

1. **lineto ( ):** This command draws a line on the screen from current cursor position to the x, y position.
   Syntax: lineto (x, y);
2. **line ( ):** This command draws line on screen.
   Syntax: line(x1, y1, x2, y2);
3. **circle ( ):** Draws a circle on screen.
   Syntax: circle(x, y, r);
4. **rectangle ( ):** Draws a rectangle on screen.
   Syntax: rectangle(x1,y1,x2,y2);
5. **ellipse ( ):** Draws ellipse on screen.
   Syntax: ellipse (x, y, start, end, xrad, yrad);
   x, y are the co-ordinates of center point while start, end are starting and ending angles of ellipse. xrad, yrad are x-axis and y axis radius respectively.
6. **drawpoly ( ):** It outline of a polygon having a specified no of sides.
   Syntax: drawpoly (n, array),
   Where n is number of vertices of polygon. Array is integer array name that stores co-ordinates of vertices of a polygon.
   For example
   drawpoly (4,p), int p[8]=[10,10,40,40,60,60,100,100]

1.8.3 Text Mode Function

We had seen, the text mode screen is divided into two character's positions. The screen is mapped as no of rows and no of columns.

1. **Window:** This function specifies a window on screen.
   Syntax: Window (left, top, right, bottom);
2. **putch( ):** it displays a single character at a cursor position.
   Syntax: putch("char◎)
3. **clrscr( ):** It clears the entire screen and locates the cursor in top left corner of screen.
   Syntax: clrscr( ):

4. **gotoxy( ):** It positions the cursor to the specified location on screen, where location is specified by the x, y co-ordinates of the point.
   Syntax: gotoxy(x, y).
5. **puts( ):** It displays string at cursor position.
   Syntax: puts (s1);
6. **delline( ):-** It deletes a line specified by cursor position. After deletion, all subsequent lines will be pushed up by one line.
   Eg. gotoxy(4,5); delline( );
7. **textcolor( ):-** It sets the color for text. Any text display after this command will be displayed in colour specified by this command.
   Syntax: textcolor(color);
   Eg. : int col=2; textcolor(col);
8. **inline( ):** It inserts a blank line at current cursor position.
   Eg. gotoxy(4,5);inline();
9. **textbackground( ):** It changes background colour of text. The valid colours for CGA are from 0 to 6 in above table.
10. **moveto( ):** It moves cursor to the location specified by int(x, y) co-ordinates.
11. **outtextxy( ):** It displays text within quotation mark at specified location with latest set colour style.
    Eg. outtextxy(x, y "sentence");

Tabel 1.3: Colour Constant and their Name

Colour Constant	*Colour Name*	*Colour Constant*	*Colour Name*	*Colour Constant*	*Colour Name*
0	BLACK	**6**	BROWN	**12**	LIGHTRED
1	BLUE	**7**	LIGHTGRAY	**13**	LIGHTMAGENTA
2	GREEN	**8**	DARKGRAY	**14**	YELLOW
3	CYAN	**9**	LIGHTBLUE	**15**	WHITE
4	RED	**10**	LIGHTGREEN		
5	MAGENTA	**11**	LIGHTCYAN		

1.9 GRAPHICS INPUT DEVICE

To enter data into a computer, an input device is required. It can be defined as an electromechanical device that allows the user to enter data into the computer for analysis and storage and to give commands to the computer. An input device is a piece of hardware used to provide data to a computer used for interaction and control. It allows the input of raw data to the computer for processing. Some examples of input devices are Keyboard, Mouse, Scanner, etc.

- **Keyboard :** The keyboard is one of the primary input devices used to input data and commands. It has function keys, control keys, arrow keys, a keypad, and the keyboard itself with letters, numbers, and commands.
- **Mouse :** It is an input device used to control the cursor and coordinates. It can be wired or wireless. Mouse is small size hand-held box used to position screen cursor. Wheel or roller or optical sensor is directing pointer on the according to movement of mouse. Three buttons are placed on the top of the mouse for signaling the execution of some operation. Now a day's more advance mouse is available which are very useful in graphics application for example Z mouse.
- **Microphone:** It is an input device that allows users to input audio into their computers.
- **Scanner:** It is an input device that reads an image and converts it into a digital file. A scanner is connected to a computer through a USB.
- **Touch screen:** It is an input device that allows users to interact with a computer using their fingers. It is used widely in laptop monitors, Smartphone, tablets, cash registers, and information kiosks.
- **Light pens:** Light pens are pencil-shaped device used to select positions by detecting light coming from points on the CRT screen. Activated light pens pointed at a spot on the screen as the electron beam lights up that spot and generate electronic pulse that causes the coordinate position of the electron beam to be recorded.
- **Barcode Reader :** This is an example of an input device used to read information contained in barcodes
- **Joy Stick:** Joy Stick is a pointing device used to move an object on a screen in any direction. It employs a vertical rod mounted on a base with one or two buttons. Joysticks are often used to control video games and usually have one or more push button whose state can also be read by the computer.
- **Optical Mark Reading (OMR):** Optical Mark Reading (OMR) is a method of entering data into a computer system. Optical Mark Readers read pencil or pen marks made in pre-defined positions on paper forms as responses to questions or tick list prompts.
- **Visual Display Unit:** A Visual Display Unit is a device for displaying input signals as characters on a screen. The monitor is an example of VDU.
- **MIDI:** Musical Instrument Digital Interface (MIDI) controller it is a way to connect devices that make and control sounds — such as synthesizers, samplers, and computers — so that they can communicate with each other.
- **Frame buffer:** Frame buffer is a special area of memory in raster displays which is dedicated to graphics. It holds the set of intensity values for all the screen points. The stored intensity values are retrieved from frame

buffer and displayed on the screen one row (scan line) at the time. Each screen point is referred to as a pixel or pel (shortened forms of picture element). Each pixel on the screen can be specified by its row and column number. Thus, by specifying row and column number we can specify the pixel position on the screen.

- **Video basics:** Video or moving image in general, is created from a sequence of small images called frames. By recording and then playing back frames in quick succession, an illusion of movement is created. Video can be edited by removing some frames and combining sequences of frames, called clips, together in a timeline.

OBJECTIVE QUESTIONS

1. Which of the following devices have relative origin?
   (a) Joystick (b) Track ball
   (c) Mouse (d) None of the above
2. Which is NOT an input device?
   (a) Touch Screen (b) Keyboard
   (c) Mouse (d) Plotter
3. Refresh rate below this value results in picture flickering:
   (a) 85 Hz (b) 35 Hz
   (c) 50 Hz (d) 25 Hz
4. Which of the following is an example of an input device?
   (a) Speaker (b) Digital Light Processing Projector
   (c) Barcode Reader (d) Bubble Jet Printer
5. Which of the following printers are non-impact printers?
   (a) Laser Printer and Drum Printer
   (b) Bubble Jet Printer and Daisy Wheel Printer
   (c) Inkjet Printers and Dot Matrix Printers
   (d) Laser Printers and Inkjet Printers
6. Which of the following is a lever that can be moved in several directions to control the movement of an image on a computer monitor or similar display screen?
   (a) Joystick (b) Optical Mark Reader
   (c) Visual Display Unit (d) MIDI Devices
7. Which of the following is not an example of emissive display?
   (a) Plasma Panel (b) Liquid Crystal Device
   (c) Light Emitting Diode
   (d) Thin Film Electroluminescent Display

8. If an image has a width of 4 inch and an aspect ratio of 3: 2, then what is its height?
   (a) 16/3 inch (b) 8/3 inch
   (c) 4/3 inch (d) 2/3 inch
9. What does a pixel mask mean?
   (a) string containing only 1's (b) string containing only 0's
   (c) string containing two 0's (d) string containing 1's & 0's
10. The terms HD, SD, VGA etc. are related to:
    (a) Quality Performance (b) Sound Quality
    (c) Memory Capacity (d) Processing Power
11. On what factor does the quality of image depends?
    (a) number of lines used by an image
    (b) number of pixels used by an image
    (c) number of resolutions used by an image
    (d) size of the screen
12. GUI stands for :-
    (a) Graphic Utility Input (b) Graphical User Interface
    (c) Graphics Use Input (d) None of the above
13. Which of the given options best describes the truthfulness of the following statements?
    i. In 1-bit images, each pixel is stored as a single byte.
    ii. A 1-bit image with a resolution of 640 × 480 needs a storage space of 640+480 bits.
    (a) (i) false, (ii) true (b) (i) True, (ii) False
    (c) (i) True, (ii) True (d) (i) False, (ii) False
14. A frame buffer on a black and white system with one bit per pixel is commonly called:
    (a) Grayscale (b) Pixmap
    (c) Bitmap (d) Multi map
15. Computer graphics models are now commonly used for making
    (a) Motion pictures (b) Music videos
    (c) Television shows (d) All of above

ANSWERS

1. (c)	4. (c)	7. (b)	10. (a)	13. (d)
2. (d)	5. (d)	8. (b)	11. (b)	14. (c)
3. (d)	6. (a)	9. (d)	12. (b)	15. (d)

EXERCISES

1. What is computer-graphics? Explain important applications of computer-graphics.
2. What do you understand by computer graphics? Explain the basic components of a computer graphics display.
3. What is computer graphics? Indicate five practical applications of computer graphics.
4. What do you mean by interactive graphics? Explain the framework for interactive graphics.
5. Explain briefly the classification of computer graphics.
6. Discuss the various types of computer-graphics.
7. Explain the refresh rate.
8. What are a pixel and a frame buffer?
9. Write a note on any two interactive graphics input devices.
10. How is colour depth and resolution of an image related to the video memory requirement
11. How the size of frame buffer pixel and resolution are related to each other?
12. Explain frame buffer and video basics. Also, explain the terms: Pixel, Aspect ratio, and resolution.

2

Devices for Computer Graphics

Computer graphics is a branch of computer science that focuses on the creation of visual images such as line drawings and photorealistic representations of natural objects. The production of these images requires both software and hardware. Various specialized hardware are used to generate and display graphic images. This chapter provides an overview of graphic input and output devices, and explains how these devices function logically. Input/output devices are essential for communication between computer systems and the outside world. Both input and output devices have certain properties that are necessary for computer graphics to operate effectively. The majority of computer graphics systems use some form of CRT display, and most of the fundamental display concepts are based on CRT display technology. The three most common types of CRT display technologies are DVST displays, Calligraphic refresh displays / random scan displays, and Raster scan refresh displays. Plasma panels are also sometimes used. The direct view storage tube display and calligraphic refresh display are line drawing displays, while the third is a point-plotting device.

2.1 INTRODUCTION TO OUTPUT DEVICES

Display devices are also known as output devices. The most commonly used output device in a graphics system is a video monitor. The operation of most video monitors is based on the standard Cathode Ray Tube (CRT). CRT is a device that converts electrical signals into visuals signal. Classification of output devices are shown in Figure 2.1.

2.2 CATHODE-RAY TUBES

The operation of CRT is very simple, the electron gun emits a beam of electrons (cathode rays). The electron beam passes through focusing and deflection systems that direct it toward specified positions on the phosphor-coated screen. When the beam hits the screen, the phosphor emits a small spot of light at each position contacted by the electron beam. It redraws the picture by directing the electron beam back over the same screen points quickly. This type of display is called a refresh CRT. The Structure of the Cathode-Ray Tube is given in Figure 2.2.

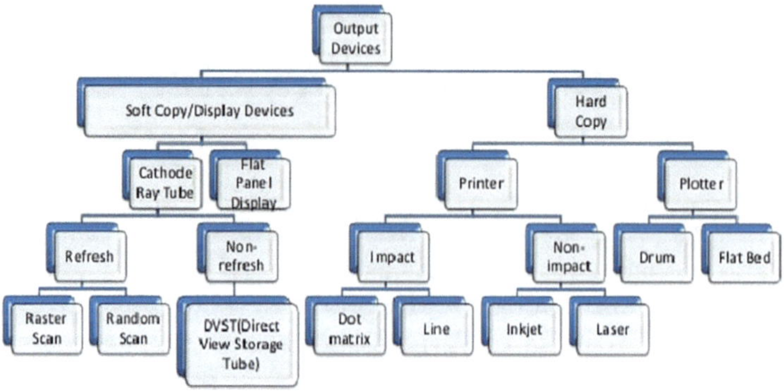

Figure 2.1: Classifications of Output Devices

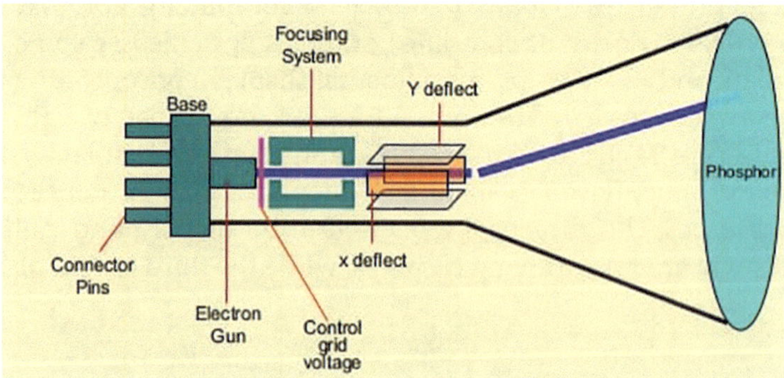

Figure 2.2: Structure of Cathode Ray Tube

Primary Component of CRT

- **Electron Gun :** The primary components of an electron gun in a CRT are the heated metal cathode and a control grid. The cathode is responsible for generating huge amounts of cathode rays (electron beam).
- **Control grid:** It is responsible for controlling the intensity or illumination in the screen by controlling the intensity of the electron beam strikes in the screen.
- **Focusing System :** The focusing system in a CRT is needed to force the electron beam to converge into a small spot as it strikes the phosphor. Otherwise, the electrons would repel each other, and the beam would spread out as it approaches the screen.

- **Deflection System :** To show the picture, the electron beam must be deflected horizontally and vertically on the screen. The deflection system is responsible for this purpose.
- **Phosphor-Coated Screen :** Spots of light are produced on the screen by the transfer of the CRT beam energy to the phosphor. There are two ways (Random scan and Raster scan) by which we can display an object on the screen.

Property of Video Monitors

- **Persistence :** Persistence refers to how long the phosphor continues to emit light after the CRT beam is removed. Persistence is defined as the time it takes for the light emitted from the screen to decay to one-tenth of its original intensity. Low Persistence Phosphorus requires high refresh rates to maintain a picture on the screen without flicker. It is useful in animations. High-persistence phosphors require low refresh rates to maintain a picture on the screen without flicker. This is useful for displaying highly complex, static images. Graphics monitors are usually constructed with persistence in the range of 10 to 60 microseconds.
- **Aspect Ratio :** Gives the ratio of horizontal points (or width) to vertical points (or height) necessary to produce equal-length lines in both directions on the screen. An aspect ratio of 3/4 means that a horizontal line plotted with three points has the same length as a vertical line plotted with four points. So 3:4 ratio (most common) means that a horizontal line plotted with 3 points has the same length as a vertical line plotted with 4 points.
- **Refresh Rate :** The light emitted by the phosphor fades, so it is necessary to repeatedly redraw the image and direct the electron beam back to the same point for the photograph to continue to glow. The number of times an image is redrawn per second to give the feeling of non-flickering images is called the refresh rate. If the refresh rate is decreased, flicker develops. Current raster-scan displays provide refresh rates of 60 to 80 frames per second, although some systems now have refresh rates of up to 120 frames per second.
- **Resolution :** The maximum number of points that can be displayed horizontally and vertically without overlapping on the display screen is called resolution. Resolution is the number of dots per inch (dpi/pixels per inch) that can be plotted horizontally and vertically. The sharpness of the image on the display depends on the resolution and size of the monitor.eg, 1280 × 1024 pixels.

2.3 CRT DISPLAY PRINCIPLE

There are two ways Random scan and Raster scan by which we can display an object on the CRT screen

2.3.1 Random Scan Display

It is also called vector display, stroke-writing display, or calligraphic display. It is a technique used for producing images on the screen. In this technique, the electron beam is directed only to the part of the screen where the image is to be drawn. Picture definitions are stored as a set of line-drawing commands in an area of memory referred to as a refresh display file or display program. To display a specified picture, the system cycles through a set of commands in the display file, drawing each component line in turn. After all the line-drawing commands are processed, the system cycles back to the first line command in the list, as given in Figure 2.3.

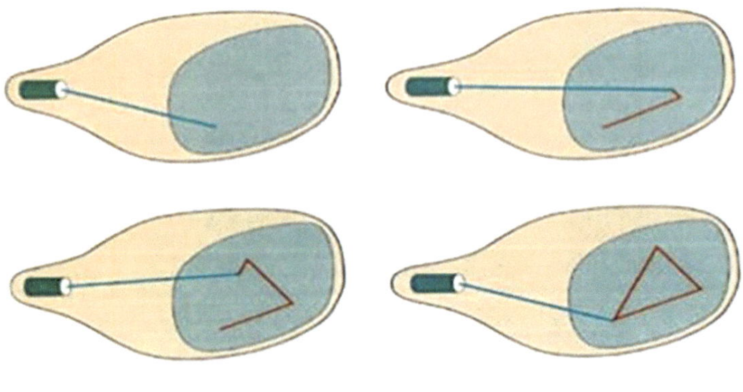

Figure 2.3: Random Scan Display

Architecture of Vector Display Device

It consists of a display controller, a central processing unit (CPU), display buffer memory, and a CRT. A display controller is connected as an I/O peripheral to the central processing unit. The display buffer memory stores the 'Display List' which contains point and line plotting commands with (x, y) or (x, y, z) coordinates as well as character plotting commands. Figure 2.4 shows the architecture of the vector display device.

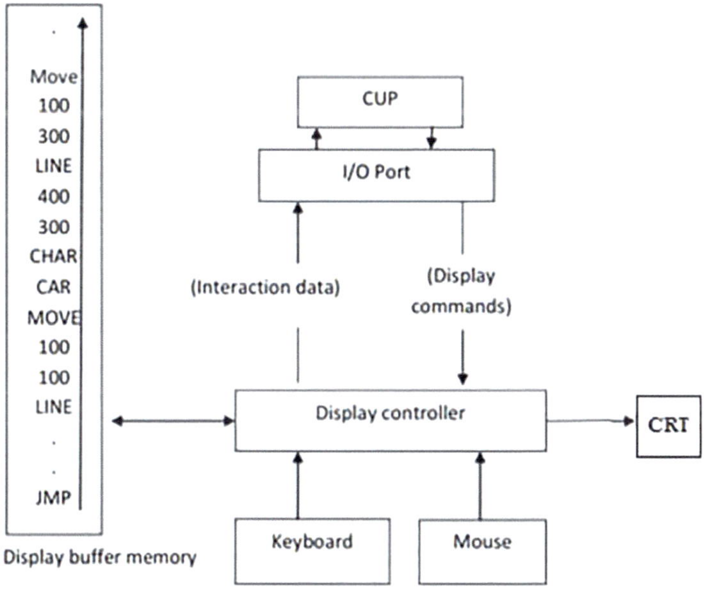

Figure 2.4: Architecture of Vector Display

The display controller (Display Adapter) interprets commands for plotting points, lines, and characters and sends digital and point coordinates to a vector generator. The vector generator then converts the digital coordinate values to analog voltages for beam-deflection circuits that displace an electron beam writing on CRT's phosphor coating. The phosphor light decays after a few milliseconds so we have to refresh the phosphor at least 30-60 times per second i.e. 30- 60 FPS (frame per second).

Advantages of a Random Scan Display

- A CRT has the electron beam directed only to the parts of the screen where an image is to be drawn.
- Need less memory to store picture definition.
- Produce smooth line.
- Higher Resolution than Raster Scan Display.

Disadvantages of a Random Scan Display

- Random-Scan monitors cannot display realistic shade scenes.
- Limitation on color to be displayed- max 4 color.
- Depend on how deep the beam penetrates.

2.3.2 Raster Scan Display

In a raster-scan system, the electron beam is swept across the screen, one row at a time from top to bottom. As the electron beam moves across each row, the beam intensity is turned ON and OFF to create a pattern of illuminated spots. Here, the picture definition is stored in a memory area called the refresh buffer or frame buffer used for redrawing. This frame buffer holds the set of intensity values for all the screen points. Stored intensity values are then retrieved from the refresh buffer and "painted" on the screen one row at a time is called a scan line as given in Figure 2.5.

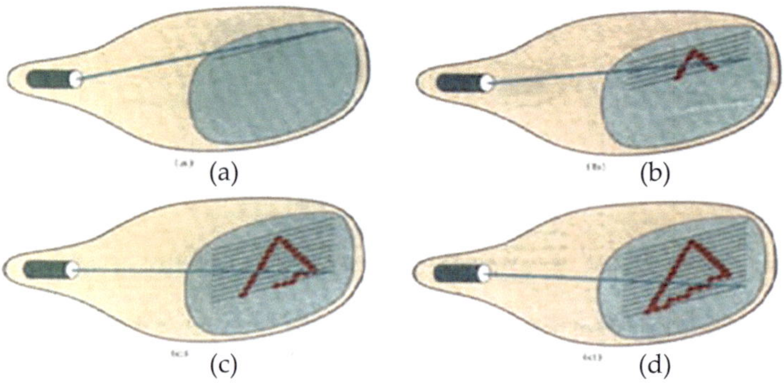

Figure 2.5: Raster Scan Display

Each screen point is referred to as a pixel or picture element. The intensity range for pixel positions depends on the capability of the raster system. In a simple black-and-white system, each screen point is either ON or OFF, So only one bit per pixel is needed to control the intensity of screen positions. On a black-and-white system with one bit per pixel, the frame buffer is commonly called a bitmap. For a bi-level system, a bit value of 1 indicates that the electron beam is to be turned ON at that position, and a value of 0 indicates that the beam intensity is to be OFF. In systems with multiple bits per pixel, the frame buffer is often referred to as a pixmap. Refreshing on raster scan displays is carried out at the rate of 60 to 80 frames per second. Refresh rates are described in units of cycles per second or Hertz (Hz).

Architecture of Raster Scan Display

Raster Scan display consists of a display controller, central processing unit (CPU), refresh buffer or frame buffer, video controller, and a CRT. Figure 2.6 show the architecture of the Raster scan display.

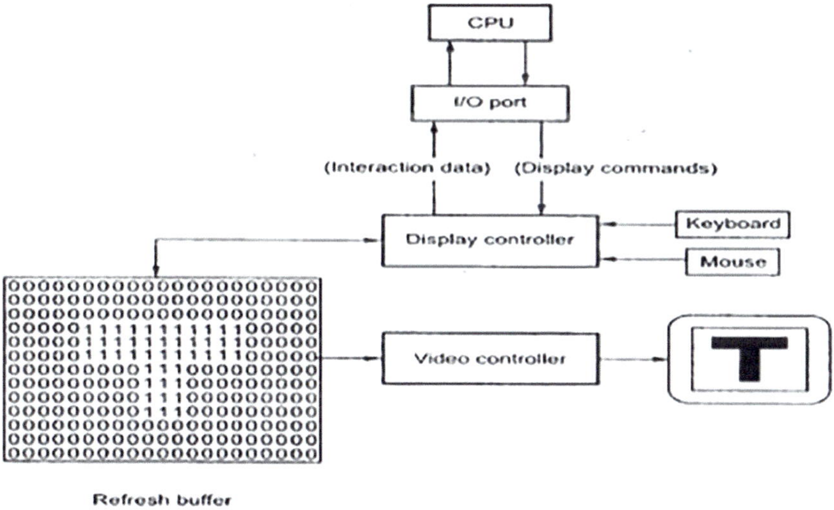

Figure 2.6: Architecture of Raster Scan Display

The displayed image is stored in the form of 1s and 0s in the refresh buffer. The images that are to be displayed are stored in a frame buffer in the form of a matrix of intensity values. The frame buffer contains the image stored in binary form as a matrix of 0's and 1's which represent the pixel. 0 indicates the darkness and 1 indicates the image. The Frame Buffer holds the set of intensity values for all the screen points. The intensity values stored in a Frame Buffer are retrieved and painted on a screen one row at a time. This row is called a scan line. The video controller reads the refresh buffer and produces the actual image on the screen. It does this by scanning one scan line at a time, from top to bottom and then back to the top. The comparative study of raster scan and random scan display is given in Table 2.1.

Advantages

- Realistic image
- Million Different colors to be generated
- Shadow Scenes are possible.

Disadvantages

- Low Resolution
- Expensive

Table 2.1: Differences between Raster and Random Scan Display

Differences	*Raster Scan Display*	*Random Scan Display*
Electronic Beam	**Electron beam** is directed from top to bottom and one row at a time on screen, but electron beam is directed to whole screen.	**Electron beam** is directed only to that part of screen where picture is required to be drawn, one line at a time so also called **vector display.**
Picture Definition	It stores picture definition in **refresh buffer also called frame buffer.**	It stores picture definition as a set **of line command called refresh display file**.
Resolution	It has **less resolution** because picture deflation is stored as a intensity value.	It has **high resolution** because it stores picture definition as a set of line commands.
Refresh Rate	Are **60 to 80 frames per second?**	It depends on the number of lines to be displayed i.e. **30 to 60 frames per second.**
Line drawing	**Zig - Zag line** is produced because plotted values are discrete.	**Smooth line** is produced because directly the line path is followed by electron beam.
Realism in display	It contains shadow, advanced shading and hidden surface technique so gives a **realistic display** of scenes.	It does not contain shadow and hidden surface technique so **it cannot give realistic display of screens.**
Image drawing	It uses **pixels** along scan lines for drawing an image.	It is designed for **line drawing applications** and uses various mathematical functions to draw.
Cost	It is **less** expensive	It is **costlier** than raster scan

2.4 RETRACE IN RASTER SCAN DISPLAY

At the end of each scan line, the electron beam is returned to the left side of the screen to display the next scan line. The return to the left of the screen, after refreshing each scan line, is called the horizontal retrace of the electron beam. At the end of each frame, the electron beam returns to the top left corner of the screen and begins the next frame is called vertical retrace. Retrace in raster scan display is given in Figure 2.7.

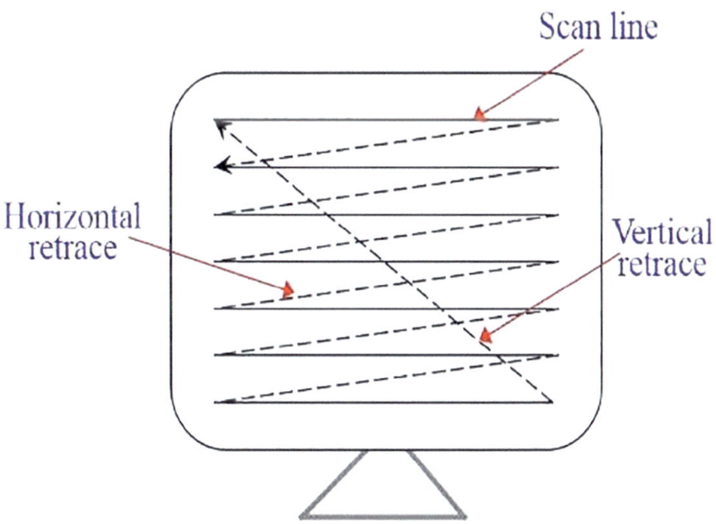

Figure 2.7: Retrace in Rater Scan Display

Interlaced V/S Non-interlaced Scan

Raster Scan may use non-interlace or interlace techniques to display pictures. In Interlaced scanning, each horizontal line of the screen is traced from top to bottom. Due to which fading (flicker) of display of object may occur. This problem can be solved by Non-Interlaced scanning. Interlacing is primarily used with slower refreshing rates.

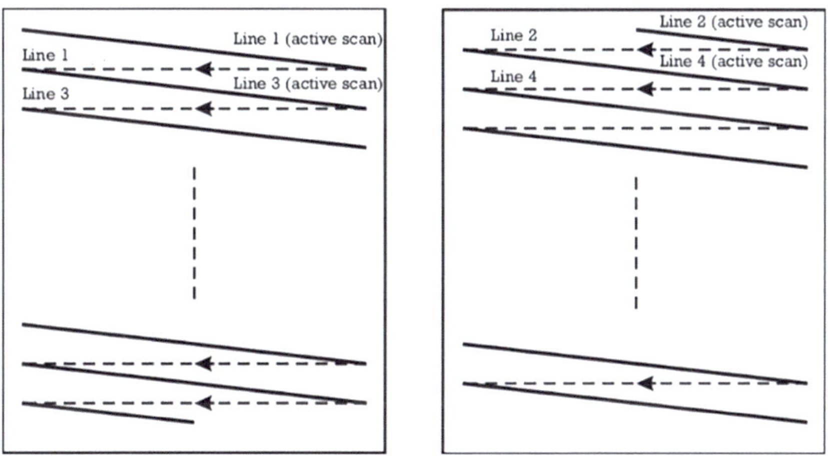

Figure 2.8: Interlaced Scanning

In Non-Interlaced scanning, each frame is displayed in two passes. In the first pass, all odd-numbered lines are traced or visited by an electron beam from top to bottom, then in the next circle, an even number of lines are located. Figure 2.8 is defining the interlaced scanning while Figure 2.9 describe the non-interlaced scanning process in the raster scan display.

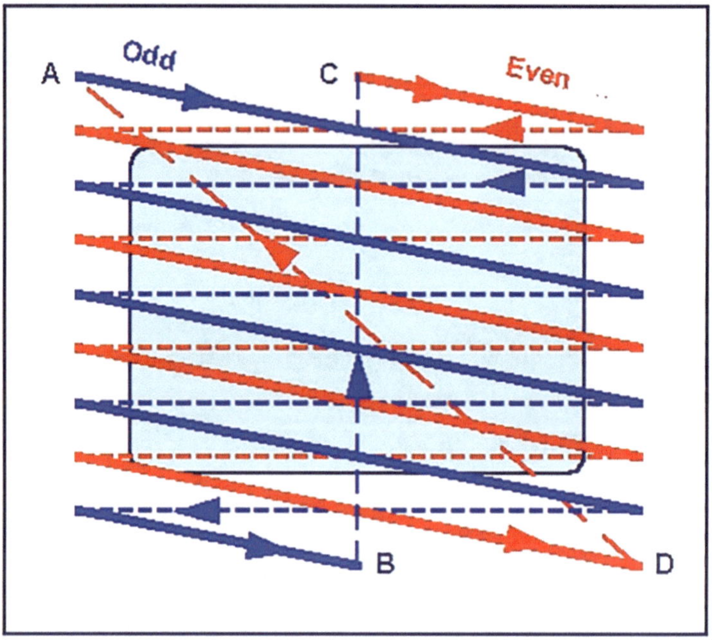

Figure 2.9: Even and odd interlaced scanning

Even and odd fields are scanned out alternately to produce an interlaced image. For non-interlaced display refresh rate of 30 frames per second is used. But it gives flickers. For interlaced display refresh rate of 60 frames per second is used.

2.5 COLOUR CRT MONITOR

A Color CRT can display colour pictures by using a combination of phosphor that emits different colored lights. Different colors are produced by combining emitted color light from different phosphors. The normal CRT can generate images of single colour due to the limitation of phosphor coating. It generates a range of colour by combining the emitted light from multilayered phosphor coated color CRT. The two basic techniques used for producing colour display on CRT are Beam Penetration techniques and Shadow Mask CRT.

2.5.1 Beam Penetration Techniques

It is used with random scan monitors. In this, a normal CRT screen is coated with two phosphor layers usually red and green. The displayed colour depends on how far the electron beam penetrates into the phosphor layers. A beam of slow electrons excites only the outer red layer. A beam of very fast electrons penetrates through the red layer and excites the inner green layer. At intermediate beam speeds, combinations of red and green light are emitted and two additional colors, orange and yellow displayed. The beam acceleration voltage controls the speed of the electrons and hence the screen colour at any point on the screen.

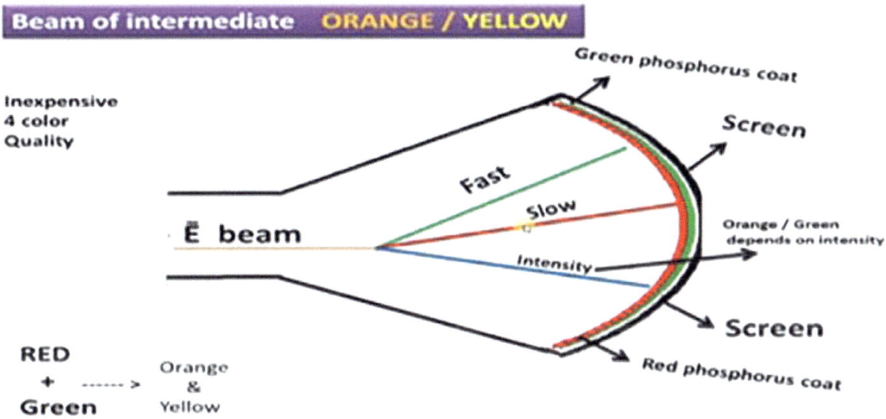

Figure 2.10: Beam Penetration Techniques

Advantages of the Beam Penetration Techniques

- Better Resolution
- Half cost
- Inexpensive

Disadvantages of the Beam Penetration Techniques

- Only four possible colors
- Time Consuming

2.5.2 Shadow–Mask Techniques

It is used with a raster scan monitor for displaying pictures. It has more range of colors than the beam penetration method. It is used in television sets and monitors. This type of CRT has three electron guns, one for each color dot, and a shadow mask grid just behind the phosphor-coated screen, named "Shadow-Mask." The shadow mask grid consists of holes aligned with dot patterns. It has three phosphorus color dots at each position of the pixel. One phosphor dot emits a red light, another emits a green light, and the third emits a blue light. The three beams are deflected and focused as a group onto the shadow mask, and when they pass through a hole they activate a dot triangle. In a dot triangle, three phosphor dots are arranged so that each electron beam can activate only its corresponding color dot when it passes through the shadow mask. By varying the intensity of the three electron beams we can obtain different colors in the shadow mask CRT. By turning off the red and green guns, we get only the color coming from the Blue phosphor. By turning off the green and blue guns, we get only the color coming from the Red phosphor. By turning off the red and blue guns, we get only the color coming from the Green phosphor. All three dots with equal intensity activate we get white.

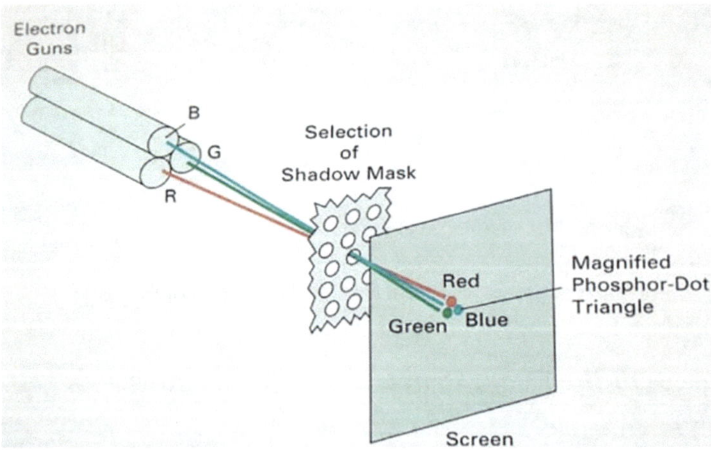

Figure 2.11: Shadow-Mask Techniques

All three dots with equal intensity are inactivated we get Black. When blue and green are activated equally we get Cyan. When green and red dots are activated equally we get Yellow. When blue and red dots are activated equally we get Magenta.

Advantages of the Shadow Mask Technique

- The image is more real as compared to other RGB filtering methods.
- Tailored, that is this technique is customizable.
- And is relatively less expensive compared to other techniques.

Disadvantages of the Shadow Mask Technique

- Use of very limited colors, only three to four colors usage.
- Other methods available provide much better results in terms of the quality of the picture.

Table 2.2: Differences between Beam Penetration and Shadow Mask Techniques

	Beam Penetration Technique	*Shadow Mask Technique*
Where Used	It is used with **Random Scan System** to display color.	It is Used With **Raster Scan System** to display color.
Colors produced	It can displays Only **four colors** i.e. Red, Green, Orange and Yellow	It can display **Millions** of colors.
Color Dependency	**Fewer colors are available** because the colors in Beam Penetration depend on the speed of the electron beam.	**Millions of colors are available** because colors in the Shadow Mask depends on the type of the ray
Cost	It **is Less Expensive** as compared to Shadow Mask.	It **is More Expensive** than other methods.
Picture Quality	**Quality of picture is not so good** i.e. Poor with Beam Penetration Method.	Shadow Mask gives realism to pictures with shadow effects and millions of colors.
Resolution	It gives **Low Resolution.**	It gives **High Resolution.**
Criteria	In Beam Penetration method, Color display depends on how far electron criteria outer Red layer and then Green layer.	In Shadow Mask Method, there are no such criteria for producing colors. It is in computers, in color TV etc.

2.6 DIRECT VIEW STORAGE TUBES

DVST stands for direct view storage tube. In the raster scan display, we do refreshing of the screen to maintain a screen image. The DVST gives an alternate method of maintaining the screen image. A DVST uses the storage grid which stores the picture information as a charge distribution just behind the phosphor coated screen. DVST consists of two guns a primary gun and a flood gun as shown in Figure 2.12. A primary gun stores the picture pattern and the flood gun maintains the picture display. A primary gun produces high speed electrons which strike on the storage grid to draw the picture pattern. As electron beam strikes on the storage grid with high speed, it knocks out electrons from the storage grid keeping the net positive charge. The knocked out electrons are attracted towards the collector. The positive charge on the storage grid is nothing but the picture pattern. The low-speed electrons from the flood gun continuously pass through the control grid and are attracted to the positively charged regions of the storage grid. The low-speed electrons then enter the storage grid and strike the phosphor coating. During this process collector behind the storage grid smooth's out the flows of flood electrons.

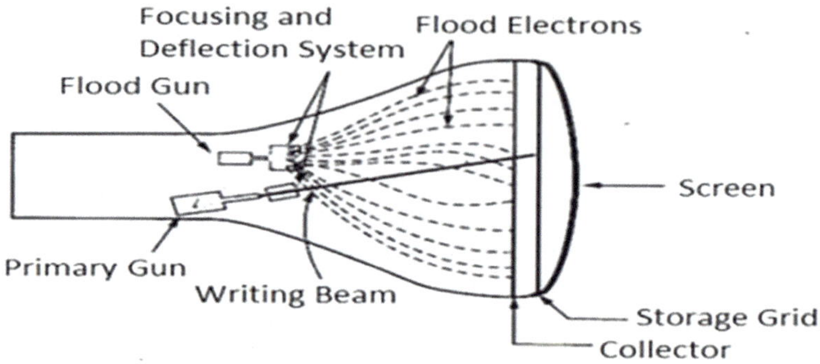

Figure 2.12: Direct View Storage Tubes

Advantages of the Direct View Storage Tubes

- No refreshing is needed.
- Complex picture can be displayed in high resolution
- Cost is very less

Disadvantages of the Direct View Storage Tubes

- It is not possible to erase the selected part of a picture.
- It is not suitable for dynamic graphics applications.
- If a part of picture is to modify, then time is consumed.
- The performance of DVST is poor in comparison to CRT

2.7 ATTRIBUTES OF OUTPUT PRIMITIVES

The Primitives are the simple geometric functions that are used to generate various Computer Graphics required by the User. The characteristics of an output primitive are known as Attributes. In other words, any parameter that affects the way a primitive is to be displayed is known as Attribute. Line Attributes, Area Fill Attributes, Color and Grayscale Levels, Character Attributes are the types of attributes.

2.7.1 Line Attributes

The basic attributes of a straight line segment are its type, its width, and its color. In some graphics packages, lines can also be displayed using selected pen or brush options.

- **Line Type :** Possible selection of line type attribute includes solid lines, dashed lines and dotted lines.

Figure 2.13: Line type

To set line type attributes in a PHIGS (Programmer's Hierarchical Interactive Graphics Standard) application program, a user invokes the function

setLinetype (lt)

Where parameter lt is assigned a positive integer value of 1, 2, 3, 4 to generate lines that are solid, dashed, and dash dotted respectively.

- **Line Width :** Implementation of line width option depends on the capabilities of the output device to set the line width attributes.

setLinewidthScaleFactor(lw)

Line width parameter lw is assigned a positive number to indicate the relative width of line to be displayed.

- **Line Color :** A polyline routine displays a line in the current color by setting this color value in the frame buffer at pixel locations along the line path using the set pixel procedure. To set the line color value in PHIGS with the function

setPolylineColourIndex (lc)

Non negative integer values, corresponding to allowed color choices, are assigned to the line color parameter lc.

- **Pen and Brush Options :** In some graphics packages, lines can also be displayed using selected pen or brush options. Options in this category include shape, size, and pattern. Example: Various line attribute commands in an applications program are given by the following sequence of statements

setLinetype(2);
setLinewidthScaleFactor(2);

```
setPolylineColourIndex (5);
polyline(n1,wc points1);
setPolylineColorIindex(6);
polyline (n2, wc points2);
```

This program segment would display two figures, drawn with double-wide dashed lines. The first is displayed in a color corresponding to code 5, and the second in color 6.

2.7.2 Fill Area Attributes

Options for filling a defined region include a choice between a solid color, a pattern fill and choices for particular colors and patterns.

- **Fill Styles :** Areas are displayed with three basic fill styles: hollow with a color border, filled with a solid color, or filled with a specified pattern or design. A basic fill style is selected in a PHIGS program with the function

  setInteriorStyle(fs)

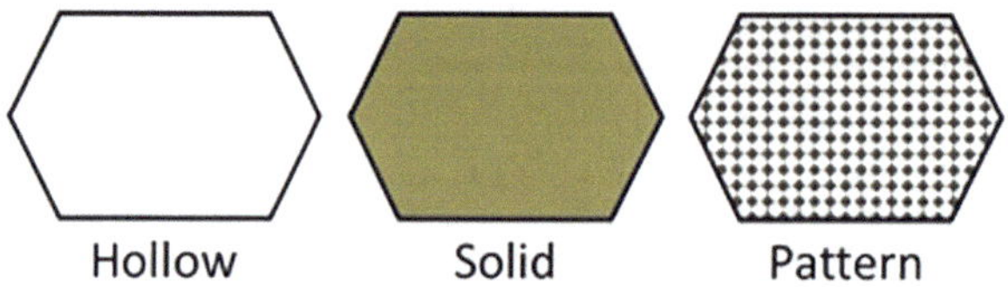

Figure 2.14: Basic Fill Styles of Area Attribute

Values for the fill-style parameter fs include hollow, solid, and pattern. Another value for fill style is hatch, which is used to fill an area with selected hatching patterns-parallel lines or crossed lines

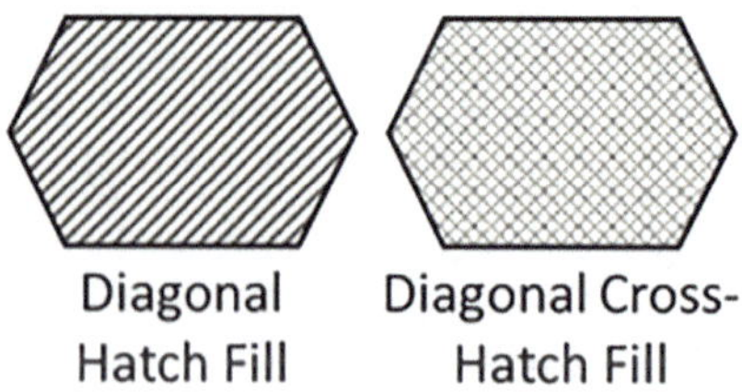

Figure 2.15: Hatch Fill Styles of Area Attribute

The color for a solid interior or for a hollow area outline is chosen with

setInteriorColourIndex(fc)

Where fill color parameter fc is set to the desired color code.

- **Pattern Fill :** We select fill patterns with

  setInteriorStyleIndex (pi)

Index(pi)	Pattern(cp)
1	$\begin{bmatrix} 4 & 0 \\ 0 & 4 \end{bmatrix}$
2	$\begin{bmatrix} 2 & 1 & 2 \\ 1 & 2 & 1 \\ 2 & 1 & 2 \end{bmatrix}$

Figure 2.16: Pattern Fill Styles of Area Attribute

Where pattern index parameter pi, specifies a table position. For example, the following set of statements would fill the area defined in the fill Area command with the second pattern type stored in the pattern table:

SetInteriorStyle(pattern)
SetInteriorStyleIndex(2);
Fillarea (n, points)

2.7.3 Text Attributes

The choice of font or typeface is a set of characters with a particular design style such as Courier, Helvetica, Times Roman, and various symbol groups. The characters in a selected font also are displayed with styles. (Solid, dotted, double) in bold face in italics, and or shadow styles.

A particular font and associated style is selected in a PHIGS program by setting an integer code for setting the font style we have the function

setTextFont (tf)

Where parameter, tf, is used to specify text font. Control of text color (or intensity) is managed with

setTextColourIndex (tc)

Where text color parameter tc specifies an acceptable color code. Text size can be adjusted without changing the width to height ratio of characters with

setCharacterHeight (ch)

Parameter ch is assigned a real value greater than 0 to set the coordinate height of capital letters. The scaling width only of text can be set with function.

setCharacterExpansionFactor (cw)

Where parameter, cw is set to a positive real value that scales the body width of character. Spacing between characters is controlled separately with setCharacterSpacing (cs)

Where parameter cs can be assigned any real value. The orientation for a displayed character string is set according to the direction of the character up vector

setCharacterUpVector (upvect)

Parameter upvect assigned two values that specify the x and y vector components. For example, with upvect = (1, 1), the direction of the up vector is 45o and text would be displayed. To arrange character strings vertically or horizontally

setTextPath (tp)

Can be assigned the value: right, left, up, or down. Alignment attributes are set with

setTextAlignment (h,v)

Where, parameters h and v control horizontal and vertical alignment. Horizontal alignment is set by assigning h a value of left, center, or right. Vertical alignment is set by assigning v a value of top, cap, half, base or bottom. A precision specification for text display is given with

setTextPrecision (tpr)

tpr is assigned one of values string, char or stroke.

2.7.4 Marker Attributes

A marker symbol is a single character that can be displayed in different colors and different sizes. To select a particular character to be the marker symbol with

setMarkerType (mt)

Where parameter mt is set to an integer code Typical codes for marker type are the integers 1 through 5, specifying, respectively, a dot (.) a vertical cross (+), an asterisk (*), a circle (o), and a diagonal cross (X). To set the marker size with

setMarkerSizeScaleFactor (ms)

Where parameter ms is assigned a positive number. This scaling parameter is applied to the nominal size for the particular marker symbol. Values greater than 1 increase the marker size and values less than one reduce the marker size. Marker color is specified with

SetPolymarkerColourIndex (mc)

Where parameter mc is stored in the current attribute list and used to display subsequently specified marker primitives, overall summary of output primitive attribute is describe in Table 2.3.

Table 2.3: Attribute of Output Primitive

Output primitive types	*Associated attributes*	*Attribute setting function*
Line	Type Width Color	setLinetype setLinewidthScaleFactor setPolylineColourIndex
Fill Area	Fill Styles Fill Color Pattern	setInteriorStyle setInteriorColourIndex setInteriorStyleIndex setPatternRepresentation setPatternSize setPatternReferencepoint
Text	Font Color Size Orientation	setTextFont setTextColourIndex setCharacterHeight setCharacterExpansionFactor setCharacterUpVector setTextPath setTextAlignment
Marker	Type Size Color	setMarkerType setMarkerSizeScaleFactor SetPolymarkerColourIndex

Example 2.1

Consider the three different raster systems, systems with resolution of 640 × 480, 1280 × 1024 and 2560 × 2048. What size of the frame buffers is needed for each of these systems to store 12-bits per pixel? How much storage is required for each system if 24-bits per pixel are to be stored?

Solution:

The size of the frame buffers for each of the above raster system to store 12 bits per pixel is

Total number of pixels required = 640 × 480 pixels

Size of frame buffer required = 640 × 480 pixels

1 pixel can store 12 bits (given)

Therefore Size of frame buffer (in bits)

$$640 \times 480 \times 12 = 3686400$$

Similarly

$$1280 \times 1024 \times 12 = 15728640$$

$$2560 \times 2084 \times 12 = 64020480$$

If 24-bits per pixel are to be stored, then

$$640 \times 480 \times 24 = 44236800$$
$$1280 \times 1024 \times 24 = 188743680$$
$$2560 \times 2084 \times 24 = 768245760$$

Example 2.2

Consider the three different raster systems, systems with resolution of 640 × 480, 1280 × 1024 and 2560 × 2048. What size of the frame buffers (in bytes) is needed for each of these systems to store 12-bits per pixel? How much storage is required for each system if 24-bits per pixel are to be stored?

Solution:

Case I. When one pixel store 12 bits

For 640 × 480 resolution, we have Size of frame buffer (in bits)

$= 640 \times 480 \times 12$ bits

$= \dfrac{640 \times 480 \times 12}{8}$ bytes

$= 460800$ bytes

$= 450$ KB

For 1280 × 1024 resolution, we have Size of frame buffer (in bits)

$= 1280 \times 1024 \times 12$ bits

$= \dfrac{1280 \times 1024 \times 12}{8}$ bytes

$= 1920$ KB

For 2560 × 2084 resolution, we have Size of frame buffer (in bits)

$= 2560 \times 2084 \times 12$ bits

$= \dfrac{2560 \times 2084 \times 12}{8}$ bytes

$= 7.5$ MB

Case II. When one pixel store 24 bits

For 640 × 480 resolution, we have Size of frame buffer (in bits)

$= 640 \times 480 \times 24$ bits

$= \dfrac{640 \times 480 \times 24}{8}$ bytes

$= 921600$ bytes

$= 900$ KB

For 1280 × 1024 resolution, we have Size of frame buffer (in bits)
= 1280 × 1024 × 24 bits

$$= \frac{1280 \times 1024 \times 24}{8} \text{ bytes}$$

= 3932160 bytes
= 3840 KB

For 2560 × 2084 resolution, we have Size of frame buffer (in bits)
= 2560 × 2084 × 24 bits

$$= \frac{2560 \times 2084 \times 24}{8} \text{ bytes}$$

= 16005120 bytes
= 15630 KB
= 15.26 MB

Example 2.3

Suppose a raster system with resolution 640 by 480. How many pixels could be accessed per second in this system if the display controller refresh rate is 60 Hz? What is the access time per pixel in this system?

Solution:

Refresh rate = 60 Hz = 60 frames/sec.
Resolution of the raster = 640 × 480.
No. of pixel that could be accessed per second is 60 × 640 × 480.
Access time per pixel = 1/ (60 × 640 × 480) sec = 0.00000005 sec.

Example 2.4

In the system the resolution is 600 × 400. How many KB Does a frame buffer needs? If 1 pixel can store n bit.

Solution:

Resolution = total number of pixel
= 600 × 400
∴ 1 pixel can store n bit
Frame buffer are required (KB) = (resolution × bits per pixel × 1024) / 8
= (600 × 400 × n × 1024) / 8
= 29.29.nkb

Example 2.5

How much time is spent scanning across each row of pixels during a screen refresh of 1280 x 1024 at a refresh rate of 60 frames per second?

Solution:

Here, resolution = 1280×1024

That means system contains 1024 scan lines and each scan line contains 128 pixels

Refresh rate = 60 frame/sec.

So, 1 frame takes = 1/60 sec. $\therefore$ Resolution = 1280×1024

1 frame buffer consist of 1024 scan lines

It means then 1024 scan lines take 1/60 sec

Therefore, 1 scan line takes,

$1 / (60 \times 1024)$ Sec = 0.058 sec

Example 2.6

Calculate the refresh rate for a raster screen of 512×512 pixels with average access time for each pixel of 200 nanoseconds.

Solution:

Average access time for each pixel = 200 nanoseconds = 200×10^{-9} sec

Raster screen of 512×512 pixels

$\therefore$ Total time to access all pixels $= 512 \times 512 \times 200 \times 10^{-9}$ sec

$= 0.0524$ sec

For one frame to get refreshed, it takes 0.0524 sec. So in 1 sec, the refresh rate would be

$= 1/ (0.0524)$

$= 19$ frames /sec

OBJECTIVE QUESTIONS

1. _____ Method for displaying colour pictures is commonly used with random scan displays.
   (a) Beam penetration (b) Shadow masking
   (c) Retracing (d) Refreshing
2. The duration of phosphorescence exhibited by a phosphor is known as ______.
   (a) Fluorescence (b) Persistence
   (c) Phosphorescence (d) Deflection

3. Random scan monitors are also referred as
   (a) Stroke writing display (b) Calligraphic display
   (c) Vector display (d) All of these
4. With respect to CRT, the horizontal retrace is defined as:
   (a) The path an electron beam takes when returning to the left side of the CRT.
   (b) The path an electron beam takes when returning to the right side of the CRT.
   (c) The technique of turning the electron beam off while retracing.
   (d) The technique of turning the electron beam on/off while retracing
5. In a raster scan display, the frame buffer holds:
   (a) Line drawing commands (b) Scanning instructions
   (c) Image Resolution (d) Intensity information
6. The phenomenon of having a continuous glow on the screen even after it is removed is called
   (a) Fluorescence (b) Persistence
   (c) Phosphorescence (d) Incandescence
7. Aspect ratio is generally defined as the ratio of
   (a) Vertical to horizontal points
   (b) Horizontal to vertical points
   (c) Vertical to (horizontal + vertical) points
   (d) Either (a) or (b) depending on the convention followed
8. ___________ will free the CPU from graphics chores.
   (a) Display processor (b) Monitor
   (c) ALU (d) Video controller
9. Which of the following is CRT based display devices?
   (a) Raster scan display device (b) Direct View Storage Tube (DVST)
   (c) Calligraphic or vector based or random scan display device
   (d) all of the above
10. _______ is responsible for accessing the frame buffer to refresh the screen.
    (a) Graphics package (b) Video controller
    (c) CPU (d) Monitor
11. The brightness of a spot on the screen depends upon
    (a) Number of electrons striking the phosphor coating (screen)
    (b) Distance between cathode and screen
    (c) Speed of electrons striking the screen
    (d) Type of phosphor coating

12. Interactive graphics are useful in
    (a) Training pilots (b) Computer-aided design
    (c) Process control (d) All of these
13. The aspect ratio of an image describes the proportional relationship between its _____ and its _____.
    (a) Length, Breadth (b) Width, Depth
    (c) Width, Height (d) Breadth, Height
14. PHIGS stands for
    (a) Programmer's Hierarchical Interface Graphics Standard
    (b) Programmer's Hierarchical Interactive Graphics Standard
    (c) Programmer's Hierarchical Interest Graphics Standard
    (d) None of these
15. Which Color producing technique is more suitable for raster scan system?
    (a) Beam penetration technique (b) Shadow mask technique
    (c) All of these (d) None of these

ANSWERS

1. (a)	4. (a)	7. (d)	10. (b)	13. (c)
2. (b)	5. (d)	8. (a)	11. (a)	14. (b)
3. (d)	6. (b)	9. (d)	12. (d)	15. (b)

EXERCISES

1. Explain the working principle of a Refresh CRT monitor with suitable diagrams.
2. Draw the architecture and explain working of raster scan display system.
3. Compare Raster Scan system and Random Scan System.
4. Explain the working of a random scan display system with suitable diagram.
5. Explain the advantages of raster scan display over random scan display.
6. Explain the architecture of raster graphics system with suitable diagrams.
7. Differentiate between DVST & Refresh CRT.
8. Explain the working of a beam penetration CRT.
9. With a suitable figure, Explain the working of a delta-delta shadow mask CRT.
10. Explain the working of Direct View Storage Tube (DVST) as well as merit and demerit of DVST.

11. Compare Plasma display with LCD display on the basis of parameters in tabular form.

12. Explain Graphics Standards, and Explain Graphics Software.

13. Compare and contrast the raster and random scan systems. Mention some applications of raster scan system.

14. What is the fundamental difference in the method of operation of a monochrome CRT and a colour CRT?

15. Define:

(A) Aspect Ratio

(B) Persistence

(C) Frame Buffer.

16. What is refresh buffer? Identify the contents and the organization of the refresh buffer for the case of raster display and vector display.

17. What do you understand by the aspect ratio and resolution of a display screen in a raster scan display?

18. How much time is spent scanning across each row of pixels during a screen refresh of 1280 x 1024 at a refresh rate of 60 frames per second?

19. What do you understand by the aspect ratio and resolution of a display screen in a raster scan display?

20. Consider a raster system with a resolution of 2560 x 2048. Determine the frame buffer size (in bytes) needed for the system to store 12-bits per pixel. How much storage is required if 24-bits per pixel are to be stored?

21. Suppose you have a raster system designed using an 8 inches × 10 inches screen with a resolution of 100 pixels per inch in each direction. What frame buffer size is required if 6 bits are stored per pixel in the buffer?

22. Consider a raster system with a resolution of 2560 x 2048. Determine the frame buffer size (in bytes) needed for the system to store 12-bits per pixel. How much storage is required if 24-bits per pixel are to be stored?

23. Consider a raster system with resolution of 1280 by 1024. What size of frame buffer is needed for given system to store 24bits per pixel? How many colors are possible in given system? What is the access time per pixel if refreshing rate is 60 frames per second?

3

Scan Conversion

When creating graphics on a computer screen, an object is displayed by selecting which pixel of the screen should be highlighted. This process can be used to create patterns and more complex objects like cubes, cones, circles, and ellipses. Different algorithms have been developed to generate these objects, and a computer can use them to produce raster images on raster devices by turning the appropriate pixels ON or OFF. This process of representing continuous graphics objects as a collection of discrete pixels is known as scan conversion or rasterization. Scan conversion is the process of converting vertical or horizontal scan frequency of video signals for different purposes and applications. Scan converters are the devices that perform the scan conversion, and the instrument used for scan conversion is known as a scan converter. Scan conversion acts as a bridge between TV and computer graphics technology. This chapter explains the procedures followed in drawing complex objects, as well as various line drawing algorithms, such as Bresenham's line drawing and circle drawing algorithm. Additionally, it covers the mathematical and algorithmic aspects of scan conversion.

3.1 INTRODUCTION OF SCAN CONVERSION

The process of representing continuous graphics objects as a collection of discrete pixels is called Scan Conversion. For example, a line is defined by its two end points and the line equation, whereas a circle is defined by its radius, centre position and circle equation. It is the responsibility of graphics system or the application program to convert each primitive (point, line, circle, ellipse, Polygon) from its geometric definition into a set of pixels that make up the primitive in image space. This conversion task is generally referred to as a scan conversion or Rasterization.

The term pixel is a short form of the picture element. It is also called a point or dot. It is the smallest picture unit accepted by display devices. A picture is constructed from hundreds of such pixels. Each pixel has some intensity value which is represented in the memory of the computer called a frame buffer. Inside the buffer, the image is stored as a pattern of binary digits either 0 or 1. So there is an array of 0 or 1 used to represent the picture. In black and white monitors, black pixels are represented using 1's and white pixels are represented using 0's. In the case of systems having one bit per pixel frame buffer is called a Bitmap. In systems with multiple bits per pixel, it is called a Pixmap.

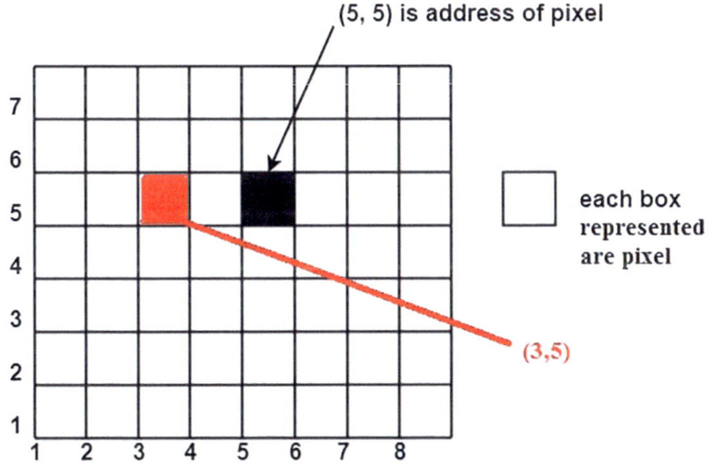

Figure 3.1: Pixel Representation

Point P (5, 5) is used to represent a pixel in the 5th row and the 5th column. In the case of line, it can be possible that any pixel may have any floating value like (2.7, 5) which will not be considered by the system as shown in Figure 3.1. Therefore, the process of making these coordinates according to the system's assumption i.e. (3, 5) to plot the pixel is scan conversion.

3.2 SCAN CONVERSION ALGORITHMS

Scan conversion algorithms are of different types. Some of them are scan conversion of point, scan conversion of line, scan conversion of circle and scan conversion of ellipse.

3.3 SCAN CONVERSION OF POINT

A mathematical point (x, y) where x and y are real numbers within an image area, needs to be scan-converted to a pixel at location (x′, y′). This may be done by making x′ and y′ to be the integer part of x and y, that is

$$x' = \text{Floor}(x) \text{ and } y' = \text{Floor}(y)$$

The floor is a function that returns the largest integer that is less than or equal to the argument. The origin is at the lower left corner of the pixel grid. All points that satisfy $x' < x < x'+1$ and $y' < y < y'+1$ are mapped to pixel (x′, y′) as represented in Figure 3.2 (a).

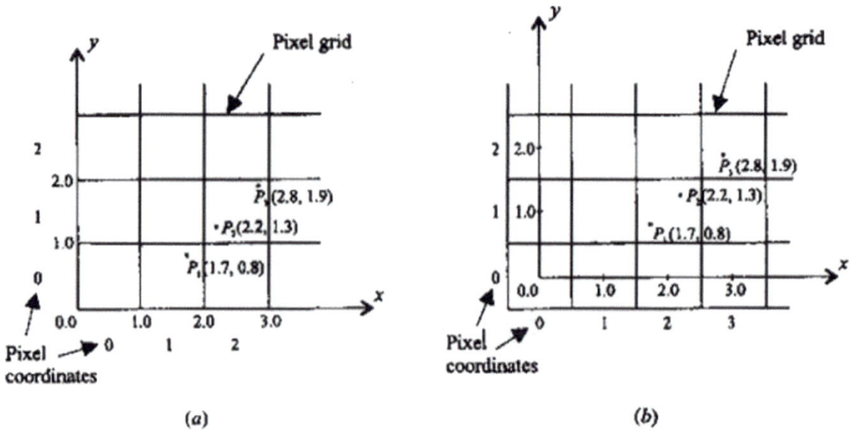

Figure 3.2: Scan conversion of Point

For example, P1 (1.7, 0.8) is represented by pixel (1, 0). P2 (2.2, 1.3) and P3 (2.8, 1.9) are both represented by pixels (2, 1). Another approach, in Figure 3.2 (b) is to scan convert (x, y) by making

$$x' = \text{Floor}(x + 0.5) \text{ and } y' = \text{Floor}(y+0.5).$$

This essentially places the origin of the coordinate system for (x, y) at the center of the pixel (0, 0).

$$x'-0.5< x < x'+0.5 \text{ and } y'- 0.5 < y <y'+0.5$$

All point that satisfies is mapped to (x', y'). This means that points P1 and P2 are now both represented by pixel (2, 1), whereas point P3 is represented by pixel (3, 2). To load the specified colour into the frame buffer at a particular position, we will assume we have an available low-level procedure of the form setpixel(x, y). To retrieve the current frame buffer intensity, we assume to have the procedure getpixel (x, y, color) or putpixel(x, y, color).

Program to draw a pixel

```
#include <graphics.h>
#include <conio.h>
#include <stdio.h>
#include <math.h>
void main( )
{
clrscr( );
int gdriver=DETECT, gmode;   /* request auto detection */
initgraph (&gdrive, &ggmode,"c://tc//bgi"); /* initialize graphics & local
variable */
int x, y;
```

```
printf ("Enter the value of x and y");
scanf("%d%d", &x, &y);
putpixel(x, y, color)
getch( );
closegraph( );
return 0;
}
```

3.4 SCAN CONVERSION OF LINE

A line in computer graphics typically refers to a line segment, which is a portion of a straight line that extends indefinitely in the opposite direction. It is defined by its two endpoints and the slope intercepts equation for a line:

$$y = mx + b \quad (1)$$

Where, m = slope of the line

b = the y-intercept of a line

The two endpoints of a line segment are specified at positions (x1, y1) and (x2, y2).

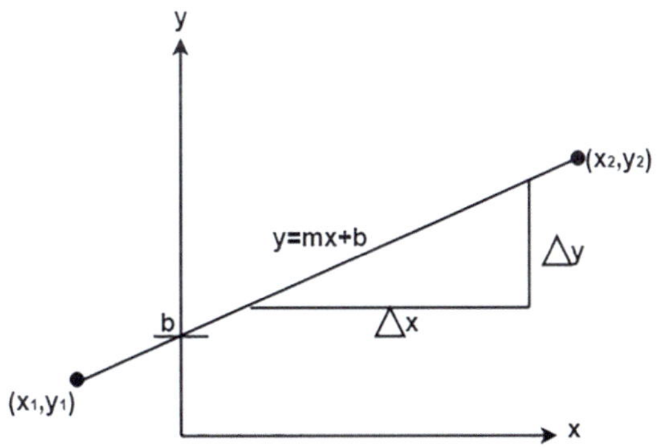

Figure 3.3: Line Segment

Line Drawing Algorithms are of different types, some of the line drawing algorithms are DDA algorithm and Bresenham's algorithm. The following are the properties that a line must hold in any line-drawing algorithm,

- Line must be straight.
- Line must terminate accurately.
- Line must have constant density.
- Density must be independent of its length.
- Line must be drawn very fast.

3.4.1 Direct use of Line Equation

It is the simplest form of conversion. We can determine the value for slope m & b intercept as

$$m = \frac{y_2 - y_1}{x_2 - x_1} \qquad (2)$$

$$b = y_1 - mx_1 \qquad (3)$$

For any given x interval Δx, we can compute the corresponding y interval Δy as:

$$\Delta y = m\Delta x \qquad (4)$$

Similarly, we can obtain x interval Δx as:

$$\Delta x = \frac{\Delta y}{m} \qquad (5)$$

Case I. If | m | > 1, then for every integer value of y between and excluding y1 and y2, calculate the corresponding value of x using equation $\Delta x = {}^{\Delta y}\!/_{m}$ and scan convert (x, y), that is $x = x + \frac{1}{m}$ and $y = y + 1$.

Case II. If | m | ≤ 1, then for every integer value of x between and excluding x1 and x2, calculate the corresponding value of y using equation Δy = m Δx and scan convert (x, y), that is $x = x + 1$ and $y = y + m$.

Example 3.1

The endpoints of a line are (0, 0) and (6, 18), Compute each value of y as x steps from 0 to 6 and plot the result

Solution:

First point (0, 0) and last point (6, 18)

x1 = 0 , y1 = 0

x2 = 6 , y2 = 18

We know equation of line is

y = m x + b

y = 3x + b (1)

Put value of x from initial point in equation (1),

The value of x = 0, y = 0 so

y = 3x + b

0 = 3 x 0 + b

0 = b ⇒ b=0

Put b = 0 in equation (1)

$$y = 3x + 0$$

$$y = 3x$$

Now calculate intermediate points

Let $x = 1 \Rightarrow y = 3 \times 1 \Rightarrow y = 3$

Let $x = 2 \Rightarrow y = 3 \times 2 \Rightarrow y = 6$

Let $x = 3 \Rightarrow y = 3 \times 3 \Rightarrow y = 9$

Let $x = 4 \Rightarrow y = 3 \times 4 \Rightarrow y = 12$

Let $x = 5 \Rightarrow y = 3 \times 5 \Rightarrow y = 15$

Let $x = 6 \Rightarrow y = 3 \times 6 \Rightarrow y = 18$

So points are P1 (0, 0)

P2 (1, 3)

P3 (2, 6)

P4 (3, 9)

P5 (4, 12)

P6 (5, 15)

P7 (6, 18)

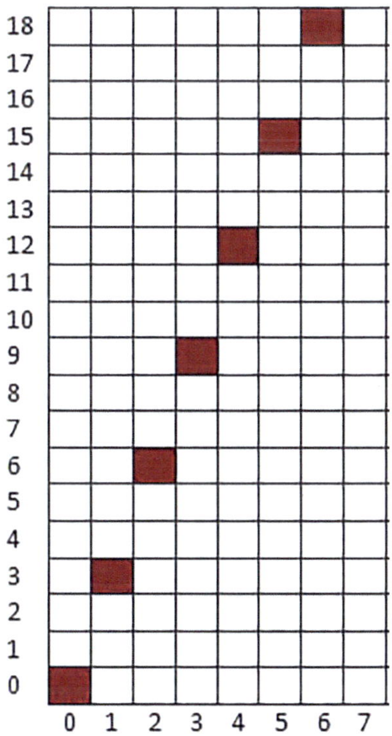

Figure 3.4: Rasterization of a line

Disadvantages of Direct Use of Line Equation

While this approach is mathematically sound, it involves floating-point computation (multiplication and addition) in every step that uses the line equation since m and b are generally real numbers. The challenge is to find a way to achieve the same goal as quickly as possible. So

- To draw a line on the screen, first, we have to determine which pixels are to be switched ON.
- The process of determining which combination of pixels provides the best approximation to the desired line is known as Rasterization.
- The choice of pixels is determined by the orientation of the line which is to be drawn.
- There is little difficulty in selecting the pixels for horizontal, vertical and diagonal lines. For any other orientation of lines, the selection of pixels is a difficult process.
- Therefore, we must sample a line at discrete positions and determine the nearest pixel to the line at each sample position.

3.4.2 DDA Algorithm

In Digital Differential Analyzer algorithm samples the line at unit intervals in one coordinate and determines corresponding integer values nearest the line path for the other coordinate. DDA stands for Digital Differential Analyzer. It is an incremental method of scan conversion of lines. In this method calculation is performed at each step but by using results of previous steps. Let the equation of the line as

$$y = mx + b$$

Where m is the slope of the line and b is the intercept. We also know that

$$m = {}^{\Delta y}\!/_{\Delta x}$$

Now, we consider one point (x_k, y_k) and the next point is (x_{k+1}, y_{k+1}) then

$$m = (y_{k+1} - y_k) / (x_{k+1} - x_k)$$

Now, we have to find the slope between the starting point and ending point. There can be the following three cases to discuss:

Case I. If x is incrementing faster ($m < 1$) this implies x parallel more than y or $\frac{dy}{dx} < 1$ then we sample at unit increment in x-direction and compute each successive y value as $y_{k+1} = y_k + m$.

Case II. If $m = 1$ then x and y coordinates tend to unit interval $x_{k+1} = x_k + 1$ and $y_{k+1} = y_k + 1$.

Case III. If y is incrementing faster ($m > 1$) this implies y parallel more than x or $\frac{dy}{dx} > 1$ then we sample at unit increment in y direction and compute each successive x value as $x_{k+1} = \Delta x + {}^{1}\!/_{m}$. The position of slope is given in Figure 3.5.

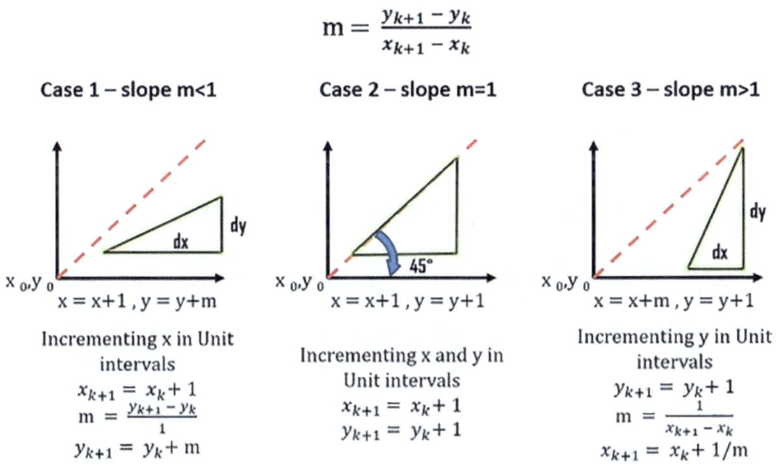

Figure 3.5: Position of Slope

When a straight line $y = mx + b$ is given, the different situations of angle and slope are defined in Figure 3.6 and Figure 3.7, respectively.

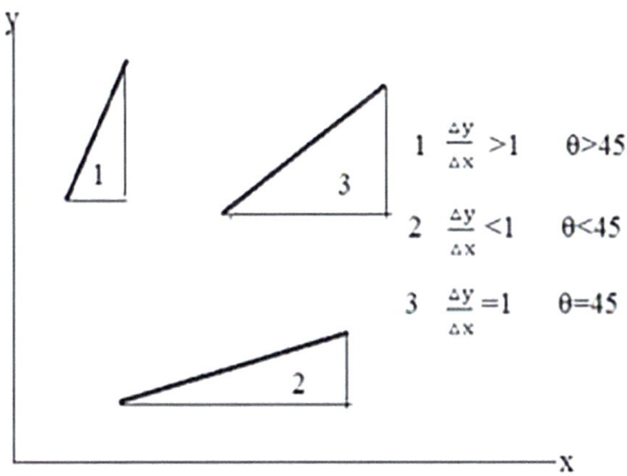

Figure 3.6: Different Situations of Angle

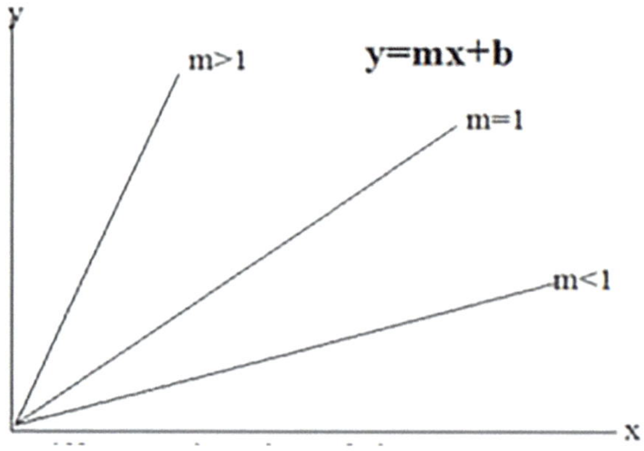

Figure 3.7: Different Situations of Slope

Algorithm for Digital Differential Analyzer algorithm

Step 1. Read the input of the two end points of the line as (x1, y1) and (x2, y2) such that x1! = x2 and y1! = y2

Step 2. Calculate *dx* = x2 – x1 and dy = y2 – y1

Step 3. if (abs (*dx*) ≥ abs (*dy*))
length = abs (*dx*)
else
length = abs (*dy*)

Step 4. xin = dx/length
yin = dy/length

Step 5. x = x1 + 0.5
y = y1 + 0.5

Step6. for (k = 0; k < length; k++)

```
{
    putpixel(x, y)
    x = x + xin
    y = y + yin
}
```

Advantages of Digital Differential Analyzer

- It is a simple algorithm to implement.
- It is a faster algorithm than the direct line equation.
- It avoids using the multiplication operation that makes it faster than the direct use of the line equation.

Disadvantages of Digital Differential Analyzer

- The floating-point arithmetic implementation is time-consuming.
- It uses a round-off ( ) function that increases the complexity of the algorithm.
- Sometimes the point position is not accurate.

Example 3.2

Consider a line from (5, 4) to (12, 7). Use the DDA algorithm to rasterized this line.

Solution

(x1, y1) = (5, 4)

(x2, y2) = (12, 7).

dx = x2 – x1 = 12 – 5 = 7

dy = y2 – y1 = 7 - 4 = 3

length = dx = 7

xin = dx / length = 7/7 = 1

yin = dy / length =3/7 = 0.42

x = x + xin= 5 + 1 = 6

y = y + yin = 4 + 0.42 = 4.42

Since $m = \frac{dy}{dx}$ = 3/7 = 0.42 that is (m ≤ 1) therefore $y_{k+1} = yk + m$

The next calculation is given in Figure 3.8(a).

i	$x_{i+1} = x_i + 1$	$y_{i+1} = y_i + m$	*Setpixel* (x_{i+1}, y_{i+1})
0	5	4	
1	6	4.42	(5, 4)
2	7	4.84	(6, 4)
3	8	5.26	(7, 5)
4	9	5.68	(8, 5)
5	10	6.1	(9, 6)
6	11	6.52	(10, 6)
7	12	6.94	(11, 6)
			(12, 7)

Figure 3.8(a): Rasterization of a line

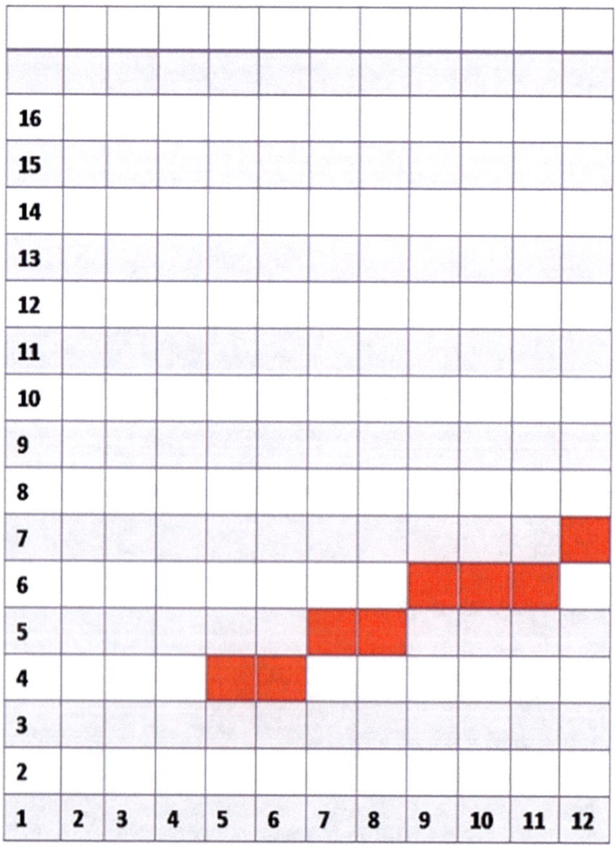

Figure 3.8(b) Rasterization of a line

Example 3.3

Consider a line from (5, 10) to (15, 30). Use the DDA algorithm to rasterized this line.

Solution

(x1, y1) = (5, 10)
(x2, y2) = (15, 30).
dx = x2 – x1 = 15 – 5 = 10
dy = y2 – y1 = 30 – 10 = 20
length = dx = 20
xin = dx / length =10/20 = 0.5
yin = dy / length =20/20 = 1
x = x + xin= 5 + 0.5 = 5.5
y = y + yin = 10 + 1 = 11

Since m = $\frac{dy}{dx}$ = 20/10 = 2 that is (m ≥ 1) therefore $x_{k+1} = x + \frac{1}{m}$.

i	$x_{k+1} = x + \frac{1}{m}$	$y_{i+1} = y_i + 1$	*Setpixel* (x_{i+1}, y_{i+1})
0	5	10	
1	5.5	11	(5, 10)
2	6	12	(5, 11)
3	6.5	13	(6, 12)
4	7	14	(6, 13)
5	7.5	15	(7, 14)
6	8	16	(7, 15)
7	8.5	17	(8,16)
8	9	18	(8, 17)
9	9.5	19	(9, 18)
10	10	20	(9, 19)
11	10.5	21	(10, 20)
12	11	22	(10, 21)
13	11.5	23	(11, 22)
14	12	24	(11, 23)
15	12.5	25	(12,24)
16	13	26	(12, 25)

Contd.

Figure 3.9: (a) Rasterization of a line

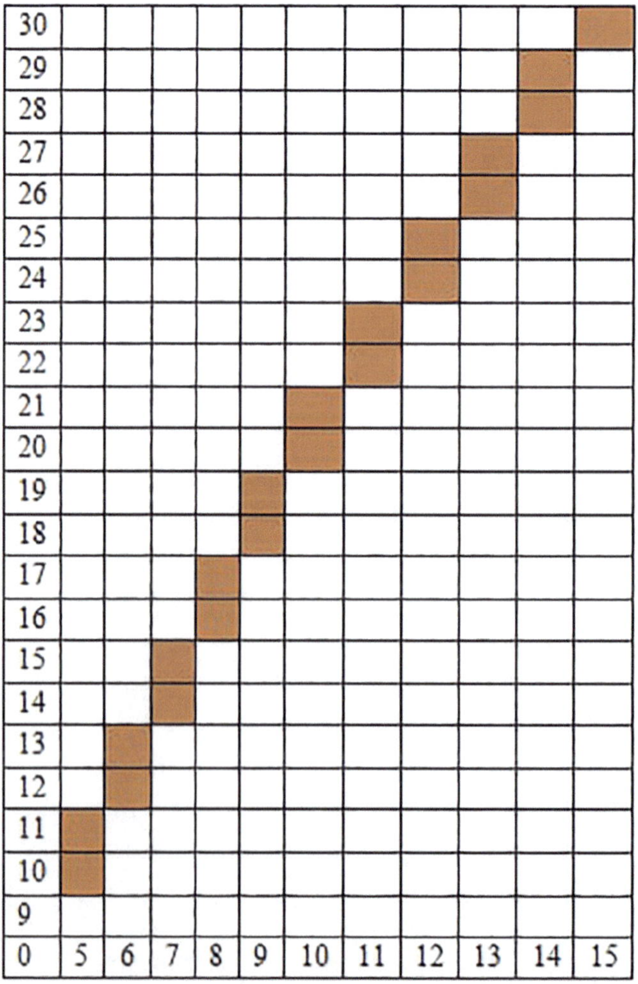

Figure 3.9: (b) Rasterization of a line

Program for DDA Line Drawing Algorithm in C

```
#include <graphics.h>
#include <stdio.h>
#include <math.h>
#include <dos.h>
void main( )
{
      float x,y,x1,y1,x2,y2,dx,dy,step;
      int i,gd=DETECT,gm;
      initgraph(&gd,&gm,"c:\\turboc3\\bgi");
      printf("Enter the value of x1 and y1 : ");
      scanf("%f%f",&x1,&y1);
      printf("Enter the value of x2 and y2: ");
      scanf("%f%f",&x2,&y2);
      dx=abs(x2-x1);
      dy=abs(y2-y1);
      if(dx>=dy)
length = dx;
else
      length=dy;
      dx=dx/length;
      dy=dy/length;
      x=x1;
      y=y1;
      i=1;
      while(i<=length)
            {
               putpixel(x,y,5);
               x=x+dx;
               y=y+dy;
               i=i+1;
               delay(100);
            }
      closegraph();
}
```

3.4.3 Bresenham's Algorithm

Bresenham's algorithm is another incremental scan conversion algorithm. The advantage of this algorithm is that it uses only integer calculations. The basic idea behind the algorithm is to find decision variables. It is defined as the distance between the actual line location and the nearest pixel. The algorithm increments x or y by one unit based on the slope of the line. Once this is done, increment in other variables is calculated based on the decision variable. The following figure indicates the expected line.

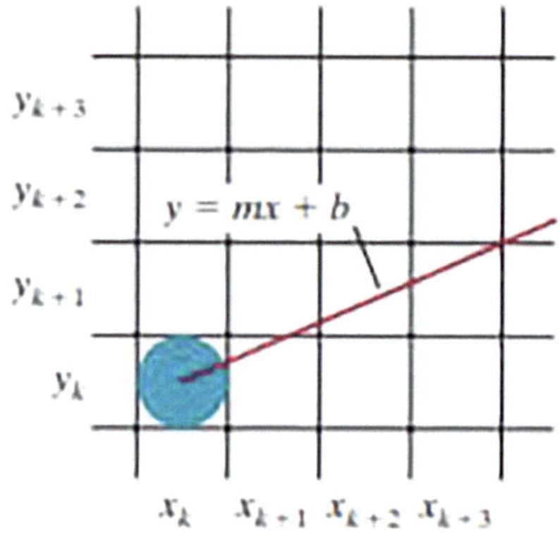

Figure 3.9: Expected Straight Lines

Now, we select those pixels which are close to the expected line, but how to find this closed pixel. Well, we make use of the decision variable for this purpose. To illustrate Bresenham's approach, we first consider the scan-conversion process for lines with a positive slope less than 1 i.e. m < 1.

Pixel positions along a line path are determined by sampling at unit x intervals. Starting from the left endpoint (x0, y0) of a given line, we step to each successive column (x position) and plot the pixel whose scan-line y value is closest to the line path. Assuming we have determined that the pixel at (x_k, y_k) is to be displayed, next we need to decide which pixel to plot in column x_{k+1}. Our choices are the pixels at positions (x_{k+1}, y_k) and (x_{k+1}, y_{k+1}) .

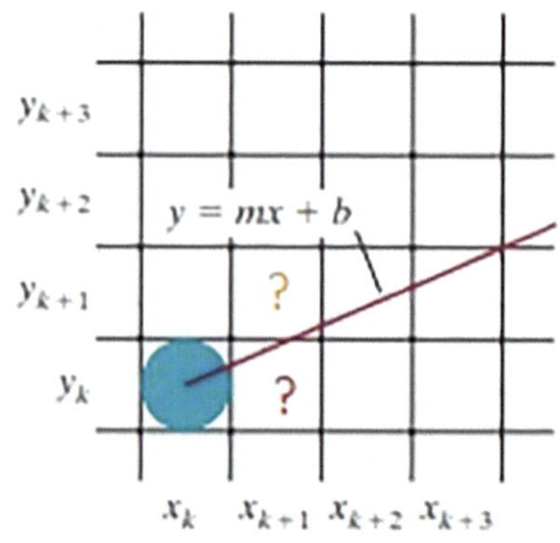

Figure 3.10: Position of the line on a grid

At sampling position x_{k+1}, we label vertical pixel separations from the mathematical line path as d1 and d2.

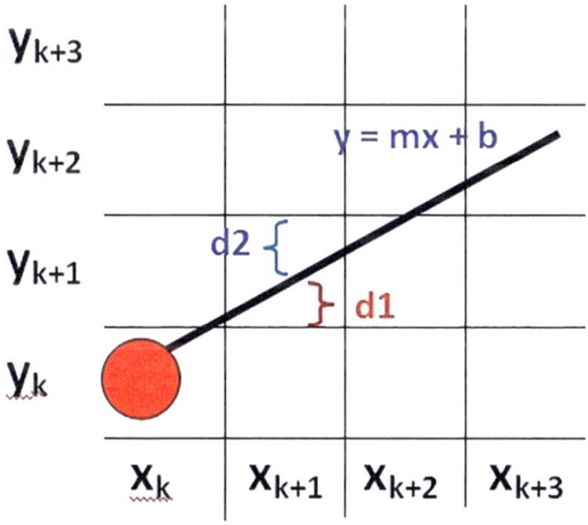

Figure 3.11: Decision Parameter

The y coordinate on the mathematical line at pixel column position x_{k+1} is calculated as

$$y = m(x_{k+1}) + b$$

Then

$$d1 = y - y_k$$
$$= m(x_{k+1}) + b - y_k$$

and

$$d2 = (y_{k+1}) - y$$
$$= y_{k+1} - m(x_{k+1}) - b$$

The difference between these two separations is

$$d1 - d2 = 2m(x_{k+1}) - 2y_k + 2b - 1$$

Suppose we use the decision parameter p_k, kth step is the line algorithm by rearranging the above equation so that it is in values integer calculation. By substituting m = Δx/Δy, Where Δx, Δy are vertical and horizontal separations of the end point position then we get

$$p_k = \Delta x\,(d1 - d2)$$
$$= 2\Delta y.x_k - 2\Delta x.y_k + c \qquad (1)$$

The sign of p_k is the same as the sign of d1 – d2 since Δx > 0. Therefore Δx (d1 – d2) can be used as a decision parameter for choosing the pixel (x_{k+1}, y_{k+1}) next to (x_k, y_k).

We call this Δx (d1 – d2) as a parameter pk.

- If $p_k > 0$ then d1 > d2 hence we select the coordinate (x_{k+1}, y_{k+1}).
- If $p_k < 0$ then d1 < d2 hence we select the coordinate (x_{k+1}, y_k).

Therefore we can obtain the value of successive parameters using increment integer calculation at step k + 1 the decision parameter is evaluated at

$$p_{k+1} = 2\Delta y(x_{k+1}) - 2\Delta x\,(y_{k+1}) + c$$
$$p_{k+1} - p_k = 2\Delta y\,(x_{k+1} - x_k) - 2\Delta x\,(y_{k+1} - y_k)$$

As $x_{k+1} = x_k + 1$

$$p_{k+1} = p_k + 2\Delta y - 2\Delta x\,(y_{k+1} - y_k)$$

The $y_{k+1} - y_k$ is either 0 or 1 depending on the sign of parameter p_k. First parameter p0 is evaluated from the equation (1), at starting point (x0, y0) and m is evaluated as $\Delta x / \Delta y$, then

$$p_o = 2\Delta y - \Delta x$$

The actual competitions are explained below. We will initially set the decision parameter as

$$p_o = 2\Delta y - \Delta x$$

Where
$$\Delta x = x2 - x1$$
$$\Delta y = y2 - y1$$

Now the further start with computing the new decision value

- If $p_k > 0$ then x, y are incremented, that is (x_{k+1}, y_{k+1}).
  $p_{k+1} = p_k + 2\Delta y - 2\Delta x\,(y_{k+1} - y_k)$ since $y_{k+1} - y_k$ is 1 so
  $p_{k+1} = p_k + 2\Delta y - 2\Delta x$
- If $p_k < 0$ then only increment x value, that is (x_{k+1}, y_k).
  $p_{k+1} = p_k + 2\Delta y - 2\Delta x\,(y_{k+1} - y_k)$ since $y_{k+1} - y_k$ is 0 so
  $p_{k+1} = p_k + 2\Delta y$.

Bresenham's Line Drawing Algorithm for $|m| < 1$

Step 1. Input the two line endpoints and store the left endpoint in (x_0, y_0).

Step 2. Set the color for frame-buffer position (x_0, y_0); that is plot the point.

Step 3. Calculate the constants Δx, Δy, $2\Delta y$, $2\Delta y - \Delta x$ and obtain the starting value for the decision parameter as $p_0 = 2\Delta y - \Delta x$

Step 4. At each x_k along the line, starting at k = 0, perform the following test.
If $p_k < 0$, the next point to plot is (x_{k+1}, y_k) and

$$p_{k+1} = p_k + 2\Delta y.$$

Otherwise, the next point to plot is (x_{k+1}, y_{k+1}) and

$$p_{k+1} = p_k + 2\Delta y - 2\Delta x$$

Step 5. Perform step 4 Δx - 1 times.

Program for Bresenham's Line Drawing Algorithm in C

```
#include<stdio.h>
#include<graphics.h>
```

```
void drawline(int x0, int y0, int x1, int y1)
{
   int dx, dy, p, x, y;
   dx=x1-x0;
   dy=y1-y0;
    x=x0;
   y=y0;
    p=2*dy-dx;
while(x<x1)
   {
        if(p>=0)
        {
                putpixel(x,y,7);
                    y=y+1;
                p=p+2*dy-2*dx;
        }
   else
{
putpixel(x,y,7);
   p=p+2*dy;
   }
   x=x+1;
   }
   }
int main()
{
int gdriver=DETECT, gmode, r, x0, y0, x1, y1;
initgraph(&gdriver, &gmode, "c:\\turboc3\\bgi");
printf("Enter co-ordinates of first point: ");
scanf("%d%d", &x0, &y0);
printf("Enter co-ordinates of second point: ");
scanf("%d%d", &x1, &y1);
drawline(x0, y0, x1, y1);
return 0;
}
```

Example 3.3

Using Bresenham's Line Algorithm Draw the line with endpoints (20, 10) to (30, 18).

Solution

The line has the slope m = (18 - 10)/ (30 - 20) = 8/10 = 0.8

$\Delta x = 10$

$\Delta y = 8$

The initial decision parameter has the value p0 = $2\Delta y - \Delta x = 6$ and the increments for calculating successive decision parameters are

$2\Delta y = 16$

$2\Delta y - 2\,\Delta x = -4$

We plot the initial point (x0, y0) = (20, 10) and determine successive pixel positions along the line path from the decision parameter as given in Table 3.2.

Table 3.2: Solution of Example 3

k	p_k	(x_{k+1}, y_k)	(x_{k+1}, y_{k+1})
0	6		(21, 11)
1	2		(22, 12)
2	-2	(23, 12)	
3	10		(24, 13)
4	14		(25, 14)
5	6		(26, 15)
6	2		(27, 16)
7	-2	(28, 16)	
8	14		(29, 17)
9	10		(30, 18)

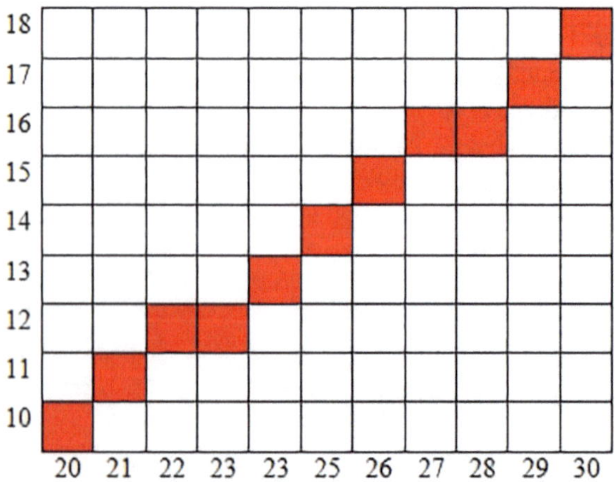

Figure 3.12: Rasterization of a line

Advantages of Bresenham's Line Drawing

- Algorithm is fast.
- Uses only integer calculations which are subtraction and multiplication.
- The points generated by this algorithm are more accurate than DDA Algorithm.

Disadvantages of Bresenham's Line Drawing

- It is meant only for basic line drawing.
- Resultant line may not be smooth.

Table 3.3: Comparisons between DDA and Bresenham's Line Algorithm

S. No.	*DDA Algorithm*	*Bresenham's Line Algorithm*
Arithmetic	It uses floating point, i.e., Real Arithmetic.	It uses fixed point, i.e., Integer Arithmetic.
Operations	It uses multiplication and division in its operation.	It uses only subtraction and addition operation.
Speed	It is slowly than Bresenham's Line Algorithm in line drawing because it uses real arithmetic (Floating Point operation).	It is faster than DDA Algorithm in line because it involves only addition & subtraction in its calculation and uses only integer arithmetic.
Accuracy & Efficiency	It is not accurate and efficient as Bresenham's Line Algorithm.	It is more accurate and efficient at DDA Algorithm.
Drawing	It can draw circles and curves but are not accurate as Bresenham's Line Algorithm.	It can draw circle and curves with more accuracy than DDA Algorithm.
Round off	DDA algorithm round off the coordinates to an integer that is nearest to the line.	Bresenham's algorithm does not round off but takes the incremental value in its operation.

3.5 SCAN CONVERSION OF CIRCLE

To draw a circle we need two things, the coordinates of the centre and the radius of the circle. The radius of a circle is the length of the line from the centre to any point on its edge and for any point on the circle (x, y) and the centre at point (x_c, y_c), the equation of the circle is

$$(x-x_c)^2+(y-y_c)^2-r^2=0$$

Here r is the radius of the circle. If the circle has an origin (0, 0) as its centre then the above equation can be reduced to

$$x^2 + y^2 = r^2$$

A circle is a geometric figure which is round and can be divided into 360 degrees. A circle is a symmetrical figure which follows 8-way symmetry.

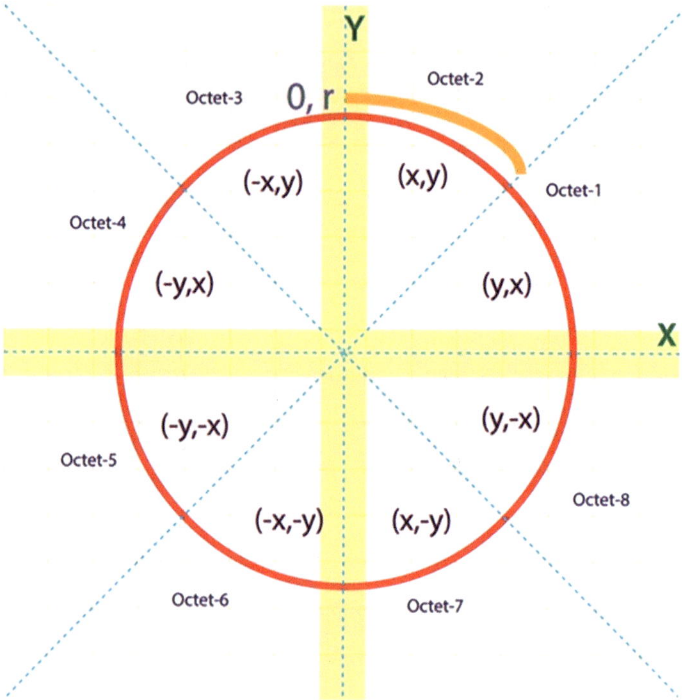

Figure 3.13: Symmetry for a circle generation

8-Way symmetry: Any circle follows 8-way symmetry. This means that for every point (x, y) 8 points can be plotted.

Plot $(y + x_c, x + y_c)$ octet-1
Plot $(x + x_c, y + y_c)$ octet-2
Plot $(-x + x_c, y + y_c)$ octet-3
Plot $(-y + x_c, x + y_c)$ octet-4
Plot $(-y + x_c, -x + y_c)$ octet-5
Plot $(-x + x_c, -y + y_c)$ octet-6
Plot $(x + x_c, -y + y_c)$ octet-7
Plot $(y + x_c, -x + y_c)$ octet-8

For any point $(x + a, y + b)$, points (x ± a, y ± b) and (y ± a, x ± b) also lie on the same circle. So it is sufficient to compute only 1/8 of a circle, and all the other points can be computed from it. If the centre is zero that is if $(x_c, y_c) = (0,0)$ then

(x, y) Octet-1
(y, x) Octet-2
(-y, x) Octet-3
(-x, y) Octet-4
(-x,-y) Octet-5
(-y,-x) Octet-6
(y,-x) Octet-7
(x,-y) Octet-8

There are the following two algorithms used to draw a circle Bresenham's Circle drawing Algorithm and Mid-point Circle Drawing Algorithm.

3.5.1 Mid-point Circle Drawing Algorithm

Principal: We have two pixels $U(x_{k+1}, y_k)$ and $L(x_{k+1}, y_{k-1})$. We need to select which of these pixels is close to the true circle and in this algorithm; we find the midpoint between the two pixels. The midpoint pixel M is given by $\left(x_{k+1}, y_k - \frac{1}{2}\right)$ that is the midpoint of the upper and lower pixel is M.

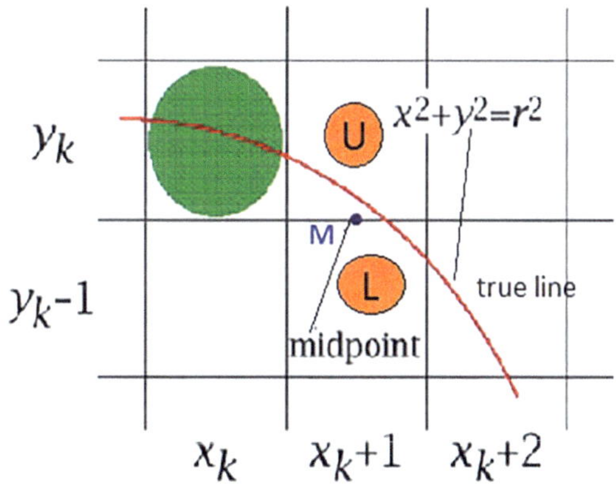

Figure 3.14: Midpoints Inside or Outside of a Circle

Now to select the next pixel, it depends on the midpoint pixel like.

Midpoint	*Plot*	*Condition*
On the circle	Plot U or L	=0
Outside the circle	Plot U	>0
Inside the circle	Plot L	<0

To apply the midpoint method, we define is circle function as

$$f_{circle}(x,y) = x^2 + y^2 - r^2$$

The equation evaluates as follows

$$f_{circle}(x,y) = \begin{cases} <0, \ if\,(x,y)\ is\,inside\,the\,circle\,boundary \\ =0, \ if\,(x,y)\ is\,on\,the\,circle\,boundary \\ >0, if\,(x,y)\ is\,outside\,the\,circle\,boundart \end{cases}$$

By evaluating this function at the midpoint between the candidate pixels we can make our decision

$$p_k = f_{circle}\left(x_{k+1}, y_k - \frac{1}{2}\right)$$

$$p_k = \left(x_{k+1}\right)^2 + \left(y_k - \frac{1}{2}\right)^2 - r^2$$

If p_k is negative, the midpoint is inside the circle, and we choose the pixel L. On the other hand if p_k, is positive the midpoint is outside the circle and we choose pixel U. The decision parameter for the next step is.

$$p_k + 1 = f_{circle}\left(x_{k+1} + 1, y_{k+1} - \frac{1}{2}\right)$$

since $x_{k+1} = x_k + 1$

$$= \left[\left(x_k + 1\right) + 1\right]^2 + \left(y_{k+1} - \frac{1}{2}\right)^2 - r^2$$

Or

$$p_k + 1 = p_k + 2\left(x_k + 1\right) + \left({y^2}_{k+1} - {y^2}_k\right) - \left(y_{k+1} - y_k\right) + 1$$

If pixel L is chosen (meaning $p_k < 0$) we have $y_k + 1 = y_k$ on the other hand and if pixel U is chosen (meaning $p_k \geq 0$), we have $y_k + 1 = y_k - 1$ so we have

$$p_k + 1 = \begin{cases} p_k + 2x_k + 3, & if\ p_k < 0 \\ p_k + 2\left(x_k - y_k\right) + 5, & if\ p_k > 0 \end{cases}$$

The initial value of the decision parameter p_k can be obtained by taking the value of $x_k = 0$ and $y_k = r$, so from $p_k = \left(x_k + 1\right)^2 + \left(y_k - \frac{1}{2}\right)^2 - r^2$.

$$p_k = \left(0 + 1\right)^2 + \left(r - \frac{1}{2}\right)^2 - r^2$$

$$= \left(1\right)^2 + \left(r - \frac{1}{2}\right)^2 - r^2$$

$$p_k = \frac{5}{4} - r$$

However, we can set the initial decision parameter $p_0 = 1 - r$ for integer computation.

Algorithm of Mid-Point Circle Drawing

Step 1. Input radius r of the circle and the first point on the circumference of a circle centred on the origin as $x_k = 0, y_k = r$

Step 2. Calculate the initial value of the decision parameter as $p_k = 1 - r$.

Step 3. setpixel (x_k, y_k)

Step 4. At each x position starting from the initial point perform the following test:

Step 4.1. *if* $p_k < 0$ then

$$x_{k+1} = x_k + 1$$
$$y_{k+1} = y_k$$
$$p_{k+1} = p_k + 2x_k + 3$$

Step 4.2. *if* $p_k > 0$ then

$$x_{k+1} = x_k + 1$$
$$y_{k+1} = y_k - 1$$
$$p_{k+1} = p_k + 2(x_k - y_k) + 5;$$

Step 5. Repeat step 4.1 to 4.2 until $x \leq y$.

Example 3.4

Consider an origin centered circle of radius 10. Determine the pixel that will be put ON for the first quadrant only.

Solution:

Initialization: x = 0, y = 10,
Plot (x, r) = (0, 10) = (x0, y0)
Po = 1 – r = 1 – 10 = –9
Plotting begins

Table 3.4: Solution for Example 4

Condition	*Next point*	*Next Decision Parameter*
$P_0 < 0$	$(x_1, y_1) = (1, 10)$	$P_1 = P_0 + 2x_0 + 3 = -9 + 2 * 0 + 3 = -6$
$P_1 < 0$	$(x_2, y_2) = (2, 10)$	$P_2 = P_1 + 2x_1 + 3 = -6 + 2 * 1 + 3 = -1$
$P_2 < 0$	$(x_3, y_3) = (3, 10)$	$P_3 = P_2 + 2x_2 + 3 = -1 + 2 * 2 + 3 = 6$
$P_3 > 0$	$(x_4, y_4) = (4, 9)$	$P_4 = P_3 + 2(x_3 - y_3) + 5 = 6 + 2(3 - 10) + 5 = -3$

Table 3.4: Solution for Example 4

Condition	Next point	Next Decision Parameter
$P_4 < 0$	$(x_5, y_5) = (5, 9)$	$P_5 = P_4 + 2x_4 + 3 = -3 + 2 * 4 + 3 = 8$
$P_5 > 0$	$(x_6, y_6) = (6, 8)$	$P_6 = P_5 + 2(x_5 - y_5) + 5 = 8 + 2(5 - 9) + 5 = 5$
$P_6 > 0$	$(x_7, y_7) = (7, 7)$	

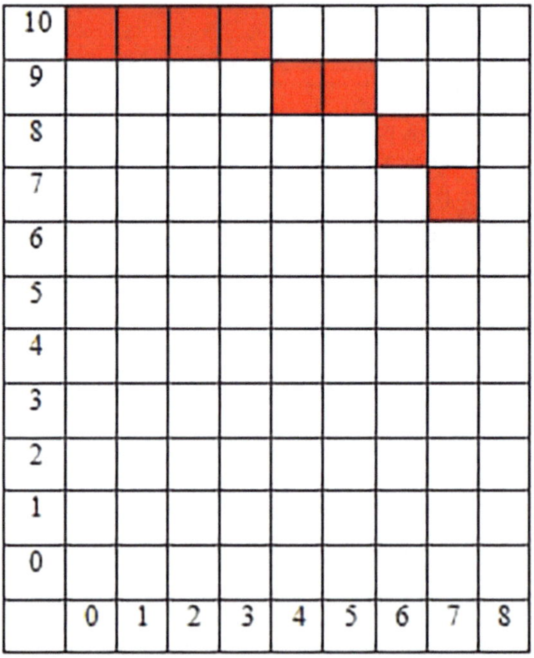

Figure 3.15: Rasterization of Circle

Advantages of Midpoint Circle Drawing Algorithm

- It is a powerful and efficient algorithm.
- The midpoint circle drawing algorithm is easy to implement.
- It is also an algorithm based on a simple circle equation ($x^2 + y^2 = r^2$).
- This algorithm helps to create curves on a raster display.

Disadvantages of Midpoint Circle Drawing Algorithm

- It is a time-consuming algorithm.
- Sometimes the points of the circle are not accurate

3.5.2 Bresenham's Circle Drawing Algorithm

The principal of Bresenham's Circle drawing Algorithm is "the best approximation of the true circle will be described by those pixels in the raster that falls the least distance from the true circle." We obtain the next pixel value using the decision variable and generate the circle with 8 symmetry properties. With this method, 1/8th of the circle is plotted from 90° to 45°. When the circle is drawn from 90° to 45° x moves in the positive direction and y moves in the negative direction.

The working of Bresenham's circle drawing algorithm is as follows: If the eight-way symmetry of a circle is used to generate a circle, points will have to be generated through 45° angles, and, if points are generated from 90° to 45°, moves will be made only in the +x and –y directions. If points are generated from 90° to 45° each new point closest to the true circle can be found by taking either of two actions:

- Move in the x direction one unit or
- Move in the positive x direction by one unit and in the negative y direction by one unit as well.

Assume that (x_k, y_k) are the coordinates of the last scan-converted pixel upon entering step i. Let the distance from the origin to pixel T squared minus the distance to the true circle squared, that is D (T) = $t^2 - r^2$. Let the distance from the origin to pixel S squared minus the distance to the true circle squared, that is D(S) = $s^2 - r^2$. Coordinates of T is (x_{k+1}, y_k) and S is (x_{k+1}, y_{k-1}).

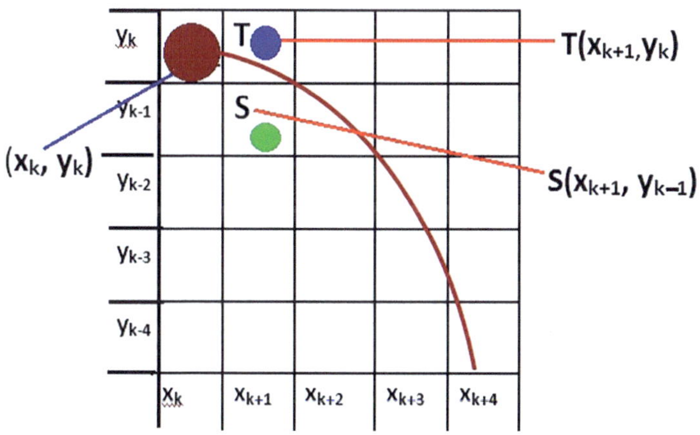

Figure 3.16: Point Inside or Outside of a Circle

Since D (T) is always +ve (T is outside the circle) and D(S) will always be –ve (S is inside the true circle), a decision variable p_k can be defined as:

$$p_k = D(T) - (-D(S)) = D(T) + D(S)$$

Where $D(T) = (x_{k\ 1})^2 + (y_k)\ - r^2$

$$D(S) = (x_{k+1})^2 + (y_{k-1})^2 - r^2$$

Therefore,

$$p_k = 2(x_{k+1})^2 + (y_k)^2 + (y_{k-1})^2 - 2r^2$$

When $p_k < 0$, we have | D (T) | < | D(S) | and pixel T is chosen and When $p_k > 0$, we have | D (T) | > | D(S) | and pixel S is selected. The decision variable for next step:

$$p_k + 1 = 2(x_{k+1} + 1)^2 + (y_{k+1})^2 + (y_{k+1} - 1)^2 - 2r^2$$

Hence,

$$p_{k+1} - p_k = (2x_{k+1} + 1)^2 + (y_{k+1})^2 + (y_{k+1} - 1)^2 - 2(x_{k+1})^2 + (y_k)^2 + (y_{k-1})^2$$

Since $x_{k+1} = x_k + 1$, we have

$$p_{k+1} = p_k + 4x_k + 2(y_{k+1}{}^2 - y_k{}^2) - 2(y_{k+1} - y_k) + 6$$

If T is chosen pixel (meaning that $p_k < 0$) then

$y_{k+1} = y_k$ and decision variable is

$$p_k + 1 = p_k + 4x_k + 6$$

If S is chosen (meaning that $p_k > 0$) then

$y_{k+1} = y_{k-1}$ and decision variable is

$$p_{k+1} = p_k + 4(x_k - y_k) + 10$$

Finally, we set (0, r) to the starting pixel coordinates and compute p_0 from the original definition of p_k:

$$x = 0,\ y = r$$

$$p_k = 2(x_{k+1})^2 + (y_k)^2 + (y_{k-1})^2 - 2r^2$$

$$p_k = 2(0 + 1)^2 + (r)^2 + (r - 1)^2 - 2r^2$$

$$p_k = 3 - 2r$$

Bresenham's Circle Drawing Algorithm

Step 1. First, we allot the starting coordinates (x1, y1) as follows:

$$x_k = 0$$

$$y_k = r$$

Step 2. Now, we calculate the initial decision parameter

$$p_0 = 3 - 2 \times r$$

Step 3. setpixel (x_k, y_k)

Step 4. : wile $(x_k \le y_k)$ //plot 8 points

putpixel $(y + x_c, x + y_c, 15)$

putpixel $(x + x_c, y + y_c, 15)$

$$putpixel\ (-x + x_c, y + y_c, 15)$$
$$putpixel\ (-y + x_c,\ x + y_c, 15)$$
$$putpixel\ (-y + x_c, -x + y_c, 15)$$
$$putpixel\ (-x + x_c, -y + y_c, 15)$$
$$putpixel\ (x + x_c, -y + y_c, 15)$$
$$putpixel\ (y + x_c, -x + y_c, 15)$$

Step 5. At each x_k, $k = 0$ perform the following test

Case 1 :If

$p_k < 0$

then

$x_{k+1} = x_{k+1}$

$y_{k+1} = y_k$

$p_{k+1} = p_k + 4x_k + 6$

Case 2 : If

$p_k > 0$

then

$x_{k+1} = x_k + 1$

$y_{k+1} = y_{k-1}$

$p_{k+1} = p_k + 4(x_k - y_k) + 10$

Step 6. Stop.

Example 3.5

Plot 6 points of a circle using Bresenham's Algorithm. When the radius of a circle is 10 units and a circle has a centre (20, 20).

Solution:

Let r = 10 (Given)

Step 1: Take the initial point (0, 10)

$p_0 = 3 - 2r$
$= 3 - 2 * 10$
$= -17$

$p_0 < 0$

$\therefore \quad p_1 = p_0 + 4x + 6$
$= -17 + 4\ (0) + 6$
$= -11$

Step 2: Plot (1, 10)

$$p_2 = p_1 + 4x + 6 \ (\because p_1 < 0)$$
$$= -11 + 4\,(1) + 6$$
$$= -1$$

Step 3: Plot (2, 10)

$$p_3 = p_2 + 4x + 6 \ (\because p_2 < 0)$$
$$= -1 + 4 \text{ x } 2 + 6$$
$$= 13$$

Step 4: Plot (3, 9)

$$p_3 > 0 \text{ so } x = x + 1, y = y - 1$$
$$p_4 = p_4 + 4\,(x - y) + 10 \ (\because p_3 > 0)$$
$$= 13 + 4\,(3 - 9) + 10$$
$$= 13 + 4\,(-6) + 10$$
$$= 23 - 24 = -1$$

Step 5: Plot (4, 9)

$$p_5 = p_4 + 4x + 6 \ (\because p_4 < 0)$$
$$= -1 + 4\,(4) + 6$$
$$= 21$$

Step 6: Plot (5, 8)

$$p_6 = p_5 + 4(x - y) + 10 \ (\because p_5 > 0)$$
$$= 21 + 4\,(5-8) + 10$$
$$= 21 - 12 + 10 = 19$$

So
P1 (0, 10)$\Rightarrow$(20, 30)
P2 (1, 10)$\Rightarrow$(21, 30)
P3 (2, 10)$\Rightarrow$(22, 30)
P4 (3, 9)$\Rightarrow$(23, 29)
P5 (4, 9)$\Rightarrow$(24, 29)
P6 (5, 8)$\Rightarrow$(25, 28)

Table 3.5: Solution of Example 5

k	p_k	(x_{k+1}, y_k)	(x_{k+1}, y_{k-1})	Setpixel (x, y)
0	-17			(0, 10)
1	-11	(1, 10)		(1, 10)
2	-1	(2, 10)		(2, 10)
3	13		(3, 9)	(3, 9)
4	-1	(4, 9)		(4, 9)
5	21		(5, 8)	(5, 8)
6	19		(6, 7)	(6, 7)

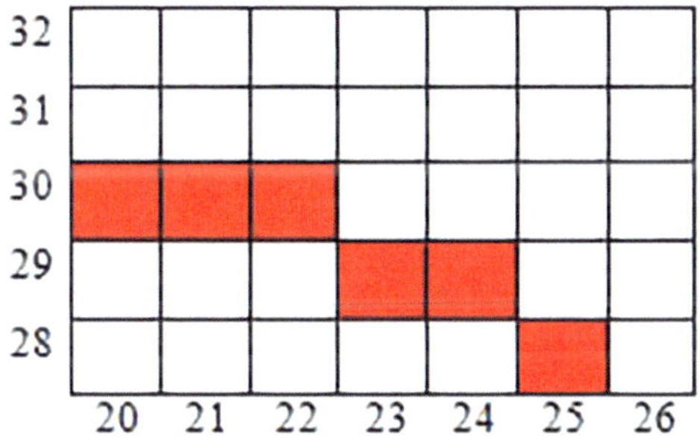

Figure 3.17: Rasterization of a circle

3.6 SCAN CONVERSION OF ELLIPSE

The ellipse is another important geometric entity. It is a symmetric entity with its major axis and minor axis. An origin-centered ellipse divided into 4 parts. This property of an ellipse (symmetric about its major axis and minor axis) can be used in the generation of an ellipse with minimum codes. Out of the four parts, only the first part is to be generated; the remaining three quarter parts are generated by using the symmetry of ellipse. Generation starts from point (0, R_y) where R_y is the semi-minor axis of the ellipse.

3.6.1 Midpoint Ellipse Generation Algorithm

Step 1. Take input radius along x axis and y axis and obtain center (x_c, y_c) of ellipse.

Step 2. Initially, we assume ellipse to be centered at origin and the first point as:

$$\left(x_1, y_1\right) = \left(0, R_y\right)$$

Step 3. Obtain the initial decision parameter for region 1 as:

$$p1 = R_y^2 - R_y.R_x^2 + \frac{1}{4}R_x^2$$

Step 4. For every x_k position in region 1 :

If $p1 < 0$ then the next point along the is $\left(x_{k+1}, y_k\right)$ and

$$p1_{k+1} = p1 + 2R_y^2\, x_{k+1} + R_y^2$$

Else, the next point is $\left(x_{k+1}, y_{k-1}\right)$ and

$$p1_{k+1} = p1 + 2R_y^2 x_{k+1} - 2R_x^2 y_{k+1} + R_y^2$$

Continue loop until $2R^2{}_y x \geq 2R^2{}_x y$

Step 5. Obtain the initial value in region 2 using the last point (x_1, y_1) of region 1 as:

$$p2 = R^2_y\left(x_1 + \frac{1}{2}\right)^2 + R^2_x(y_1 - 1)^2 - R^2_x R^2_y$$

Step 6. At each y_k in region 2 starting at $k = 0$ perform the following task. $p2 > 0$ the next point is (x_k, y_{k-1}) and

$$p2_{k+1} = p2 + 2R^2_x y_{k+1} + R^2_x$$

Else, the next point is (x_{k+1}, y_{k-1}) and

$$p2_{k+1} = p2 + 2R^2_y x_{k+1} - 2R^2_x y_{k+1} + R^2_x$$

Step 7. Now obtain the symmetric points in the three quadrants and plot the coordinate value as: $x = x + x_c$, $y = y + y_c$

Step 8. Repeat the steps for region 1 until $2R^2_y x \geq 2R^2_x$

Example 3.6

Generate an ellipse using Bresenham's midpoint algorithm with the center of the ellipse (15, 17) and $R_x = 9$ and $R_y = 7$.

Solution

Generation of part (1)

$x_c = 15, y_c = 17, R_c = 9$ and $R_y = 7$.

$p_1 = R^2_y - R_y.R^2_x = 49 - 81 \times 7 = -518$

Table 3.6 Solution for part (1)

P	x	$R^2_y.x$	$x + x_c$	Y	$R^2_x.y$	$y + y_c$	$(x_c + y_c)$
– 518	0	0	15	7	518	24	(15, 24)
371	1	49	16	7	518	24	(16, 24)
– 28	2	98	17	7	518	24	(17, 24)
413	3	147	18	7	518	24	(18, 24)
142	4	196	19	6	486	23	(19, 23)
131	5	245	20	5	405	22	(20, 22)
380	6	294	21	4	324	21	(21, 21)
	7	343	22	3	243	20	22, 20)

Generation of Part (2)

The starting point decision parameter is

$$p_2 = R^2_x - R_x.R^2_y = 81 - 9 \times 49 = -360$$

Table 3.7: Solution for part (2)

	x	$R^2_y . x$	$x + x_c$	Y	$R^2_x . y$	$y + y_c$	(x_c , y_c)
360	9	441	24	0	0	17	(24, 17)
360 + 81 (2 + 3) = 45	9	441	24	1	81	18	(24, 18)
45 + 81 × 7 + 49 × (–14) = – 74	8	392	23	2	162	19	(23, 19)
– 74 + 81 × 9 = 655	8	392	23	3	243	20	(23, 20)
655 + 81 × 11 + 49 × (– 12) = 958	7	343	22	4	324	21	(22, 21)
	6	**294**	21	5	**405**	22	(21, 22)

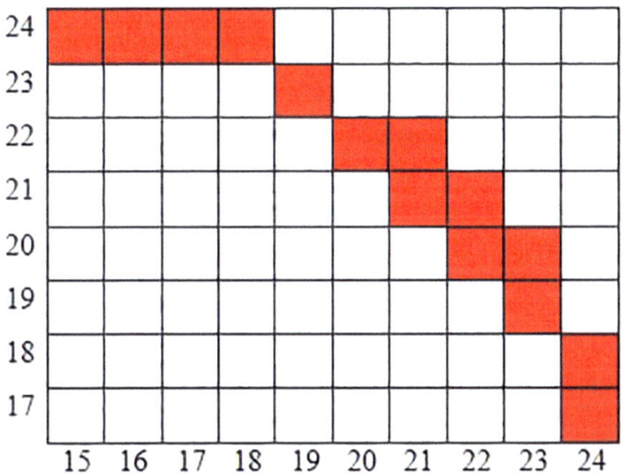

Figure 3.18: Rasterization of circle

OBJECTIVE QUESTIONS

1. If the slope of the line is less than 1, then Bresenham's line generation algorithm works on
   (a) Difference of distance between two successive horizontal points
   (b) Difference of distance between two successive vertical points
   (c) All of the above
   (d) None of the above

2. The process through which a vector image is converted into a bitmap image is called
   (a) Pixelization (b) Quantization
   (c) Rasterization (d) Ampling
3. If the slope of the line is positive and less than 1, then in Bresenham's line generation algorithm
   (a) Loop continues until loop counter ≤ |dy|
   (b) Loop continues until loop counter ≥ |dy|
   (c) Loop continues until loop counter ≤ |dx|
   (d) Loop continues until loop counter ≥ |dx|.
4. In Bresenham's midpoint circle generation,
   (a) Only 1/16th of circle is generated and remaining 15/16th by symmetry
   (b) Only 1/8th of circle is generated and remaining 7/8th by symmetry
   (c) Only 1/4th of circle is generated and remaining 3/4th by symmetry
   (d) Only 1/2th of circle is generated and remaining 1/2th by symmetry
5. Bresenham's circle generation algorithm works by checking the position of
   (a) Midpoint of two successive horizontal points
   (b) Midpoint of two successive vertical points
   (c) Midpoint of two successive diagonal points
   (d) All of the above
6. Which of the statements given below are correct? The midpoint (or Bresenham's) algorithm for rasterizing lines is optimized relative to DDA algorithm in that

   A. It avoids round-off operations.

   B. It is incremental.

   C. It uses only integer arithmetic.

   D. All straight lines can be displayed as straight (exact).

   Choose the correct answer from the options given below:
   (a) A and B only (b) A and C only
   (c) A, B, C, and D (d) A, B, and C only
7. The Liang-Barsky line clipping algorithm uses the parametric equation of a line from (x1, y1) to (x2, y2) along with its infinite extension which is given as :

$$\mathbf{x = x1 + \Delta x.u}$$
$$\mathbf{y = y1 + \Delta y.u}$$

   Where $\Delta x = x2 - x1$, $\Delta y = y2 - y1$, and u is the parameter with $0 < u < 1$. A line AB with end points A (–1, 7) and B (11, 1) is to be clipped against a rectangular window with Xmin = 1, Xmax = 9, Ymin = 2, and Ymax = 8.

The lower and upper bound values of the parameter u for the clipped line using Liang-Barsky algorithm is given as:

(a) (0, 2/3)
(b) (1/6 , 5/6)
(c) (0, 1/3)
(d) (0, 1)

8. Consider the Bresenham's circle generation algorithm for plotting a circle with centre (0, 0) and radius 'r' units in first quadrant. If the current point is (x1,y1) and decision parameter is pi then what will be the next point (xi+1,yi+1) and updated decision parameter pi+1 for pi ≥ 0

(a) xi+1 = xi + 1
yi+1 = yi
pi+1 = pi + 4xi + 6

(b) xi+1 = xi
yi+1 = yi - 1
pi+1 = pi + 4(xi - yi) + 6

(c) xi+1 = xi - 1
yi+1 = yi
pi+1 = pi + 4xi + 10

(d) xi+1 = xi + 1
yi+1 = yi - 1
pi+1 = pi + 4(xi - yi) + 10

9. Consider the Bresenham's line generation algorithm for a line with gradient greater than one, current point (xi, yi) and decision parameter, di. The next point to be plotted (xi+1, yi+1) and updated decision parameter, di+1, for di < 0 are given as.................

(a) xi+1 = xi
yi+1 = yi + 1
di+1 = di + 2 dx

(b) xi+1 = xi+1
yi+1 = yi
di+1 = di + 2 dy

(c) xi+1 = xi
yi+1 = yi + 1
di+1 = di + 2 (dx – dy)

(d) xi+1 = xi + 1
yi+1 = yi + 1
di+1 = di + 2 (dy – dx)

10. When using a Mid-Point Circle Drawing, If $p_k > 0$ then x, y are incremented that is $\left(x_{k-1}, y_{k-1}\right)$ and the decision parameter is given by

(a) $p_{k+1} = p_k + 2y_k + 3$
(b) $p_{k+1} = p_k + 2x_k + 3$
(c) $p_{k+1} = p_k + 2\left(x_k - y_k\right) + 5$
(d) $p_{k+1} = p_k + 2\left(y_k - x_k\right) + 5$

11. A line connecting the point (1, 1) and (5, 3) is to be drawn using the DDA algorithm. Find the value of X and Y increments.

(a) X-increment= 1;
y-increment =1

(b) X-increment= 0.5;
y-increment =1

(c) X-increment= 1;
y-increment =0.5

(d) None of the above

12. What will be the value of initial decision parameter, if we intend to draw a line between A (3, 6) and B (4, 9) using Bresenham's algorithm?

(a) 3
(b) 4
(c) 5
(d) 6

13. What is the rotation point in two dimensional if a point (2,-3) is rotated by 30 degree.
    (a) $(\sqrt{3}+2,1-2\sqrt{3})$
    (b) $(\sqrt{2}+2,1-2\sqrt{3})$
    (c) $(\sqrt{3}+2,1-3\sqrt{2})$
    (d) $(\sqrt{3}+2,1-2\sqrt{2})$
14. Why is the complexity of Bresenham's line drawing algorithm less than that of DDA line drawing algorithm?
    (a) It uses floating point operations over integer addition and subtraction
    (b) It considers only selected ranged inputs
    (c) It uses integer addition and subtraction over floating point operations
    (d) None of the above
15. In Bresenham's ellipse generation algorithm, 1/4th of ellipse is further divided into two parts on the basis of
    (a) Major axis and minor axis
    (b) Radius of ellipse
    (c) Center of ellipse
    (d) Slope of tangents

ANSWERS

1. (b)	4. (b)	7. (b)	10. (c)	13. (a)
2. (c)	5. (a)	8. (d)	11. (c)	14. (c)
3. (c)	6. (d)	9. (a)	12. (c)	15. (d)

EXERCISES

1. What are the criteria that should be satisfied by a good line drawing algorithm? Explain each.
2. What is Rasterization? Derive the equation for the intercept form of line.
3. What steps are required to plot a line whose slope is between 00 and 450 using the slope intercept equation?
4. What are the advantages and disadvantages of DDA line drawing algorithm?
5. Calculate value of pixels which is scan converted by DDA algorithm and endpoint of line is (4, 4) and (- 3, 0).
6. Consider a line from (0, 0) to (6, 7). Use DDA algorithm to rasterized this line.
7. Scan convert the line segment with end points (30, 20) and (15, 10) using DDA line drawing algorithm.
8. Scan convert the line segment with end points (30,20) and (15,10) using DDA line drawing algorithm

9. Write and explain Bresenham's algorithm for drawing a straight line. How does it remove the drawback of DDA algorithm? List the advantages of using Bresenham's line drawing algorithm.
10. Briefly explain Bresenham's line drawing algorithm with its advantages and disadvantages.
11. Why do you take unit steps along x-axis in Bresenham's line generation algorithm?
12. Write steps required to draw a line from point (x1, y1) to (x2, y2) using Bresenham's line drawing algorithm.
13. What steps are required to plot a line whose slope is between 00 and 450 using Bresenham's method?
14. Scan convert a line between the point (0, 2) and (4, 5) using Bresenham's approach.
15. Develop and write Bresenham's algorithm of line, also, predict the pixels on the line from (2, 2) to (12, 10) using this algorithm.
16. Illustrate the Bresenham's line generation algorithm by digitizing the line with end points (20, 10) and (30, 18).
17. Develop Bresenham's algorithm to generate a line segment with positive slope greater than one and use it to find the points need to be rasterized along the path of the line segment from (1, 2) to (3, 10).
18. Apply the Bresenham's algorithm to turn up pixels along the line segment determined by points (5, 7) and (12, 11).
19. Compare digital differential analyzer with Bresenham's line drawing algorithm.
20. Derive the Initial decision parameter of midpoint circle drawing algorithm; also write the midpoint circle drawing algorithm.
21. Explain the property of circle and calculate the pixel position along circle path with radius r =10 centered on the origin using midpoint circle algorithm up to x=y.
22. Use mid-point circle drawing algorithm to plot a circle whose radius =20 units and centre at (50, 30).
23. Write the midpoint circle drawing algorithm. Use midpoint circle drawing algorithm to plot a circle whose radius =20 units and center is (50, 30).
24. Find the points required to plot to draw the circle with center (2, 2) and radius 3 using Bresenham's circle drawing algorithm.
25. Find the points required to plot to draw the circle with center as (100, 90) and radius 10 using Bresenham's circle drawing algorithm.
26. How 8-way symmetry of circle can be used for writing circle drawing algorithms? Write the symmetric points if (x, y) is a point on the circle with centre at origin.
27. Explain Mid-point Ellipse algorithm with example.

4

Polygon Filling

A polygon is a closed two-dimensional object or figure that has three or more sides. The process of filling the object or image area with color is called region filling. A glyph can be a numeric, alphabetic font, or some other symbol that represents an encoded character. The characteristics of a glyph are always data-driven, such as size, color, and orientation. Anti-aliasing is a technique that deceives the eye by displaying a jagged edge as a smooth end. In the previous chapter, we discussed the method of scan-converting circles, lines, ellipses, arcs, and sectors. In this chapter, we will discuss the method of scan-converting polygons, as well as provide an overview of region filling and anti-aliasing.

4.1 INTRODUCTION OF POLYGON

A polygon can be defined as a shape that is formed by line segments that are placed end to end, creating a continuous closed path.

4.2 TYPES OF POLYGON

Computer graphics used three types of polygon which are convex, concave, and complex polygon. Some other polygons are also used in computer graphics such as unfilled polygons and filled polygons.

4.2.1 Convex

When a straight line connecting ANY two points that are inside the polygon cannot intersect any edges of the polygon are called convex polygon.

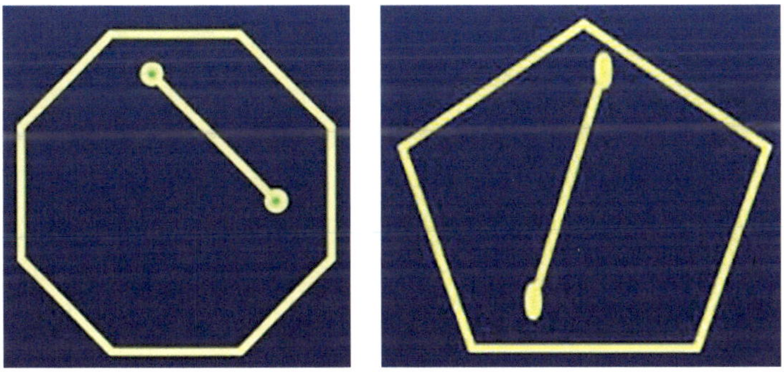

Figure 4.1: Convex Polygon

4.2.2 Concave

When straight lines connecting ANY two points that are inside the polygon intersect any edges of the polygon is called concave polygons.

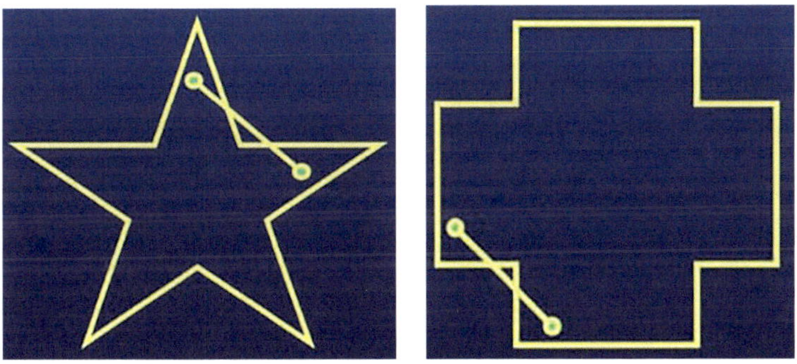

Figure 4.2: Concave Polygon

4.2.3 Complex

Complex polygons are basically concave polygons that may have self-intersecting edges.

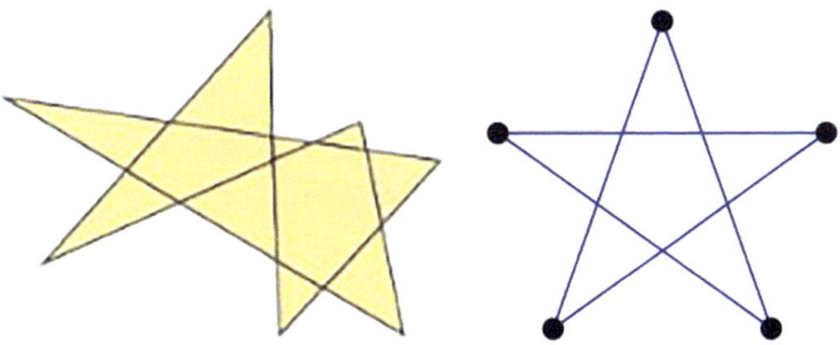

Figure 4.3: Complex Polygon

Some other polygons are unfilled polygons and Filled Polygons. When an unfilled polygon is rendered (constructed), only the points on the perimeter (edge) of the polygon are drawn, is an unfilled polygon and when a polygon is filled, the interior of the polygon must be considered. All of the pixels within the boundaries of the polygon must be set to the specified color or pattern, which is a filled polygon.

4.3 INSIDE-OUTSIDE TESTS

When filling polygons we should decide whether a particular point is interior or exterior to a polygon. Based on deciding whether a particular point is interior or exterior to a polygon can be even–odd method and the winding number method.

4.3.1 Even–Odd Method

Even-Odd method is also known as the "Crossing Number Method", construct a line segment that crosses the given polygon and then count the number of times a line crosses the polygon boundary. If the crossing number is odd then the line is inside the polygon, else outside.

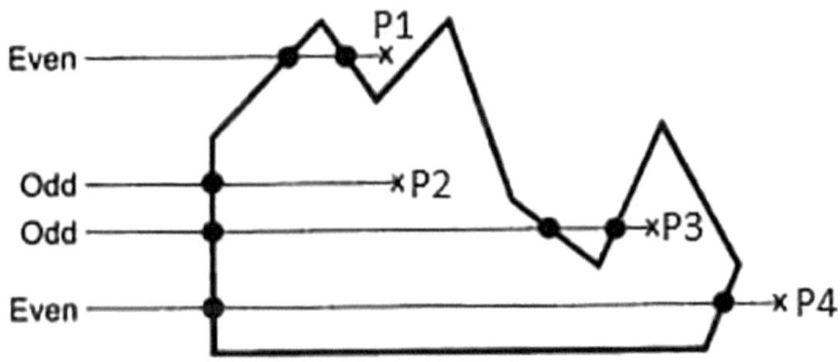

Figure 4.4: Even-Odd Method

Special Case

When a point of intersection is the vertex.

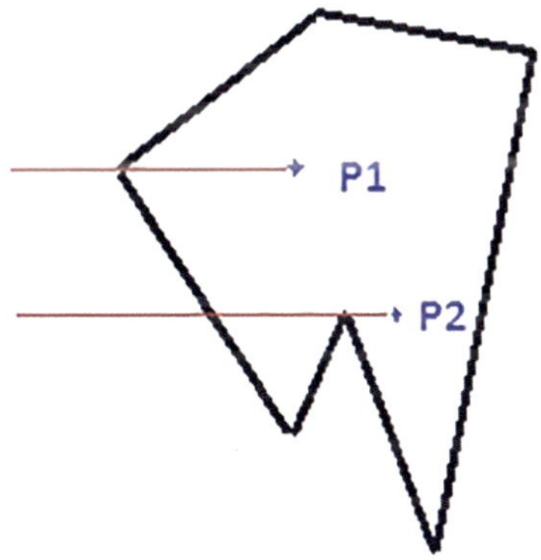

Figure 4.5: Special Cases in Even-Odd Method

Special Case Handling

Two cases:

- Case A: edges are monotonically increasing or decreasing
- Case B: edges reverse direction at the endpoint

In Case A, we should consider this as only ONE edge intersection, and in Case B, we should consider this as TWO edge intersections.

Figure 4.6: Special cases handling of Even-odd Method

4.3.2 Nonzero Winding Number Method

This method counts the number of times the polygon edges wind around a particular point in the counterclockwise direction. This count is called a winding number. In this, every point has a winding number, and the interior points of a two-dimensional object are defined to be those that have a nonzero value for the winding number.

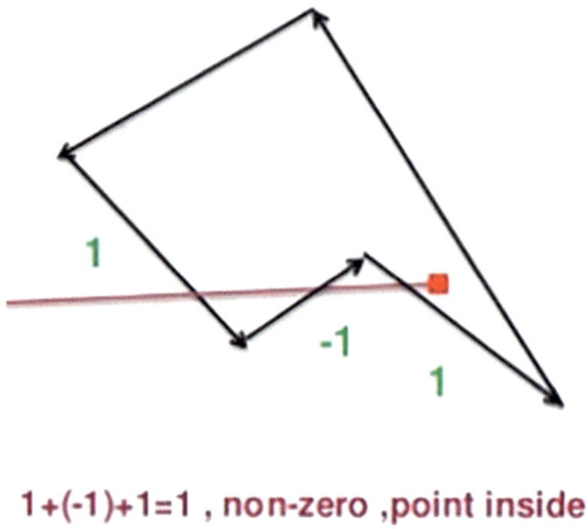

Figure 4.7: Non-Zero Winding Number Method

Rules

I. Initializing the winding number to 0.

II. Drawn a line for any position P to a distant point beyond the coordinate extents of the object.

III. We add 1 to the winding number if the edge crosses our line from bottom to top.

IV. We subtract 1 from winding number if edges cross our line from top to bottom.

V. If the edge crosses our line from left to right or right to left then no values are added.

VI. Count the number of edges that cross the line in each direction.

VII. If the sum of the winding number edges is nonzero, then P is defined to be an interior point.

VIII. Else P is taken to be an exterior point.

Example 4.1

Consider Figure 4.8, find whether the points P1 and P2 are inside or outside the polygon.

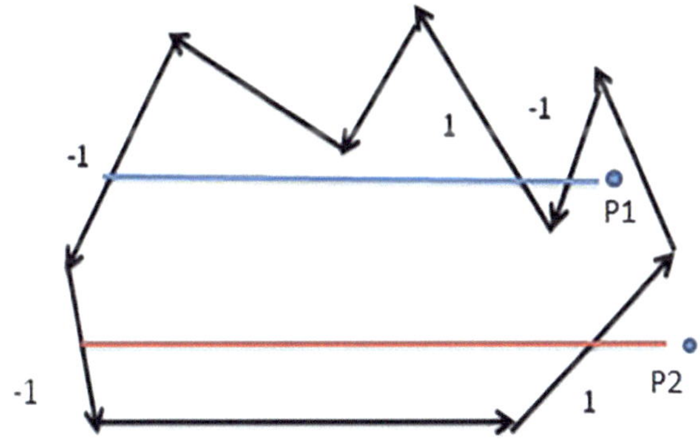

Figure 4.8: Polygon

Solution

For P1
W.N. =0-1+1-1=-1 so P1 is Nonzero so it is inside of the polygon.
For P2
W.N. =0-1+1=0 so P2 is zero so it is outside of the polygon.

4.4 POLYGON FILLING

Filling a polygon is the process of coloring every pixel that comes inside the polygon region. It fills or highlights all the pixels. There are two algorithms or methods used to fill the polygon one is seed fill method and another is scan line fill method. The seed fill method can further be divided into two parts boundary fill algorithm and flood fill algorithm.

4.4.1 Seed Fill Method

In this method, we will select a seed or starting point inside the boundary. We can further divide the seed fill into two parts.

4.4.1.1 Boundary Fill Techniques

It is used when we have to do interactive painting in computer graphics and the interior point can be selected easily. If we have a specified boundary in a single color, the fill algorithm proceeds pixel by pixel until the boundary color is encountered. To process the boundary fill techniques they used following steps.

- Start with any interior (called seed) pixel (x, y) and test neighboring pixels to determine if they are of boundary color or boundary pixel.
- If not, point the pixels with a fill color and test their neighboring pixels.

- This process continues until all pixels up to the boundary have been tested.
- There are two ways to process the next pixel. They are 4 connected and 8 connected.
- This algorithm uses the recursive method.

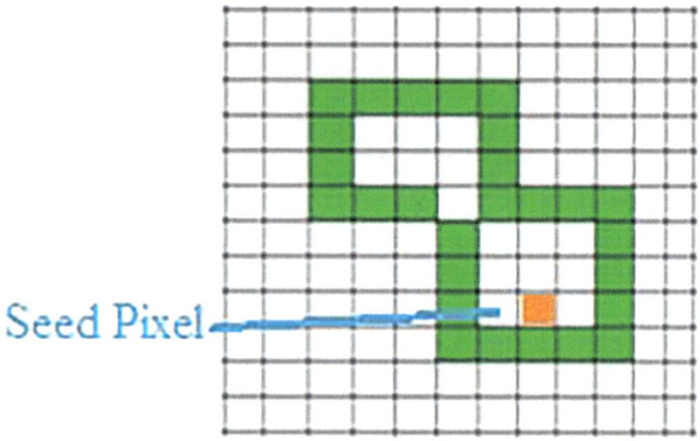

Figure 4.9: Boundary Fill Technique

Algorithm of Boundary-fill

Procedure boundary-fill (x, y, f-color, b-color: int)

Step 1. Initialize the boundary of the region.

Step 2. Get the interior pixel (x, y). Now, define an Integer called current pixel and assign it to (x, y).

int current = getpixel (x, y);

Step 3. If

(current pixel != b-color) and (current pixel != f-color)
Then
putpixel(x, y, f-color);
Boundary-fill (x +1, y, f-color, b-color);
Boundary-fill (x -1, y, f-color, b-color);
Boundary-fill (x, y +1, f-color, b-color);
Boundary-fill (x, y -1, f-color, b-color);

Step 4. End;

Note: Where f-color is fill color and b-color is a Boundary color. A getpixel () is a function used to fetch color of a pixel on the screen. A putpixel () is a function that gives color to a particular pixel.

The order of pixels that should be added to the stack using 4-connected is above, below, left, and right, and for 8-connected is above, below, left, right, above-left, above-right, below-left, and below-right.

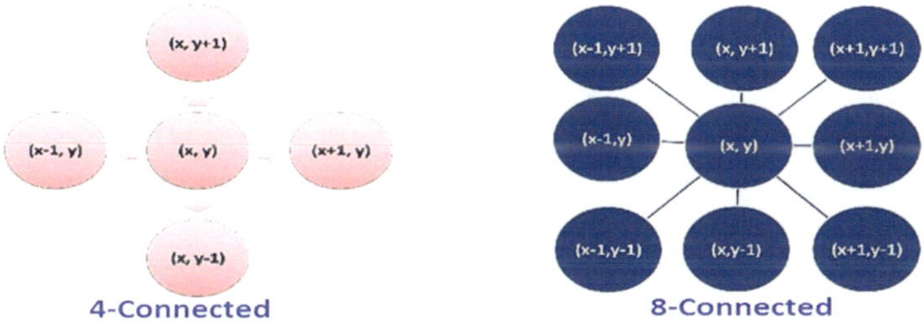

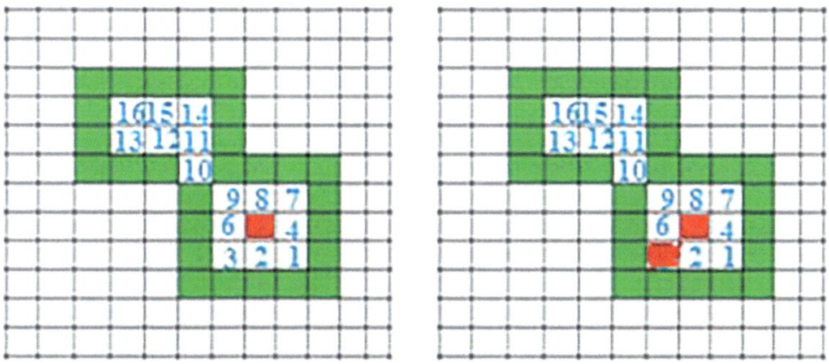

Figure 4.10: Process of Boundary fill with 8-connected

Problems with the Boundary Fill Algorithm

- If some pixel is already filled with fill color then the use of recessive call will be terminated.
- The 4-connected and 8-connected methods involve heavy recursion which can consume memory and time.
- In the 4-connected method, it does not fill corner pixels. Because it only checks the adjacent position of the pixel.

Advantages of Boundary Fill Algorithm

- This method is good for a polygon with a multicolor area and single-colored boundary.
- In this method, pixels may be visited more than once.

Disadvantages of Boundary Fill Algorithm

- It may not fill regions correctly if the same interior pixels are also displayed in fill color.
- In the 4-connected approach, there is a problem. Sometimes it does not fill the corner pixel as it checks only the adjacent position of the given pixel.

4.4.1.2 Flood Fill Techniques

It is used for filling a region with multiple boundary colors. It is used to fill the interior area of a polygon. It is used to fill an area where the boundary is not specified with a single color. We start from a specified interior point (x, y) and reassign all pixel values that are currently set to a given interior color with the desired fill color. If the area has more than one interior color, we can first reassign pixel values so that all interior pixels have the same color. Using either a 4-connected or 8-connected approach, we then step through pixel positions until all interior points have been repainted. In this algorithm, we match the color of a pixel with the background color of the object as given in Figure 4.11. We stop colors fill until we do not find a pixel where the color is not same as background color.

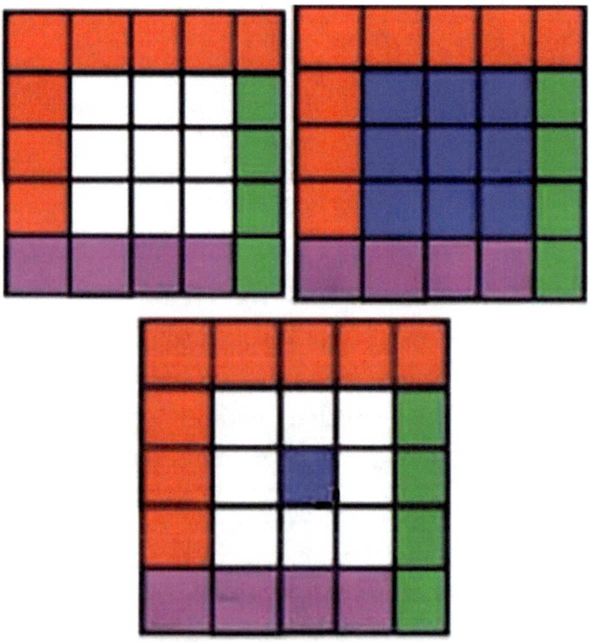

Figure 4.11: Flood Fill Technique

Algorithm of Flood-fill
Procedure flood_fill (x, y, old_color, new_color : Integer)
Var
Current: Integer
Current = getpixel (x, y)
If
(Current = old_color)
Then

```
Start
setpixel (x, y, new_color);
flood_fill (x, y +1, old_color, new_color );
flood_fill (x, y -1, old_color, new_color );
flood_fill (x +1, y, old_color, new_color );
flood_fill (x -1, y, old_color, new_color);
End;
```

Note: getpixel () defines the color of specified pixel and setpixel () set the pixel with the specified color.

Advantages of Flood-fill algorithm

- It provides an easy way to fill color in graphics.
- The Flood-fill algorithm colors the whole area through interconnected pixels by a single color.
- The algorithm fills the same color inside the boundary.

Disadvantages of Flood-fill Algorithm

- It is a more time-consuming algorithm.
- Sometimes it does not work on large polygons.
- Initial pixels required more knowledge about surrounding pixels.

Table 4.1: Differences between Boundary Fill and Flood Fill

S. No	*Boundary Fill Algorithm*	*Flood Fill Algorithm*
1.	An area filling is started inside a point within a boundary region and fill the region with specified color until it reaches the boundary.	Area filling is started from a point and it replaces old color with a new fill color.
2.	It is used in interactive packages where we can specify the region boundary easily.	It is used when we are unable to define the boundary and if there are many color boundaries in a region.
3.	Algorithm stops when the entire region is covered with a boundary in fill color.	Algorithm stopped when all old color pixel fill with new colors.
4.	It is less time consuming	It is more time consuming
5.	It searches for boundary colors.	It searches for old colors.
6.	Memory consumption is relatively low in Boundary-fill algorithm.	It requires huge amount of memory.
7.	It can only process the image containing single boundary color.	It can process the image containing more than one boundary color.

4.4.2 Scan Line Fill Method

It is used for solid color filling in polygon. For each scan line.

- Locate the intersection point of scan line with polygon edges (y-axis).
- Sort the intersection point from left to right.

Draw the interiors intersection point's pair, that is (a-b) (c-d). Fill the color within pairs, the pixels between the coordinates x and y. Intersection points are updated for each scan line. Stop when the scan line reaches y_{max}.

Example 4.2

Consider Figure 4.12 using scan line fill technique to fill the color of a polygon.

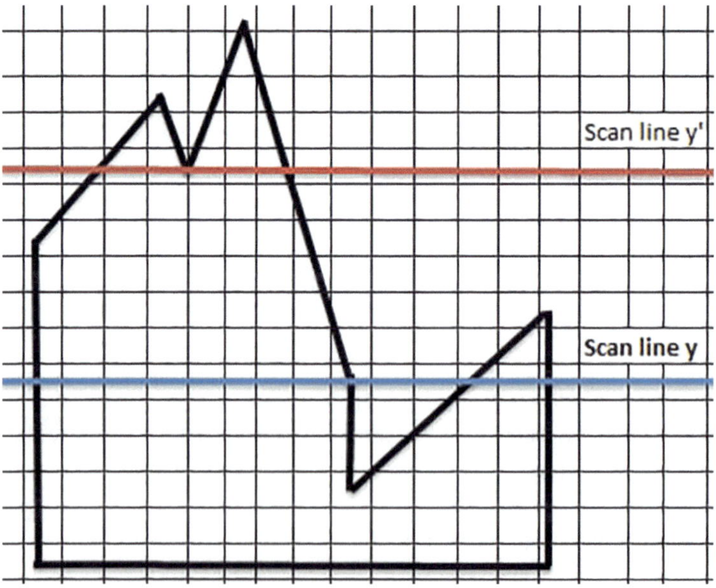

Figure 4.12: Scan Line Fill Techniques

Solution

Intersections for y′ are {(2, 12), (4, 12), (7, 12)} and

Intersections for y are {(1, 6), (9, 6), (12, 6), (14, 6)}.

Sort = {(2, 12), (4, 12), (7, 12)}, {(1, 6), (9, 6), (12, 6), (14, 6)}

Pair = {(2, 12), (4, 12)}, {(4, 12), (7, 12)}, {(1, 6), (9, 6)}, {(12, 6), (14, 6)}.

Then fill all the pixels between them with color. If we used blue color then

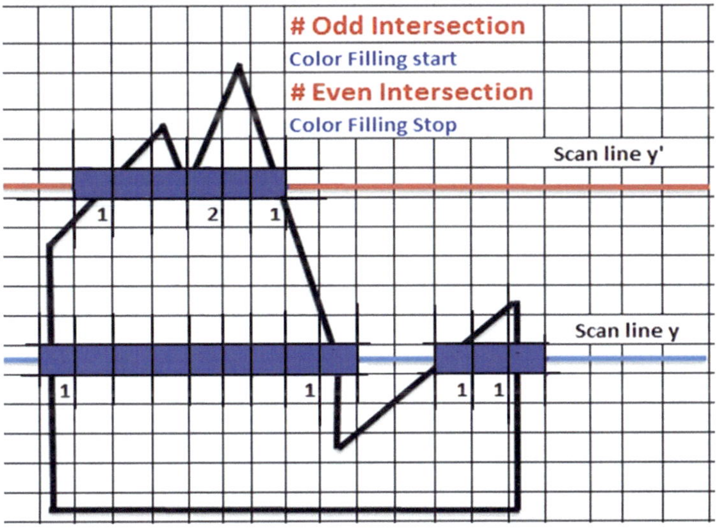

Figure 4.13: Process of Scan Line Fill Technique

Scan line intersections at polygon vertices require some special handling. If a scan line passing through a vertex intersects two polygon edges, then whether or not to count the vertices at that point twice is a problem. For example, consider Figure 3.14.

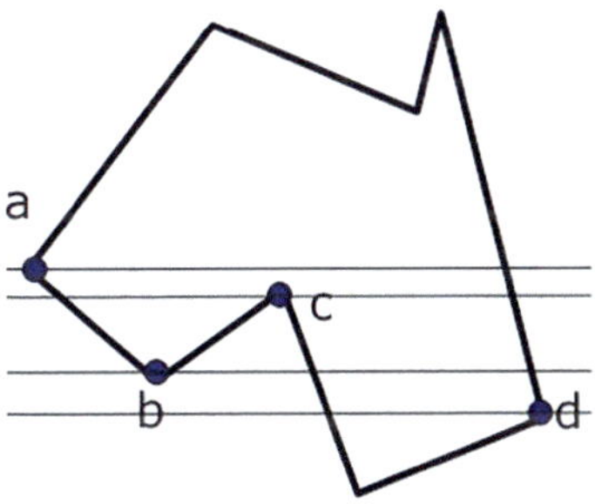

Figure 4.14: Vertex Intersects Two Polygon Edges

The vertex points a, b, c, and d is intersected by 2 line segments each. Count vertex point b, and c twice but vertex point a, and point d once. Why? When the scan line crosses the vertex (not edges) then makes a clockwise or counterclockwise traversal on edges. Check whether the direction of the edge is monotonically increasing or decreasing. If the direction of the edges changes, we have to double count the intersection point as given in Figure 4.15.

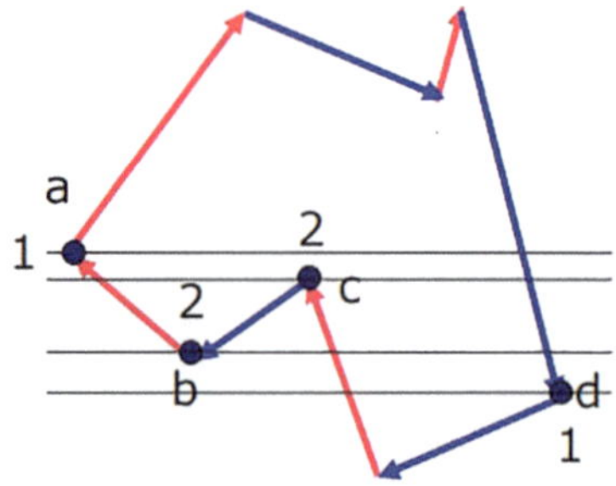

Figure 4.15: Process of Vertex Intersects Two Polygon Edges

Otherwise, there is a single intersection point with the scan lines that intersect the polygon vertices.

In the case of Figure 4.15, scan line y′ generates an even number of intersections that can be paired to correctly identify the interior pixel span. To identify the interior pixels for scan line y, we should count the vertex intersection as just one point.

4.5 ANTI-ALIASING

Anti-aliasing is a technique of reducing the aliasing i.e. elimination of jaggies or blocked patterns when we try to represent a high resolution image at a lower resolution. Aliasing is an effect due to which smooth curves are jagged across the edges because the resolution of the graphic is not high enough to represent the smooth curve. So, anti-aliasing is needed to reduce this effect.

- With anti-aliasing, curved lines can be made smooth again with the use of discoloration to the edges of the image.
- One solution to remove aliasing is to increase the resolution.
- Another solution is to add digital filtration to the image at high resolution. It is known as post-filtering. One another method is pre-filtering.

OBJECTIVE QUESTIONS

1. Anti-aliasing is important to improve the readability of text. It deals with the:
   (a) Spacing between two individual characters.
   (b) Spacing of a group of characters.
   (c) Elimination of "jaggies".
   (d) Spacing of a group of words

2. Which of the following algorithm aims to overcome the difficulties of the seed fill algorithm?
   (a) Scan line algorithm
   (b) Boundary fill algorithm
   (c) Flood fill algorithm
   (d) Line algorithm

3. Convex and Concave types of Polygon are classified on the basis of:
   (a) Where line segment joining any two points lies entirely within a polygon
   (b) Where the line segment joining any two points may not lie completely within the polygon.
   (c) Both (a) and (b)
   (d) Where the line segment joining any two points lies

4. Algorithm that fills interior defined region are called ___ algorithm, those that fill boundary defined region are called ___ algorithm.
   (a) Flood Fill, Boundary Fill
   (b) Flood Fill, Edge Fill
   (c) Boundary Fill, Edge Fill
   (d) Both (a) and (b)

5. The boundary is specified in a single color, and the algorithm proceeds pixel by pixel until the boundary color is encountered is known.
   (a) Scan-line fill algorithm
   (b) Boundary-fill algorithm
   (c) Entire fill algorithm
   (d) Slide curve algorithm

6. If we want to recolor an area that is not defined within a single color boundary is known as
   (a) Boundary-fill algorithm
   (b) Parallel curve algorithm
   (c) Flood-fill algorithm
   (d) (a) and (b)

7. Scan line algorithm for filling polygon is ______ algorithm.
   (a) Recursive
   (b) Non-recursive
   (c) (a) and (b)
   (d) None of these

8. Which approaches are used for determine whether a particular point is inside or outside of a polygon____________.
   (a) Even-odd method
   (b) Winding number method
   (c) Both (a) and (b)
   (d) None of these

9. Which of these is false for Boundary-fill algorithm?
   (a) Recursive algorithm
   (b) Begins with a starting point called seed
   (c) It checks for any pixel to be boundary color
   (d) Works only for rectangles and circles

10. The functions of the scan line polygon fill algorithm are:
   (a) Find the intersection point of the boundary of the polygon and scan line
   (b) Find the intersection point of the boundary of polygon and point

(c) (a) and (b) both
(d) None of these

11. Algorithms that fill the interior, that define regions are called ___.
(a) Boundary Fill algorithm (b) Flood Fill algorithm
(c) Scan line algorithm (d) Fill area algorithm

12. If the line connecting two interior points of the polygon lies completely inside the polygon, is said to be ___________.
(a) Convex (b) Pixel
(c) Concave (d) Bitmap

13. Which of the following is a not a attributes of output primitives
(a) Line Attributes (b) Area Fill Attributes
(c) Circle Levels Attributes (d) Character Attributes

14. Which of the following is also known as forest- fire fill algorithm because it spreads from a seed in all the directions?
(a) Boundary Fill (b) Flood Fill
(c) Scan Line Fill (d) Polygon Scan Line Fill

15. Consider the following statements with respect to approaches to fill area on raster system:
P: To determine the overlap intervals for scan lines that cross the area.
Q: To start from a given interior position and paint outward from this point until we encounter the specific boundary conditions.
Select the correct answer from the options given below:
(a) P only (b) Q only
(c) Both P and Q (d) Neither P nor Q

ANSWERS

1. (c)	4. (d)	7. (b)	10. (a)	13. (c)
2. (a)	5. (b)	8. (b)	11. (b)	14. (b)
3. (d)	6. (c)	9. (d)	12. (a)	15. (c)

EXERCISES

1. What is do you understand by polygon? Define convex and concave polygon.
2. Define Concave and Convex polygon with example. Also explain how to split concave polygon.
3. What is inside -outside test? List out the method for inside -outside test.
4. Describe the relevance and various methods of inside-outside test used in polygon filling.

5. Explain the non-zero winding number rule to identify interior regions of a polygon.
6. What are the steps required to fill a polygon using flood-fill or boundary fill?
7. Explain the boundary fill algorithm using 4-connected approach. What are the merits and demerits of Boundary fill algorithms
8. Write the boundary fill algorithm for filling a polygon using eight connected approach.
9. Compare and contrast boundary fill algorithm and flood fill algorithm.
10. Write the flood fill algorithm for filling a polygon, What are the merits and demerits of flood-fill algorithms
11. Write the scan line algorithm for filling a polygon.
12. Write procedure to fill polygon using Flood fill.
13. Write the Scan Line fill algorithm for filling a polygon, What are the merits and demerits of Scan line fill algorithms

5

Two Dimensional Transformations

Manipulating the orientation, size, or shape of an entity is often necessary in many practical applications. These changes are carried out using mathematical techniques called transformations. When applied to two-dimensional shapes like circles and triangles, they are referred to as 2D transformations. To carry out a 2D transformation, the coordinate values of the 2D object are represented in matrix form. This chapter discusses various transformations such as translation, scaling, reflection, and shearing that can be applied to 2D objects. For instance, translation transformation moves an object from one position to another in 2D space by multiplying the coordinate values with the corresponding transformation matrix. Scaling transformation is used to resize and reshape the object, while reflection transformation produces the mirror image of the object. Rotation transformation allows the object to be rotated clockwise or counterclockwise with respect to the origin. Shear transformation, on the other hand, is used to slant the image in the X and Y directions of the 2D space. The homogeneous transformation matrix is derived from the homogeneous coordinate system, which represents 2D objects as 3D objects by adding a non-zero third element. By multiplying the transformation matrices, the homogeneous transformation matrix can combine any two transformations. Linear transformations such as translation, scaling, reflection, rotation, and shearing are known as affine transformations.

5.1 INTRODUCTION 2D TRANSFORMATION

The process of changing of sizes, orientations or positions of objects by mathematical operation is called transformation. These changes are carrying out by geometric transformation and coordinate transformation methods.

Geometric Transformation

In which an object itself is transformed relative to the stationary coordinate system. In other word in this view point Object transformation takes place in a relatively stationary coordinate system or background.

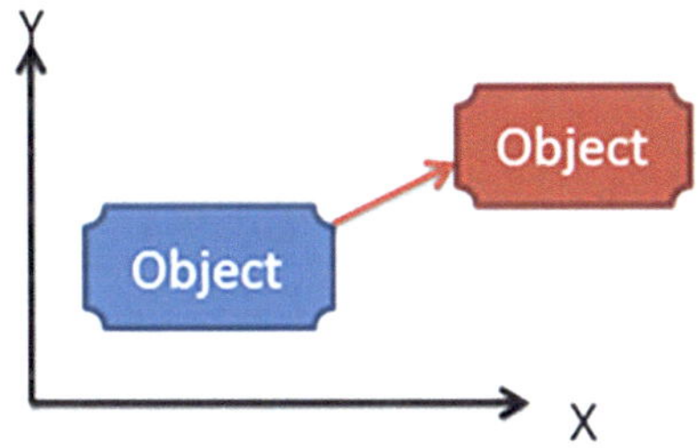

Figure 5.1: Geometric Transformation

Coordinate Transformation

In which an object is held stationary while a coordinate system is transformed relative to the object. In other word in this view point, coordinate system is transformed instead of object.

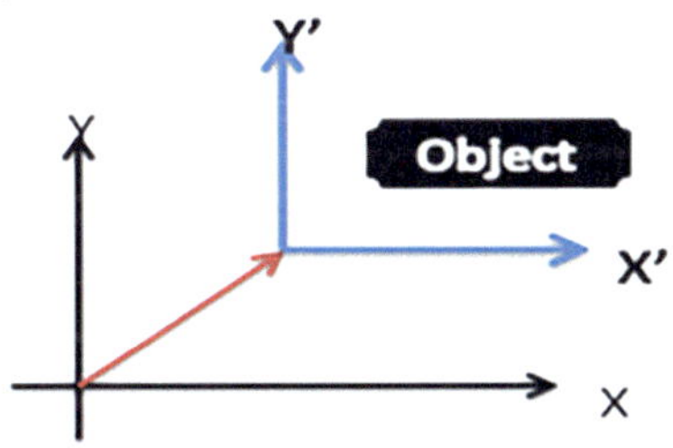

Figure 5.2: Coordinate Transformation

5.2 TYPE OF 2D GEOMETRIC TRANSFORMATION

Geometric transformations are two type's basic transformation and special transformation.

5.3 BASIC TRANSFORMATION

Basic transformation includes three transformations translation, rotation and scaling. These transformations are known as basic transformations because, with a combination of these three transformations, we can obtain any transformation.

5.3.1 Translation Transformation

2D Translation is a process of moving an object from one position to another in a two dimensional plane, that is, the repositioning of the coordinates of an object along a straight line path is called as translation. The translation transformation is done by adding translation distance t_x and t_y to the original coordinate position (x, y) to obtain new a position (x′, y′).

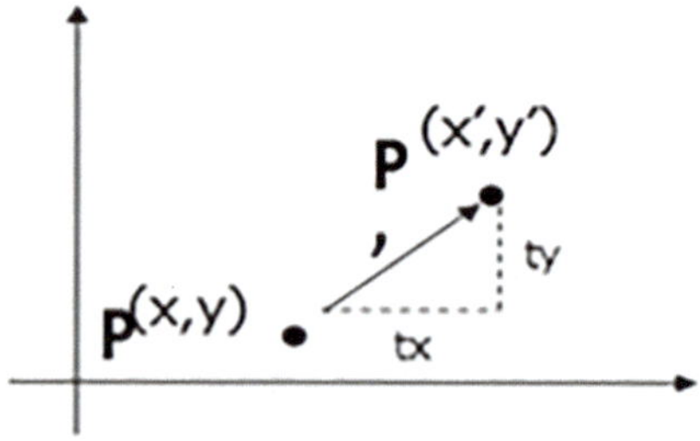

Figure 5.3: Translation Transformation

$$x' = x + t_x$$

$$y' = y + t_y$$

The pair (t_x t_y) is called as translation vector or shift vector. In the matrix form, it can be written as P′ = P + T

Where

$$P' = \begin{bmatrix} x' \\ y' \end{bmatrix}$$

$$P = \begin{bmatrix} x \\ y \end{bmatrix}$$

$$T = \begin{bmatrix} t_x \\ t_y \end{bmatrix}$$

Or in column major Matrix form

$$\begin{bmatrix} x' \\ y' \end{bmatrix} = \begin{bmatrix} x \\ y \end{bmatrix} + \begin{bmatrix} t_x \\ t_y \end{bmatrix}$$

Example 5.1

Translate a triangle with the coordinates (10, 20), (10, 10), and (20, 10) by 5 units in x direction and 10 units in y direction.

Solution: We compute as followings:

Give that $t_x = 5$ $t_y = 10$ and we know that

$$\begin{bmatrix} x' \\ y' \end{bmatrix} = \begin{bmatrix} 10 & 10 & 20 \\ 20 & 10 & 10 \end{bmatrix} + \begin{bmatrix} 5 \\ 10 \end{bmatrix}$$

$$\begin{bmatrix} x' \\ y' \end{bmatrix} = \begin{bmatrix} 15 & 15 & 25 \\ 30 & 20 & 20 \end{bmatrix}$$

The resultant coordinates of the triangle vertices are (15, 30), (15, 20), and (25, 20) respectively.

5.3.2 Scaling Transformation

It is defined as a process of changing the size and shape of an object in x and y directions. Scaling with respect to origin can be done by multiplying co-ordinate value (x, y) of each vertex of a polygon or each endpoint of a line by scaling factor s_x and s_y respectively to produce the new co-ordinate (x′, y′). Scaling means resizing the object, either to maximize or minimize the object. If s_x and s_y is between 0 and 1 the size of object will decrease. If s_x and s_y is greater than 1 the size of object will increase. If s_x and s_y are equal it is also called Uniform Scaling. If s_x and s_y are not equal then it is called Differential Scaling. Let P(x, y) is a point before scaling and P′ (x′, y′) is a point after scaling.

Then

$x' = x^* s_x$

$y' = y^* s_y$

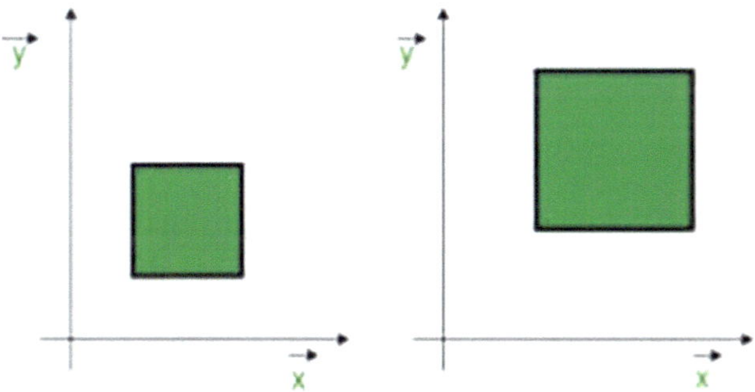

Figure 5.4: Scale Transformation

These equations can be represented in column vector matrix equation as:

$$P' = S \bullet P$$

$$\begin{bmatrix} x' \\ y' \end{bmatrix} = \begin{bmatrix} s_x & 0 \\ 0 & s_y \end{bmatrix} \cdot \begin{bmatrix} x \\ y \end{bmatrix}$$

Example 5.2

Scale a triangle with respect to the origin, with vertices at original coordinates (10, 20), (10, 10), (20, 10) by $s_x = 2$, $s_y = 1.5$.

Solution

Given A (10, 20), B (10, 10) and C (20, 10) and $s_x = 2$, $s_y = 1.5$ and we have

$$\begin{bmatrix} A1' & B1' & C1' \\ A2' & B2' & C2' \end{bmatrix} = \begin{bmatrix} s_x & 0 \\ 0 & s_y \end{bmatrix} \cdot \begin{bmatrix} A1 & B1 & C1 \\ A2 & B2 & C2 \end{bmatrix}$$

$$\begin{bmatrix} A1' & B1' & C1' \\ A2' & B2' & C2' \end{bmatrix} = \begin{bmatrix} 2 & 0 \\ 0 & 1.5 \end{bmatrix} \cdot \begin{bmatrix} 10 & 10 & 20 \\ 20 & 10 & 10 \end{bmatrix}$$

$$\begin{bmatrix} A1' & B1' & C1' \\ A2' & B2' & C2' \end{bmatrix} = \begin{bmatrix} 20 & 20 & 40 \\ 30 & 15 & 15 \end{bmatrix}$$

Therefore new coordinates values are (20, 30), (20, 15), and (40, 15)

5.3.3 Rotation Transformation

In the rotation, we need an angle θ to rotate the object about the origin. An angle may be clockwise or in an anticlockwise direction. Positive values for the rotation angle define counterclockwise rotations about the origin. Negative values rotate objects in the clock direction. To rotate an object we need rotation axis (the axis the shape will be rotated around), rotation direction (direction: clockwise or counterclockwise) and rotation angle (number of degrees the shape will be rotated).

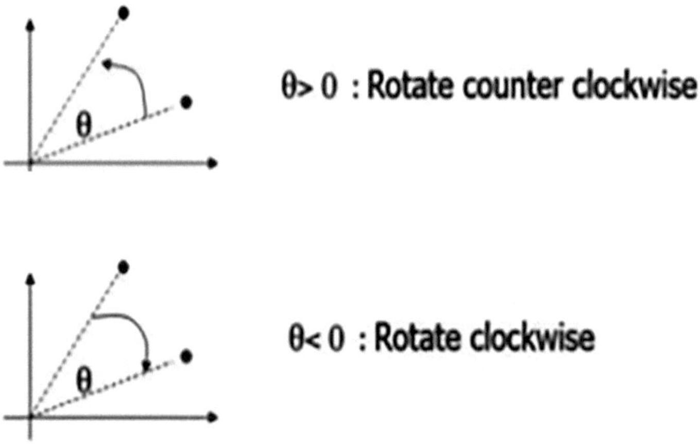

Figure 5.5: Direction of Rotation

Let co-ordinate before rotation of a point P is (x, y) and after counterclockwise rotation by amount of Ø is P′(x, y). If initially, P is at Ø angle form x axis then

$$\text{Cos } Ø = x/r$$

$$x = r \text{ Cos } Ø \quad (1)$$

Similarly

$$\text{Sin } Ø = y/r$$

$$y = r \sin Ø \quad (2)$$

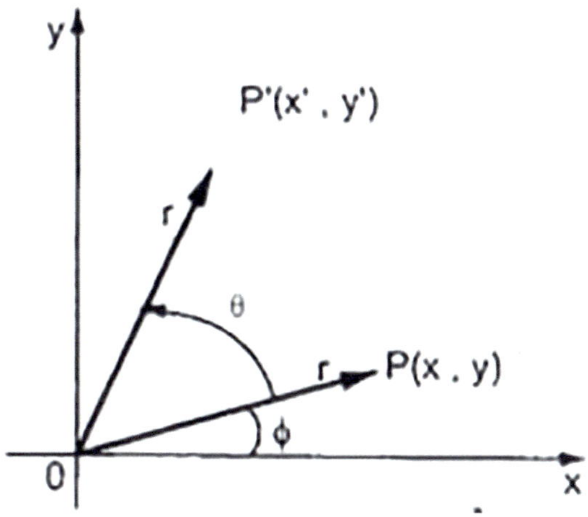

Figure 5.6: Rotation Transformation

After rotation the point from point p to p′ new angle formed is (Ø + θ) so

$$x' = r \cos (Ø + \theta)$$

We know

$$\cos(A + B) = \cos(A)\cos(B) - \sin(A)\sin(B)$$

$$\sin(A + B) = \sin(A)\cos(B) + \cos(A)\sin(B)$$

Therefore

$$x' = r \cos Ø \cos \theta - r \sin Ø \sin \theta$$

Using equation (1) and equation (2) then

$$x' = x \cos \theta - y \sin \theta$$

Similarly

$$y' = r \text{ Sin } (Ø + \theta)$$

$$y' = r \sin Ø \cos \theta + r \cos Ø \sin \theta$$

$$y' = y \cos \theta + x \sin \theta$$

Therefore the mathematical expression for rotation is

$$x' = x \cos \theta - y \sin \theta$$
$$y' = y \cos \theta + x \sin \theta$$

We can write it in the form of column major matrix equation as;

$$P' = R.\ P$$

$$\begin{bmatrix} x' \\ y' \end{bmatrix} = \begin{bmatrix} \cos\theta & -\sin\theta \\ \sin\theta & \cos\theta \end{bmatrix} \begin{bmatrix} x \\ y \end{bmatrix}$$

Example 5.3

Given a triangle with corner coordinates (0, 0), (6, 0) and (3, 3). Rotate the triangle by 90 degree anticlockwise direction about origin and find out the new coordinates.

Solution

Given A (0, 0), B (6, 0) and C (3, 3) and angle θ = 90 degree

We know that

$$\begin{bmatrix} A1' & B1' & C1' \\ A2' & B2' & C2' \end{bmatrix} = \begin{bmatrix} \cos 90 & -\sin 90 \\ \sin 90 & \cos 90 \end{bmatrix} \begin{bmatrix} 0 & 6 & 3 \\ 0 & 0 & 3 \end{bmatrix}$$

$$\begin{bmatrix} A1' & B1' & C1' \\ A2' & B2' & C2' \end{bmatrix} = \begin{bmatrix} 0 & -1 \\ 1 & 0 \end{bmatrix} \begin{bmatrix} 0 & 6 & 3 \\ 0 & 0 & 3 \end{bmatrix}$$

$$\begin{bmatrix} A1' & B1' & C1' \\ A2' & B2' & C2' \end{bmatrix} = \begin{bmatrix} 0 & 0 & -3 \\ 0 & 6 & 3 \end{bmatrix}$$

Therefore new coordinates values are A (0, 0), B (0, 6) and C (-3, 3)

5.4 HOMOGENEOUS COORDINATE SYSTEMS

It turns out that the transformation can be described in matrix form. The difference is the translation transformation, where you have to add the transformation matrix to the coordinates, while the other transformations (scale and rotation) must multiply them.

Translation $\begin{bmatrix} x' \\ y' \end{bmatrix} = \begin{bmatrix} x \\ y \end{bmatrix} + \begin{bmatrix} t_x \\ t_y \end{bmatrix}$

Rotation $\begin{bmatrix} x' \\ y' \end{bmatrix} = \begin{bmatrix} \cos\theta & -\sin\theta \\ \sin\theta & \cos\theta \end{bmatrix} \begin{bmatrix} x \\ y \end{bmatrix}$

Scaling $\begin{bmatrix} x' \\ y' \end{bmatrix} = \begin{bmatrix} s_x & 0 \\ 0 & s_y \end{bmatrix} \begin{bmatrix} x \\ y \end{bmatrix}$

Many graphics application involves sequence of geometric transformations. For example in design and picture construction application we perform Translation, Rotation, and scaling to fit the picture components into their proper positions. For efficient processing we will reformulate transformation sequences

For efficient utilization we must calculate all sequence of transformation in one step and for that reason we reformulate above equation to eliminate the matrix addition associated with translation matrix. To combine these three transformations into a single transformation, homogeneous coordinates are used. In homogeneous coordinate system, two-dimensional coordinate positions (x, y) are represented by triple-coordinates.

A point (x, y) can be reformulated in homogeneous coordinates as (*h, h,* h). The homogeneous parameter h is a nonzero value.

We can then write any point (x, y) as:

$$\begin{bmatrix} x' \\ y' \end{bmatrix} = \begin{bmatrix} xh \\ yh \\ h \end{bmatrix}$$

We can conveniently choose h = 1 so that (x, y) becomes:

$$\begin{bmatrix} x' \\ y' \end{bmatrix} = \begin{bmatrix} x \\ y \\ 1 \end{bmatrix}$$

Hence we can represent 2D in Homogeneous Coordinate Systems as

Translation $\begin{bmatrix} x' \\ y' \\ 1 \end{bmatrix} = \begin{bmatrix} 1 & 0 & t_x \\ 0 & 1 & t_y \\ 0 & 0 & 1 \end{bmatrix} \begin{bmatrix} x \\ y \\ 1 \end{bmatrix}$

Representation of translation transformation in row-wise matrix in homogeneous coordinate is

$$\begin{bmatrix} x' & y' & 1 \end{bmatrix} = \begin{bmatrix} x & y & 1 \end{bmatrix} \begin{bmatrix} 1 & 0 & 0 \\ 0 & 1 & 0 \\ t_x & t_y & 1 \end{bmatrix}$$

Rotation
$$\begin{bmatrix} x' \\ y' \\ 1 \end{bmatrix} = \begin{bmatrix} \cos\theta & -\sin\theta & 0 \\ \sin\theta & \cos\theta & 0 \\ 0 & 0 & 1 \end{bmatrix} \begin{bmatrix} x \\ y \\ 1 \end{bmatrix}$$

Representation of rotation transformation in row-wise matrix in homogeneous coordinate is

$$\begin{bmatrix} x' & y' & 1 \end{bmatrix} = \begin{bmatrix} x & y & 1 \end{bmatrix} \begin{bmatrix} \cos\theta & \sin\theta & 0 \\ -\sin\theta & \cos\theta & 0 \\ 0 & 0 & 1 \end{bmatrix}$$

Scaling
$$\begin{bmatrix} x' \\ y' \\ 1 \end{bmatrix} = \begin{bmatrix} s_x & 0 & 0 \\ 0 & s_y & 0 \\ 0 & 0 & 1 \end{bmatrix} \begin{bmatrix} x \\ y \\ 1 \end{bmatrix}$$

Representation of scaling transformation in row-wise matrix in homogeneous coordinate is

$$\begin{bmatrix} x' & y' & 1 \end{bmatrix} = \begin{bmatrix} x & y & 1 \end{bmatrix} \begin{bmatrix} s_x & 0 & 0 \\ 0 & s_y & 0 \\ 0 & 0 & 1 \end{bmatrix}$$

Example 5.4

Given a square with coordinate points A (0, 3), B (3, 3), C (3, 0), D (0, 0). Apply the translation with distance 1 towards X axis and 1 towards Y axis. Obtain the new coordinates of the square.

Solution

Given coordinate points of a square is A (0, 3), B (3, 3), C (3, 0), D (0, 0) and translation vector is 1 towards X axis and 1 towards Y axis. We known the representation of translation transformation matrix in homogeneous coordinate is

$$\begin{bmatrix} x' & y' & 1 \end{bmatrix} = \begin{bmatrix} x & y & 1 \end{bmatrix} \begin{bmatrix} 1 & 0 & 0 \\ 0 & 1 & 0 \\ t_x & t_y & 1 \end{bmatrix}$$

Or it may be written as

$$\begin{bmatrix} A1' & A2' & 1 \\ B1' & B2' & 1 \\ C1' & C2' & 1 \\ D1' & D2' & 1 \end{bmatrix} = \begin{bmatrix} A1 & A2 & 1 \\ B1 & B2 & 1 \\ C1 & C2 & 1 \\ D1 & D2 & 1 \end{bmatrix} \begin{bmatrix} 1 & 0 & 0 \\ 0 & 1 & 0 \\ t_x & t_y & 1 \end{bmatrix}$$

$$\begin{bmatrix} A1' & A2' & 1 \\ B1' & B2' & 1 \\ C1' & C2' & 1 \\ D1' & D2' & 1 \end{bmatrix} = \begin{bmatrix} 0 & 3 & 1 \\ 3 & 3 & 1 \\ 3 & 0 & 1 \\ 0 & 0 & 1 \end{bmatrix} \begin{bmatrix} 1 & 0 & 0 \\ 0 & 1 & 0 \\ 1 & 1 & 1 \end{bmatrix}$$

$$\begin{bmatrix} A1' & A2' & 1 \\ B1' & B2' & 1 \\ C1' & C2' & 1 \\ D1' & D2' & 1 \end{bmatrix} = \begin{bmatrix} 1 & 4 & 1 \\ 4 & 4 & 1 \\ 4 & 1 & 1 \\ 1 & 1 & 1 \end{bmatrix}$$

Thus, New coordinates of the square = A (1, 4), B (4, 4), C (4, 1), D (1, 1).

Example 5.5

Given a triangle with corner coordinates A (0, 0), B (1, 1) and C (5, 2). Rotate the triangle by 45 degree anticlockwise direction about the origin and find out the new coordinates.

Solution

We known the representation of rotation transformation matrix in homogeneous coordinate is

$$\begin{bmatrix} A1' & A2' & 1 \\ B1' & B2' & 1 \\ C1' & C2' & 1 \end{bmatrix} = \begin{bmatrix} A1 & A2 & 1 \\ B1 & B2 & 1 \\ C1 & C2 & 1 \end{bmatrix} \begin{bmatrix} \cos\theta & \sin\theta & 0 \\ -\sin\theta & \cos\theta & 0 \\ 0 & 0 & 1 \end{bmatrix}$$

We have 45 degree anticlockwise direction

$$\begin{bmatrix} A1' & A2' & 1 \\ B1' & B2' & 1 \\ C1' & C2' & 1 \end{bmatrix} = \begin{bmatrix} 0 & 0 & 1 \\ 1 & 1 & 1 \\ 5 & 2 & 1 \end{bmatrix} \begin{bmatrix} \cos 45^\circ & \sin 45^\circ & 0 \\ -\sin 45^\circ & \cos 45^\circ & 0 \\ 0 & 0 & 1 \end{bmatrix}$$

$$\begin{bmatrix} A1' & A2' & 1 \\ B1' & B2' & 1 \\ C1' & C2' & 1 \end{bmatrix} = \begin{bmatrix} 0 & 0 & 1 \\ 1 & 1 & 1 \\ 5 & 2 & 1 \end{bmatrix} \begin{bmatrix} \frac{\sqrt{2}}{2} & \frac{\sqrt{2}}{2} & 0 \\ -\frac{\sqrt{2}}{2} & \frac{\sqrt{2}}{2} & 0 \\ 0 & 0 & 1 \end{bmatrix}$$

$$\begin{bmatrix} A1' & A2' & 1 \\ B1' & B2' & 1 \\ C1' & C2' & 1 \end{bmatrix} = \begin{bmatrix} 0 & 0 & 0 \\ 0 & \sqrt{2} & 0 \\ \frac{3\sqrt{2}}{2} & \frac{7\sqrt{2}}{2} & 1 \end{bmatrix}$$

Thus, New coordinates of the triangle = A (0, 0), B $\left(0, \sqrt{2}\right)$, C $\left(\frac{3\sqrt{2}}{2}, \frac{7\sqrt{2}}{2}\right)$.

Example 5.6

Given a square object with coordinate points A (0, 3), B (3, 3), C (3, 0), D (0, 0). Apply the scaling parameter 2 towards X axis and 3 towards Y axis and obtain the new coordinates of the object.

Solution

We known the representation of scaling transformation matrix in homogeneous coordinate is

$$\begin{bmatrix} A1' & A2' & 1 \\ B1' & B2' & 1 \\ C1' & C2' & 1 \\ D1' & D2' & 1 \end{bmatrix} = \begin{bmatrix} 0 & 3 & 1 \\ 3 & 3 & 1 \\ 3 & 0 & 1 \\ 0 & 0 & 1 \end{bmatrix} \begin{bmatrix} s_x & 0 & 0 \\ 0 & s_y & 0 \\ 0 & 0 & 1 \end{bmatrix}$$

We have scaling parameter 2 towards X axis and 3 towards Y axis

$$\begin{bmatrix} A1' & A2' & 1 \\ B1' & B2' & 1 \\ C1' & C2' & 1 \\ D1' & D2' & 1 \end{bmatrix} = \begin{bmatrix} 0 & 3 & 1 \\ 3 & 3 & 1 \\ 3 & 0 & 1 \\ 0 & 0 & 1 \end{bmatrix} \begin{bmatrix} 2 & 0 & 0 \\ 0 & 3 & 0 \\ 0 & 0 & 1 \end{bmatrix}$$

$$\begin{bmatrix} A1' & A2' & 1 \\ B1' & B2' & 1 \\ C1' & C2' & 1 \\ D1' & D2' & 1 \end{bmatrix} = \begin{bmatrix} 0 & 9 & 1 \\ 6 & 9 & 1 \\ 6 & 0 & 1 \\ 0 & 0 & 1 \end{bmatrix}$$

Thus, New coordinates of the square = A (0, 9), B (6, 9), C (6, 0) and (0, 0).

5.5 SPECIAL TRANSFORMATION

Some package provides few additional transformations which are useful in certain applications. Two such transformations are reflection and shear.

5.5.1 Reflection Transformation

A reflection is a transformation that produces a mirror image of an object. The mirror image for a two dimensional reflection is generated relative to an axis of reflection by rotating the object 180° about the reflection axis. Reflection gives image based on position of axis of reflection. Some types of reflection transformation matrix are discussed here.

Reflection about the x-axis or Line Y = 0

This transformation keeps x values same but flips (changes the sign) y values of co-ordinate positions. We can represent the reflection along x-axis by following equation-

$$x' = x$$

$$y' = -y$$

We can also represent reflection in column major matrix form –

$$\begin{bmatrix} x' \\ y' \\ 1 \end{bmatrix} = \begin{bmatrix} 1 & 0 & 0 \\ 0 & -1 & 0 \\ 0 & 0 & 1 \end{bmatrix} \begin{bmatrix} x \\ y \\ 1 \end{bmatrix}$$

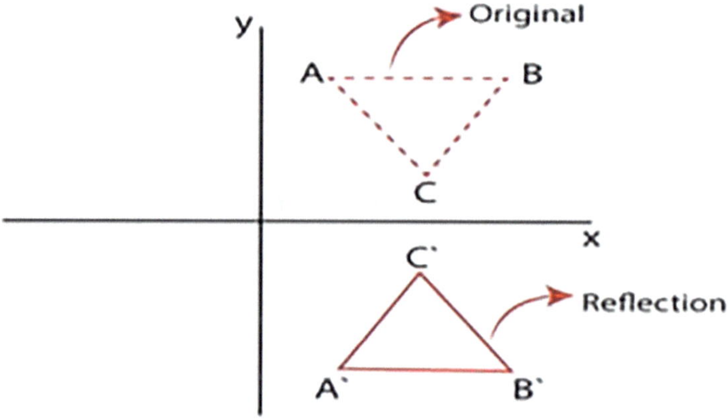

Figure 5.7: Reflection along with x-axis

Example 5.7

A triangle is given with the coordinates p (5 4), q (2 2), r (5 6) we need to reflect it along x-axis.

Solution

Given the coordinates of a triangle are p (5 4), q (2 2), r (5 6) we need to reflect it along x-axis. So

$$\begin{bmatrix} p1' & q1' & r1' \\ p2' & q2' & r2' \\ 1 & 1 & 1 \end{bmatrix} = \begin{bmatrix} 1 & 0 & 0 \\ 0 & -1 & 0 \\ 0 & 0 & 1 \end{bmatrix} \begin{bmatrix} p1 & q1 & r1 \\ p2 & q2 & r2 \\ 1 & 1 & 1 \end{bmatrix}$$

$$\begin{bmatrix} p1' & q1' & r1' \\ p2' & q2' & r2' \\ 1 & 1 & 1 \end{bmatrix} = \begin{bmatrix} 1 & 0 & 0 \\ 0 & -1 & 0 \\ 0 & 0 & 1 \end{bmatrix} \begin{bmatrix} 5 & 2 & 5 \\ 4 & 2 & 6 \\ 1 & 1 & 1 \end{bmatrix}$$

$$\begin{bmatrix} p1' & q1' & r1' \\ p2' & q2' & r2' \\ 1 & 1 & 1 \end{bmatrix} = \begin{bmatrix} 5 & 2 & 5 \\ -4 & -2 & -6 \\ 0 & 0 & 1 \end{bmatrix}$$

After reflecting the triangle about the x-axis point p, q, r becomes p′, q′, r′: p (5, 4) = p′(5, -4), q (2, 2) = q′(2, -2), and r (5, 6) = r′(5, - 6).

Reflection about the y-axis or Line X=0

This transformation keeps the y values same but flips (changes the sign) the x values of coordinate positions. We can represent the Reflection along y-axis by following equation.

$x' = -x$

$y' = y$

We can also represent Reflection in column major Matrix form –

$$\begin{bmatrix} x' \\ y' \\ 1 \end{bmatrix} = \begin{bmatrix} -1 & 0 & 0 \\ 0 & 1 & 0 \\ 0 & 0 & 1 \end{bmatrix} \begin{bmatrix} x \\ y \\ 1 \end{bmatrix}$$

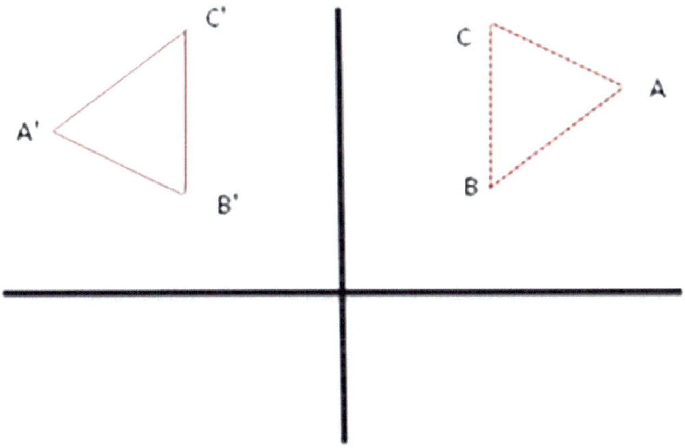

Figure 5.8: Reflection along with y-axis

Example 5.8

A triangle is given with the coordinates p (5 4), q (2 2), r (5 6) we need to reflect it along Y-axis.

Solution

Given the coordinates of a triangle are p (5 4), q (2 2), r (5 6) we need to reflect it along Y-axis. So

$$\begin{bmatrix} x' \\ y' \\ 1 \end{bmatrix} = \begin{bmatrix} 1 & 0 & 0 \\ 0 & -1 & 0 \\ 0 & 0 & 1 \end{bmatrix} \begin{bmatrix} x \\ y \\ 1 \end{bmatrix}$$

$$\begin{bmatrix} p1' & q1' & r1' \\ p2' & q2' & r2' \\ 1 & 1 & 1 \end{bmatrix} = \begin{bmatrix} -1 & 0 & 0 \\ 0 & 1 & 0 \\ 0 & 0 & 1 \end{bmatrix} \begin{bmatrix} p1 & q1 & r1 \\ p2 & q2 & r2 \\ 1 & 1 & 1 \end{bmatrix}$$

$$\begin{bmatrix} p1' & q1' & r1' \\ p2' & q2' & r2' \\ 1 & 1 & 1 \end{bmatrix} = \begin{bmatrix} -1 & 0 & 0 \\ 0 & 1 & 0 \\ 0 & 0 & 1 \end{bmatrix} \begin{bmatrix} 5 & 2 & 5 \\ 4 & 2 & 6 \\ 1 & 1 & 1 \end{bmatrix}$$

$$\begin{bmatrix} p1' & q1' & r1' \\ p2' & q2' & r2' \\ 1 & 1 & 1 \end{bmatrix} = \begin{bmatrix} -5 & -2 & -5 \\ 4 & 2 & 6 \\ 0 & 0 & 1 \end{bmatrix}$$

After reflecting the triangle about the Y-axis point p, q, r becomes p′, q′, r′: p (5, 4) = p′(-5, 4) , q (2, 2) = q′(-2, 2), and r (5, 6) = r′(-5, 6)

Reflection about an Axis Perpendicular to XY Plane and Passing through the Origin

This transformations interchanges x and y values of co-ordinate positions, that is, the value of both x and y is negative. We can represent the Reflection along y-axis by following equation-

$$x' = -x$$

$$y' = -y$$

We can also represent Reflection in column major Matrix form –

$$\begin{bmatrix} x' \\ y' \\ 1 \end{bmatrix} = \begin{bmatrix} -1 & 0 & 0 \\ 0 & -1 & 0 \\ 0 & 0 & 1 \end{bmatrix} \begin{bmatrix} x \\ y \\ 1 \end{bmatrix}$$

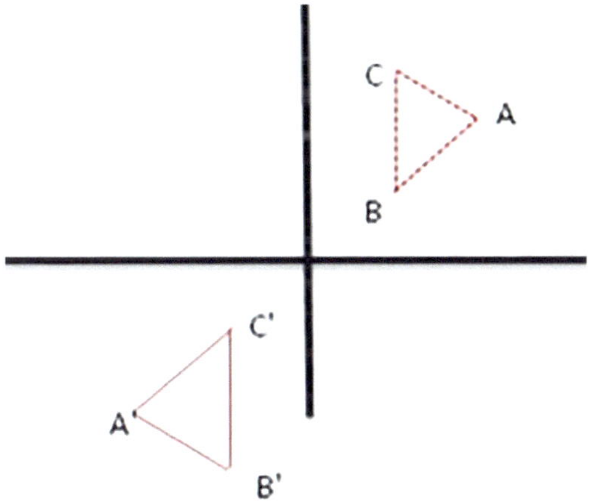

Figure 5.9: Reflection along with origin

Example 5.9

A triangle is given with the coordinates p (5 4), q (2 2), r (5 6) we need to reflect it along with origin.

Solution

Given the coordinates of a triangle are p (5 4), q (2 2), r (5 6) we need to reflect it along with origin. So

$$\begin{bmatrix} p1' & q1' & r1' \\ p2' & q2' & r2' \\ 1 & 1 & 1 \end{bmatrix} = \begin{bmatrix} -1 & 0 & 0 \\ 0 & -1 & 0 \\ 0 & 0 & 1 \end{bmatrix} \begin{bmatrix} p1 & q1 & r1 \\ p2 & q2 & r2 \\ 1 & 1 & 1 \end{bmatrix}$$

$$\begin{bmatrix} p1' & q1' & r1' \\ p2' & q2' & r2' \\ 1 & 1 & 1 \end{bmatrix} = \begin{bmatrix} -1 & 0 & 0 \\ 0 & -1 & 0 \\ 0 & 0 & 1 \end{bmatrix} \begin{bmatrix} 5 & 2 & 5 \\ 4 & 2 & 6 \\ 1 & 1 & 1 \end{bmatrix}$$

$$\begin{bmatrix} p1' & q1' & r1' \\ p2' & q2' & r2' \\ 1 & 1 & 1 \end{bmatrix} = \begin{bmatrix} -5 & -2 & -5 \\ -4 & -2 & -6 \\ 0 & 0 & 1 \end{bmatrix}$$

After reflecting the triangle about the origin point p, q, r becomes p′, q′, r′: p (5, 4) = p′(-5, -4), q (2, 2) = q′(-2, -2), and r (5, 6) = r′(-5, - 6).

Reflection about line Y = X

This transformation interchanges x and y values of the co-ordinate positions. When you reflect a point across the line y = x, the x-coordinate and y-coordinate change places. We can represent the Reflection along y-axis by following equation-

$$x' = y$$

$$y' = x$$

We can also represent Reflection in column major Matrix form –

$$\begin{bmatrix} x' \\ y' \\ 1 \end{bmatrix} = \begin{bmatrix} 0 & 1 & 0 \\ 1 & 0 & 0 \\ 0 & 0 & 1 \end{bmatrix} \begin{bmatrix} x \\ y \\ 1 \end{bmatrix}$$

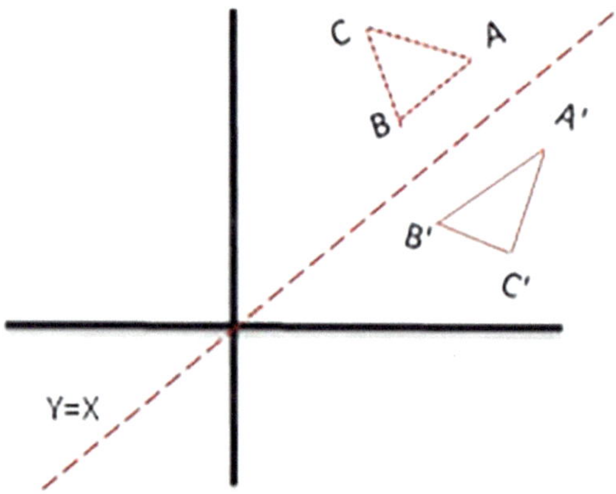

Figure 5.10: Reflection about straight line y = x

Example 5.10

A triangle is given with the coordinates p (5 4), q (2 2), r (5 6) we need to reflect it about straight line y = x.

Solution

Given the coordinates of a triangle are p (5 4), q (2 2), r (5 6) we need to reflect it about straight line y = x. So

$$\begin{bmatrix} p1' & q1' & r1' \\ p2' & q2' & r2' \\ 1 & 1 & 1 \end{bmatrix} = \begin{bmatrix} 0 & 1 & 0 \\ 1 & 0 & 0 \\ 0 & 0 & 1 \end{bmatrix} \begin{bmatrix} p1 & q1 & r1 \\ p2 & q2 & r2 \\ 1 & 1 & 1 \end{bmatrix}$$

$$\begin{bmatrix} p1' & q1' & r1' \\ p2' & q2' & r2' \\ 1 & 1 & 1 \end{bmatrix} = \begin{bmatrix} 0 & 1 & 0 \\ 1 & 0 & 0 \\ 0 & 0 & 1 \end{bmatrix} \begin{bmatrix} 5 & 2 & 5 \\ 4 & 2 & 6 \\ 1 & 1 & 1 \end{bmatrix}$$

$$\begin{bmatrix} p1' & q1' & r1' \\ p2' & q2' & r2' \\ 1 & 1 & 1 \end{bmatrix} = \begin{bmatrix} 4 & 2 & 6 \\ 5 & 2 & 5 \\ 0 & 0 & 1 \end{bmatrix}$$

After reflecting the triangle about the straight line y = x, point p, q, r becomes p′, q′, r′: p (5, 4) = p′(4, 5), q (2, 2) = q′(2, 2), and r (5, 6) = r′(6, 5).

Reflection about line Y = -X

If you reflect over the line y = -x, the x-coordinate and y-coordinate change places and are negated (the signs are changed). We can represent the Reflection along y-axis by following equation-

$$x' = -y$$
$$y' = -x$$

We can also represent Reflection in column major above Matrix form –

$$\begin{bmatrix} x' \\ y' \\ 1 \end{bmatrix} = \begin{bmatrix} 0 & -1 & 0 \\ -1 & 0 & 0 \\ 0 & 0 & 1 \end{bmatrix} \begin{bmatrix} x \\ y \\ 1 \end{bmatrix}$$

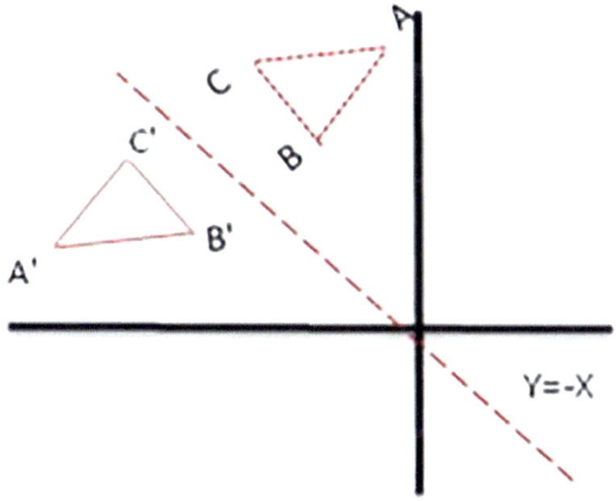

Figure 5.11: Reflection about straight line y = - x

Example 5.11

A triangle is given with the coordinates p (5 4), q (2 2), r (5 6) we need to reflect it about straight line y = - x.

Solution

Given the coordinates of a triangle are p (5 4), q (2 2), r (5 6) we need to reflect it about straight line y = - x. So

$$\begin{bmatrix} p1' & q1' & r1' \\ p2' & q2' & r2' \\ 1 & 1 & 1 \end{bmatrix} = \begin{bmatrix} 0 & -1 & 0 \\ -1 & 0 & 0 \\ 0 & 0 & 1 \end{bmatrix} \begin{bmatrix} p1 & q1 & r1 \\ p2 & q2 & r2 \\ 1 & 1 & 1 \end{bmatrix}$$

$$\begin{bmatrix} p1' & q1' & r1' \\ p2' & q2' & r2' \\ 1 & 1 & 1 \end{bmatrix} = \begin{bmatrix} 0 & -1 & 0 \\ -1 & 0 & 0 \\ 0 & 0 & 1 \end{bmatrix} \begin{bmatrix} 5 & 2 & 5 \\ 4 & 2 & 6 \\ 1 & 1 & 1 \end{bmatrix}$$

$$\begin{bmatrix} p1' & q1' & r1' \\ p2' & q2' & r2' \\ 1 & 1 & 1 \end{bmatrix} = \begin{bmatrix} -4 & -2 & -6 \\ -5 & -2 & -5 \\ 0 & 0 & 1 \end{bmatrix}$$

After reflecting the triangle about the straight line y = - x, point p, q, r becomes p′, q′, r′: p (5, 4) = p′(-4, -5), q (2, 2) = q′(-2, -2), and r (5, 6) = r′(-6, - 6).

5.5.2 Shear Transformation

A Transformation that slants (Distorting or changing) the shape of an object is called the shear transformation. Two common shearing transformations are used. One shifts the x coordinate values and other shift the y coordinate values. However in both the cases only one coordinate (x or y) changes its coordinate and other preserves its value.

Shearing in X Direction

The x shear preserves the y coordinates, but changes the x values which cause vertical lines to tilt (bend) right or left. If sh_x is shearing factor then the expression is

$$x' = x + sh_x \cdot y$$
$$y' = y$$

The Transformations matrix for x-shear is

$$\begin{bmatrix} x' \\ y' \\ 1 \end{bmatrix} = \begin{bmatrix} 1 & sh_x & 0 \\ 0 & 1 & 0 \\ 0 & 0 & 1 \end{bmatrix} \begin{bmatrix} x \\ y \\ 1 \end{bmatrix}$$

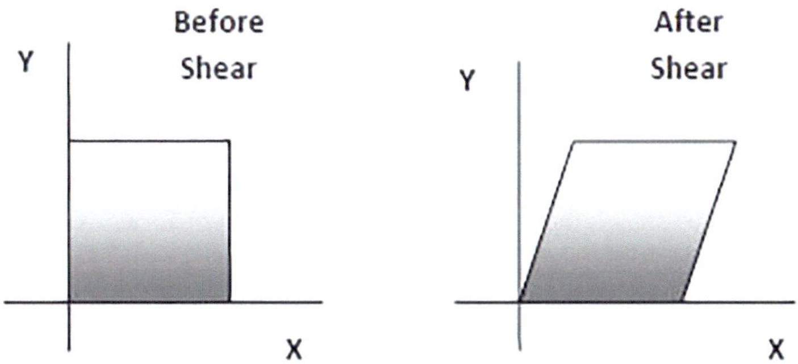

Figure 5.12: Shearing in X direction

Example 5.12

Given a triangle with points (1, 1), (0, 0) and (1, 0). Find out the new coordinates of the object along x-axis, if shearing parameter along x-axis is 4.

Solution Given points of a triangle is A (1, 1), B (0, 0) and C (1, 0) and shearing parameter along x-axis $sh_x = 4$.

$$\begin{bmatrix} A1' & B1' & C1' \\ A2' & B2' & C2' \\ 1 & 1 & 1 \end{bmatrix} = \begin{bmatrix} 1 & sh_x & 0 \\ 0 & 1 & 0 \\ 0 & 0 & 1 \end{bmatrix} \begin{bmatrix} 1 & 0 & 1 \\ 1 & 0 & 0 \\ 1 & 1 & 1 \end{bmatrix}$$

$$\begin{bmatrix} A1' & B1' & C1' \\ A2' & B2' & C2' \\ 1 & 1 & 1 \end{bmatrix} = \begin{bmatrix} 1 & 4 & 0 \\ 0 & 1 & 0 \\ 0 & 0 & 1 \end{bmatrix} \begin{bmatrix} 1 & 0 & 1 \\ 1 & 0 & 0 \\ 1 & 1 & 1 \end{bmatrix}$$

$$\begin{bmatrix} A1' & B1' & C1' \\ A2' & B2' & C2' \\ 1 & 1 & 1 \end{bmatrix} = \begin{bmatrix} 5 & 0 & 1 \\ 1 & 0 & 0 \\ 1 & 1 & 1 \end{bmatrix}$$

Therefore new coordinates values are A (5, 1), B (0, 0) and C (4, 0)

Shearing in Y Direction

The y shear preserves the x coordinates, but changes the y values which cause horizontal lines which slope up or down. If sh_y is shearing factor then the expression is

$$x' = x$$
$$y' = sh_y \; . x + y$$

The Transformations matrix for y-shear is

$$\begin{bmatrix} x' \\ y' \\ 1 \end{bmatrix} = \begin{bmatrix} 1 & 0 & 0 \\ sh_y & 1 & 0 \\ 0 & 0 & 1 \end{bmatrix} \begin{bmatrix} x \\ y \\ 1 \end{bmatrix}$$

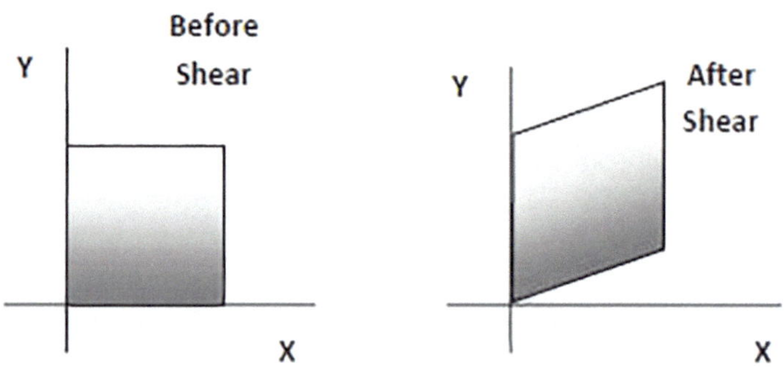

Figure 5.13: Shearing in Y direction

Example 5.13

Given a triangle with points (1, 1), (0, 0) and (1, 0). Find out the new coordinates of the object along y-axis, if shearing parameter along y-axis is 1.

Solution

Given points of a triangle is A (1, 1), B (0, 0) and C (1, 0) shearing parameter along y-axis $sh_y = 1$.

$$\begin{bmatrix} A1' & B1' & C1' \\ A2' & B2' & C2' \\ 1 & 1 & 1 \end{bmatrix} = \begin{bmatrix} 1 & 0 & 0 \\ sh_y & 1 & 0 \\ 0 & 0 & 1 \end{bmatrix} \begin{bmatrix} 1 & 0 & 1 \\ 1 & 0 & 0 \\ 1 & 1 & 1 \end{bmatrix}$$

$$\begin{bmatrix} A1' & B1' & C1' \\ A2' & B2' & C2' \\ 1 & 1 & 1 \end{bmatrix} = \begin{bmatrix} 1 & 0 & 0 \\ 1 & 1 & 0 \\ 0 & 0 & 1 \end{bmatrix} \begin{bmatrix} 1 & 0 & 1 \\ 1 & 0 & 0 \\ 1 & 1 & 1 \end{bmatrix}$$

$$\begin{bmatrix} A1' & B1' & C1' \\ A2' & B2' & C2' \\ 1 & 1 & 1 \end{bmatrix} = \begin{bmatrix} 1 & 0 & 1 \\ 2 & 0 & 1 \\ 1 & 1 & 1 \end{bmatrix}$$

Therefore new coordinates values are A (1, 2), B (0, 0) and C (1, 1)

Shearing in Both Direction

Here layers will be slide in both x as well as y direction. The sliding will be in horizontal as well as vertical direction.

The shape of the object will be distorted.

$$x' = x + sh_x.y$$
$$y' = sh_y.x + y$$

The matrix of shear in both directions is given by:

$$\begin{bmatrix} x' \\ y' \\ 1 \end{bmatrix} = \begin{bmatrix} 1 & sh_x & 0 \\ sh_y & 1 & 0 \\ 0 & 0 & 1 \end{bmatrix} \begin{bmatrix} x \\ y \\ 1 \end{bmatrix}$$

Example 5.14

Given a triangle with points (1, 1), (0, 0) and (1, 0). Find out the new coordinates of the object along xy-axis, if shearing parameter along x-axis is 4 and shearing parameter along y-axis is 1.

Solution

Given points of a triangle is A (1, 1), B (0, 0) and C (1, 0) shearing parameter along x-axis $sh_x = 4$ and shearing parameter along x-axis $sh_x = 1$.

$$\begin{bmatrix} A1' & B1' & C1' \\ A2' & B2' & C2' \\ 1 & 1 & 1 \end{bmatrix} = \begin{bmatrix} 1 & sh_x & 0 \\ sh_y & 1 & 0 \\ 0 & 0 & 1 \end{bmatrix} \begin{bmatrix} 1 & 0 & 1 \\ 1 & 0 & 0 \\ 1 & 1 & 1 \end{bmatrix}$$

$$\begin{bmatrix} A1' & B1' & C1' \\ A2' & B2' & C2' \\ 1 & 1 & 1 \end{bmatrix} = \begin{bmatrix} 1 & 4 & 0 \\ 1 & 1 & 0 \\ 0 & 0 & 1 \end{bmatrix} \begin{bmatrix} 1 & 0 & 1 \\ 1 & 0 & 0 \\ 1 & 1 & 1 \end{bmatrix}$$

$$\begin{bmatrix} A1' & B1' & C1' \\ A2' & B2' & C2' \\ 1 & 1 & 1 \end{bmatrix} = \begin{bmatrix} 5 & 0 & 1 \\ 2 & 0 & 1 \\ 1 & 1 & 1 \end{bmatrix}$$

Therefore new coordinates values are A (5, 2), B (0, 0) and C (1, 1)

5.6 COMPOSITE TRANSFORMATIONS

The process of computing the product of a matrix of several different transformations in a sequence is known as concatenation or composite transformation. The construction of products of transformation matrices is often referred to as the combination, or composition of matrices. For the column-matrix representation of the coordinate positions, we form the composite transformation by multiplying the matrices in order from right to left, that is, each successive transformation matrix multiplies the product of the preceding transformation matrix. The general pivot-point rotation and general fixed-point scaling are the types of composite transformation.

5.6.1 General Pivot-Point Rotation

We can generate rotations about an arbitrary point (x_r, y_r) by performing the following sequence of translate-rotate-translate operations:

- Translate the object so that the pivot-point position is moved to the coordinate origin.
- Rotate the object about the coordinate origin.
- Translate the object so that the pivot point is returned to its original position.

This transformation sequence is illustrated in the Figure 5.14.

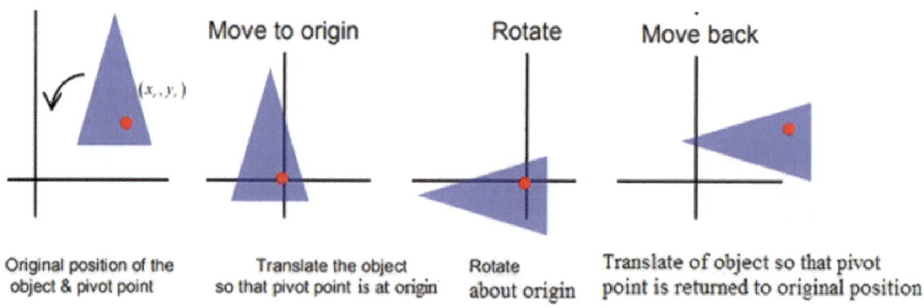

Figure 5.14: Pivot Point Rotations

The composite transformation matrix for this sequence is obtained with the concatenation.

$$P' = T(x_r, y_r) R(\theta) T(-x_r, -y_r) P$$

Where

P′ is rotated pivot point

$T(x_r, y_r)$ Translation matrix

R(θ) Rotation matrix

$T(-x_r, -y_r)$ Re-translation Matrix

P Pivot point

Therefore

$$\begin{bmatrix} x' \\ y' \\ 1 \end{bmatrix} = \begin{bmatrix} 1 & 0 & x_r \\ 0 & 1 & y_r \\ 0 & 0 & 1 \end{bmatrix} \begin{bmatrix} \cos\theta & -\sin\theta & 0 \\ \sin\theta & \cos\theta & 0 \\ 0 & 0 & 1 \end{bmatrix} \begin{bmatrix} 1 & 0 & -x_r \\ 0 & 1 & -y_r \\ 0 & 0 & 1 \end{bmatrix} \begin{bmatrix} x \\ y \\ 1 \end{bmatrix}$$

Expanding this equation we get

$$\begin{bmatrix} x' \\ y' \\ 1 \end{bmatrix} = \begin{bmatrix} \cos\theta & -\sin\theta & x_r(1-\cos\theta)+y_r\sin\theta \\ \sin\theta & \cos\theta & y_r(1-\cos\theta)-x_r\sin\theta \\ 0 & 0 & 1 \end{bmatrix} \begin{bmatrix} x \\ y \\ 1 \end{bmatrix}$$

Which are actually the equations for rotation of (x, y) from the pivot point (x_r, y_r).

Example 5.15

Rotate the triangle having coordinates (1, 2), (2, 3) and (4, 5) by 60° about (2, 3).

Solution

Given coordinate of a triangle is A (1, 2), B (2, 3) and C (4, 5) and we have 60 degree anticlockwise direction with pivot point is (2, 3) so

$$\begin{bmatrix} A1' & B1' & C1' \\ A2' & B2' & C2' \\ 1 & 1 & 1 \end{bmatrix} = \begin{bmatrix} \cos\theta & -\sin\theta & x_r(1-\cos\theta)+y_r\sin\theta \\ \sin\theta & \cos\theta & y_r(1-\cos\theta)-x_r\sin\theta \\ 0 & 0 & 1 \end{bmatrix} \begin{bmatrix} A1 & B1 & C1 \\ A2 & B2 & C2 \\ 1 & 1 & 1 \end{bmatrix}$$

$$\begin{bmatrix} A1' & B1' & C1' \\ A2' & B2' & C2' \\ 1 & 1 & 1 \end{bmatrix} = \begin{bmatrix} \cos 60° & -\sin 60° & x_r(1-\cos 60°)+y_r\sin 60° \\ \sin 60° & \cos 60° & y_r(1-\cos 60°)-x_r\sin 60° \\ 0 & 0 & 1 \end{bmatrix} \begin{bmatrix} 1 & 2 & 4 \\ 2 & 3 & 5 \\ 1 & 1 & 1 \end{bmatrix}$$

$$\begin{bmatrix} A1' & B1' & C1' \\ A2' & B2' & C2' \\ 1 & 1 & 1 \end{bmatrix} = \begin{bmatrix} \frac{1}{2} & -\frac{\sqrt{3}}{2} & 2\left(1-\frac{1}{2}\right)+3.\frac{\sqrt{3}}{2} \\ \frac{\sqrt{3}}{2} & \frac{1}{2} & 3\left(1-\frac{1}{2}\right)-2.\frac{\sqrt{3}}{2} \\ 0 & 0 & 1 \end{bmatrix} \begin{bmatrix} 1 & 2 & 4 \\ 2 & 3 & 5 \\ 1 & 1 & 1 \end{bmatrix}$$

$$\begin{bmatrix} A1' & B1' & C1' \\ A2' & B2' & C2' \\ 1 & 1 & 1 \end{bmatrix} == \begin{bmatrix} \frac{1}{2} & -\frac{\sqrt{3}}{2} & \frac{2+3\sqrt{3}}{2} \\ \frac{\sqrt{3}}{2} & \frac{1}{2} & \frac{3-2\sqrt{3}}{2} \\ 0 & 0 & 1 \end{bmatrix} \begin{bmatrix} 1 & 2 & 4 \\ 2 & 3 & 5 \\ 1 & 1 & 1 \end{bmatrix}$$

$$\begin{bmatrix} A1' & B1' & C1' \\ A2' & B2' & C2' \\ 1 & 1 & 1 \end{bmatrix} = \begin{bmatrix} \frac{3-2\sqrt{3}}{2} & -\frac{3-6\sqrt{3}}{2} & 1-\sqrt{3} \\ \frac{4-\sqrt{3}}{2} & \frac{\sqrt{3}}{2} & 4 \\ 1 & 1 & 1 \end{bmatrix}$$

$$\begin{bmatrix} A1' & B1' & C1' \\ A2' & B2' & C2' \\ 1 & 1 & 1 \end{bmatrix} = \begin{bmatrix} 6-4\sqrt{3} & -6+3\sqrt{3} & 1-\sqrt{3} \\ 2-2\sqrt{3} & 2\sqrt{3} & 4 \\ 1 & 1 & 1 \end{bmatrix}$$

Thus, New coordinates of the triangle = A $\left(6-4\sqrt{3}, 2-2\sqrt{3}\right)$, B $\left(-6+3\sqrt{3}, 2\sqrt{3}\right)$, and C$\left(1-\sqrt{3},\ 4\right)$.

5.6.2 General Fixed-Point Scaling

We can generate scaling about a fixed point (x_f, y_f) by performing the following sequence of translate-scale-translate operations:

- Translate object so that the fixed point coincides with the coordinate origin.
- Scale the object with respect to the coordinate origin.
- Use the inverse translation of step 1 to return the object to its original position.

This transformation sequence is illustrated in the Figure 5.15.

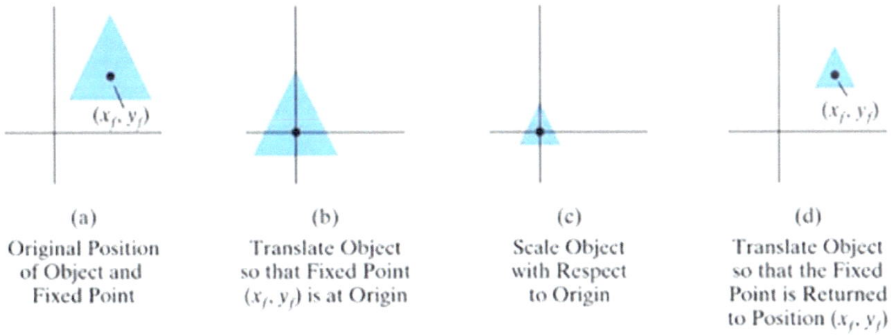

Figure 5.15: Fixed Point Scaling

The composite transformation matrix for this sequence is obtained with the concatenation.

$$P' = T(x_f, y_f) S(s_x, s_y) T(-x_f, -y_f) P$$

Where

P′ is rotated pivot point

$T(x_f, y_f)$ Translation matrix

$S(s_x, s_y)$ Scaling matrix

$T(-x_f, -y_f)$ Re-translation Matrix

P Pivot point

$$\begin{bmatrix} x' \\ y' \\ 1 \end{bmatrix} = \begin{bmatrix} 1 & 0 & x_f \\ 0 & 1 & y_f \\ 0 & 0 & 1 \end{bmatrix} \begin{bmatrix} s_x & 0 & 0 \\ 0 & s_y & 0 \\ 0 & 0 & 1 \end{bmatrix} \begin{bmatrix} 1 & 0 & -x_f \\ 0 & 1 & -y_f \\ 0 & 0 & 1 \end{bmatrix} \begin{bmatrix} x \\ y \\ 1 \end{bmatrix}$$

Expanding this equation we get

$$\begin{bmatrix} x' \\ y' \\ 1 \end{bmatrix} = \begin{bmatrix} s_x & 0 & x_f(1-s_x) \\ 0 & s_y & y_f(1-s_y) \\ 0 & 0 & 1 \end{bmatrix} \begin{bmatrix} x \\ y \\ 1 \end{bmatrix}$$

Which are actually the equations for rotation of (x, y) from the fixed point (x_f, y_f).

Example

Find the transformation matrix that transforms the given square ABCD to half its size about (2, 2,). The coordinates of the square are A (1, 1), B (3, 1), C (3, 3) and D (1, 3).

Solution

Given coordinate of a square is A (1, 1), B (3, 1), C (3, 3) and D (1, 3) .and we have half its size with fixed point is (2, 2) so

$$\begin{bmatrix} A1' & B1' & C1' & D1' \\ A2' & B2' & C2' & D2' \\ 1 & 1 & 1 & 1 \end{bmatrix} = \begin{bmatrix} s_x & 0 & x_f(1-s_x) \\ 0 & s_y & y_f(1-s_y) \\ 0 & 0 & 1 \end{bmatrix} \begin{bmatrix} A1 & B1 & C1 & D1 \\ A2 & B2 & C2 & D2 \\ 1 & 1 & 1 & 1 \end{bmatrix}$$

$$\begin{bmatrix} A1' & B1' & C1' & D1' \\ A2' & B2' & C2' & D2' \\ 1 & 1 & 1 & 1 \end{bmatrix} = \begin{bmatrix} \frac{1}{2} & 0 & 2\left(1-\frac{1}{2}\right) \\ 0 & \frac{1}{2} & 2\left(1-\frac{1}{2}\right) \\ 0 & 0 & 1 \end{bmatrix} \begin{bmatrix} 1 & 3 & 3 & 1 \\ 1 & 1 & 3 & 3 \\ 1 & 1 & 1 & 1 \end{bmatrix}$$

$$\begin{bmatrix} A1' & B1' & C1' & D1' \\ A2' & B2' & C2' & D2' \\ 1 & 1 & 1 & 1 \end{bmatrix} = \begin{bmatrix} \frac{1}{2} & 0 & 1 \\ 0 & \frac{1}{2} & 1 \\ 0 & 0 & 1 \end{bmatrix} \begin{bmatrix} 1 & 3 & 3 & 1 \\ 1 & 1 & 3 & 3 \\ 1 & 1 & 1 & 1 \end{bmatrix}$$

$$\begin{bmatrix} A1' & B1' & C1' & D1' \\ A2' & B2' & C2' & D2' \\ 1 & 1 & 1 & 1 \end{bmatrix} = \begin{bmatrix} \frac{3}{2} & \frac{5}{2} & \frac{5}{2} & \frac{3}{2} \\ \frac{3}{2} & \frac{3}{2} & \frac{5}{2} & \frac{5}{2} \\ 1 & 1 & 1 & 1 \end{bmatrix}$$

Thus, New coordinates of the square = A $\left(\frac{3}{2}, \frac{3}{2}\right)$, B $\left(\frac{5}{2}, \frac{3}{2}\right)$, C $\left(\frac{5}{2}, \frac{5}{2}\right)$, and D $\left(\frac{3}{2}, \frac{5}{2}\right)$.

OBJECTIVE QUESTIONS

1. Reflection of a point about the x-axis, followed by a counter-clockwise rotation of 90°, is equivalent to reflection about which line?
   (a) x = - y (b) y = - x
   (c) x = y (d) x + y = 1
2. Consider a triangle with co-ordinates points: A (0, 0), B (3, 3) and C (2, 5). When scaling parameter is 2 towards x-axis and 4 towards y-axis, then what are the new co-ordinates of triangle?
   (a) A(0, 0), B(6, 12), C(4, 20)
   (b) A(0, 0), B(3/2, 3/4), C(1, 5/4)
   (c) A(0, 0), B(5, 7), C(4, 9)
   (d) A(2, 4), B(5, 7), C(4, 9)
3. Consider the matrix = $\begin{bmatrix} 2 & 0 & 2 \\ 0 & 1 & 1 \\ 0 & 0 & 1 \end{bmatrix}$ representing a set of planar (2D) geometric transformations in homogeneous coordinates. Which of the following statements about the matrix M is True?
   (a) M represents first, a scaling of vector (2, 1) followed by translation of vector (1, 1)
   (b) M represents first, a translation of vector (1, 1) followed by scaling of vector (2, 1)
   (c) M represents first, a scaling of vector (3, 1) followed by shearing of parameters (−1, 1)
   (d) M represents first, a shearing of parameters (−1, 1) followed by scaling of vector (3, 1)
4. A rigid body transformation that moves objects without deformation is called _____.
   (a) Scaling (b) Augmentation
   (c) Translation (d) Rotation
5. A circle, if scaled only in one direction, becomes
   (a) Parabola (b) Hyperbola
   (c) Ellipse (d) Remains a circle
6. Two Dimensional Shearing in both directions is given by
   (a) $x' = x + sh_y x$ and $y' = sh_y x + y$
   (b) $x' = x + sh_x y$ and $y' = sh_y x + y$
   (c) $x' = x + sh_x y$ and $y' = sh_y x + y$
   (d) $x' = x + sh_x y$ and $y' = sh_y x + x$

7. Which of these are basic transformations?
   (a) Scaling (b) Rotation
   (c) Translation (d) All of the above
8. Which transformation in non-homogeneous form is captured by matrix addition?
   (a) Scaling (b) Rotation
   (c) Translation (d) Reflection
9. In a homogeneous coordinate system, all transformation is captured by matrix
   (a) Addition (b) Subtraction
   (c) Multiplication (d) Division
10. Transformation effect can be undone by
    (a) Reverse transformation (b) Forward transformation
    (c) Inverse transformation (d) None of the above
11. The process of combining or multiplying transformation matrices is called
    (a) Rasterization (b) Transformation
    (c) Concatenation (d) Reflection
12. A transformation in which object is held stationary while the co-ordinate system is transform related to the object is known as
    (a) Transformation
    (b) Geometrical Transformation
    (c) Co-Ordinate Transformation
    (d) Basic Transformation
13. The translation distance pair (t_x, t_y) in Two Dimensional Translation is also called as
    (a) Shift Vector (b) Rotation Vector
    (c) Scaling Vector (d) Reflection Vector
14. Two dimensional Matrix representation of reflection about the straight line y = - x is given as
    (a) $\begin{bmatrix} 0 & 1 \\ -1 & 0 \end{bmatrix}$ (b) $\begin{bmatrix} 0 & -1 \\ -1 & 0 \end{bmatrix}$
    (c) $\begin{bmatrix} 0 & -1 \\ 1 & 0 \end{bmatrix}$ (d) $\begin{bmatrix} 0 & 1 \\ 1 & 0 \end{bmatrix}$
15. Shear transformation is classified as a
    (a) Basic transformation (b) Special transformation
    (c) Inverse transformation (d) None of the above

ANSWERS

1. (c)	4. (c)	7. (d)	10. (d)	13. (a)
2. (a)	5. (c)	8. (c)	11. (c)	14. (b)
3. (b)	6. (b)	9. (c)	12. (c)	15. (b)

EXERCISES

1. What are the basic transformations? Describe each with their matrix representation.
2. Briefly explain the following two-dimensional basic geometric transformations?
   i. Translation ii. Scale iii. Rotation
3. Scale the rectangle ABCD with vertices A (2, 2), B (2, 6), C (5, 2) and D (5, 6) to double its size about fixed point (2, 3) then translate it using translation vector (1, 3).
4. Magnify the triangle ABC with A (0, 0), B (1, 1) and C (5, 2) to twice its size while keeping C (5, 2) fixed.
5. A triangle ABC with coordinates A (0, 0), B (6, 5), C (6, 0) is scaled with scaling factors = 2 and = 3 about the vertex C (6, 0). Find the transformed coordinate points.
6. Distinguish between Uniform Scaling and Differential Scaling.
7. Consider a triangle at A (2, 2), B (10, 2), C (2, 10). Perform the following 2D transformations in succession and find the resultant vertices.
   i. Scale with respect to (2, 2) by scaling factors (2, 2) respectively along x and y directions.
   ii. Rotate by 900 counter clockwise directions.
8. Perform the following transformations on a point (6, 4).
   i. Translate by = −2 and = 4.
   ii. Then, Scale by = 2 and = 1.
   iii. And then Rotate by 90o in clockwise direction. Determine the final coordinates of the transformed point.
9. What do you know about rotation? Derive the matrix equation for 2D rotation.
10. Derive the transformation that rotates an object point θo about the origin. Write the matrix representation for this rotation.
11. Rotate the triangle ABC with vertices A (3, 5), B (7, 2) and C (4, 9) in counterclockwise direction by 90 degree and then enlarge it to double its size.
12. Perform a 45 degree rotation of a triangle ABC having the vertices at A (0, 0), B (10, 10), and C (50, 20).
    i. About the origin.
    ii. About an arbitrary point P (-10,-10).

13. Show that uniform scaling and rotation make commutative pair, but in general scaling and rotation are not commutative.
14. What do you understand by homogenous coordinates? What are the basic advantages of using Homogeneous coordinates system.
15. What do you mean by homogeneous coordinate system? What is its significance?
16. Differentiate between the Scaling and Shearing transformation..
17. Show that the composition of two successive rotations is additive that is R (θ1). R (θ2) = R (θ1+ θ2).
18. Show that the composition of two rotation is additive by concatenating the matrix representation for R(θ1) and R(θ2).
19. Show that reflection about the line y = -x is equivalent to a reflection relative to the y-axis followed by an anticlockwise rotation of 90 degree.
20. Show that transformation matrix for reflection about a line y = x is equivalent to reflection to x-axis followed by counter clockwise rotation of 90 degree.
21. Explain the following reflection in brief:
    i. Reflection of an object about the x- axis.
    ii. Reflection of an object about the y axis Reflection axis as the diagonal line y = x.
22. Show that 2D reflection through x-axis followed by 2D reflection through the line y = - x is equivalent to a pure rotation about the origin.
23. Given a triangle A (20, 10) B (80, 20) C (50, 70). Find the co-ordinates of vertices after each of the following transformation.
    i. Reflection about the line x=y.
    ii. Rotation of the triangle ABC about vertex A in clockwise direction for an angle 90 degree.
24. What is shearing transformation? Explain with example.
25. The special case when b = 0 is called shearing in the x direction. When a = 0, we have shearing in the y direction. Illustrate the effort of these shearing transformations on the square A(0,0), B(1,0), C(1,1), and D(0,1) when a = 2 and b = 3.
26. Prove that simultaneous shearing in both direction (x and y directions) is not equal to the composition of pure shear along the x-axis followed by pure shear along the y-shear.
27. A square ABCD is given with vertices A (0, 0), B (1, 0), C (1, 1), and D (0, 1). Illustrate the effect of
    i. x-shear
    ii. y-shear
    iii. XY-shear on the given square, when = 2 and = 3.
28. What do you mean by mean by composite transformation? Explain with example.

6

Two-Dimensional Viewing Transformation and Clipping

Two-dimensional viewing is a process that allows you to view an image from a specific perspective. In this chapter, we will discuss the concepts of windows and viewports, and how they are used to map an image. We will also cover the different stages involved in the graphic pipeline. Additionally, this chapter will explain the concepts of panning and zooming. A scene consists of a collection of objects that are specified in world coordinates (x and y-axis). When a scene is displayed, you can only view the objects that are inside the viewing window (clip window) and everything outside the window is clipped. Clipping algorithms are used to identify which points and lines should be clipped and which ones should be retained. A clipping algorithm is a procedure that identifies the portions of a picture that are inside or outside the specified window frame during the clipping process. The picture region where the object is supposed to be clipped is called a clip window. Clipping algorithms are important in computer graphics as they are used to view transformations and erase picture sections in drawing and painting packages.

6.1 INTRODUCTION OF WINDOWING

The world coordinate system is used to define the position of objects in the natural world. Sometimes the complete picture of object in the World Coordinates System (WCS) is too large and complicate to clearly show on the screen, and we need to show only some part of the object. World coordinates are expressed as real numbers. You can select a rectangular subspace of world coordinates for output.

Area selected in world co-ordinate for display is called window. It defines what is to be viewed. A Window is a rectangular region in the world coordinate system. This is the coordinate system used to locate an object in the natural world.

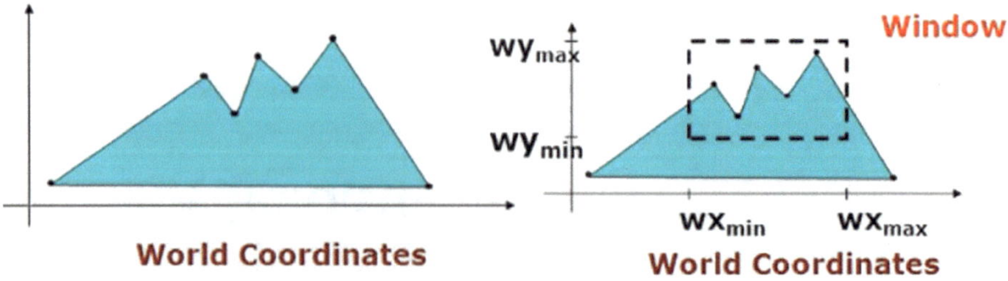

Figure 6.1: World Co-ordinates for Window

The corresponding coordinate system on the display device where the image of the picture is displayed is called the Physical Device Coordinate System (PDCS). An area on a display device in which window images is display or mapped is called a viewport. It define where it is to be displayed .The capability that show some part of object internal a specify window is called windowing and a rectangular region in a world coordinate system is called window.

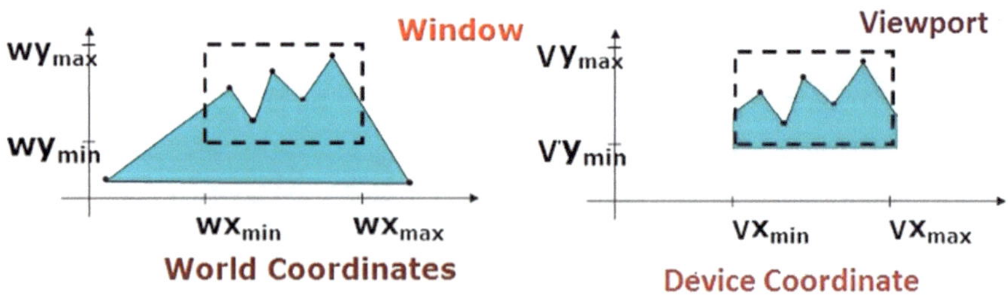

Figure 6.2: Device Coordinates for Viewport

As different display devices have different screen size measured in pixels, we need to make our program display device independent. There for device independent co-ordinate system is used to display picture on screen. Normalized device coordinate (NDC) is the display area of the virtual display device corresponding to a unit square. The lower left handed corner is the origin of the coordinate system and upper right corner is the point (1, 1). The point (0.5, 0.5) is the center of the screen. It is shown in Figure 6.3.

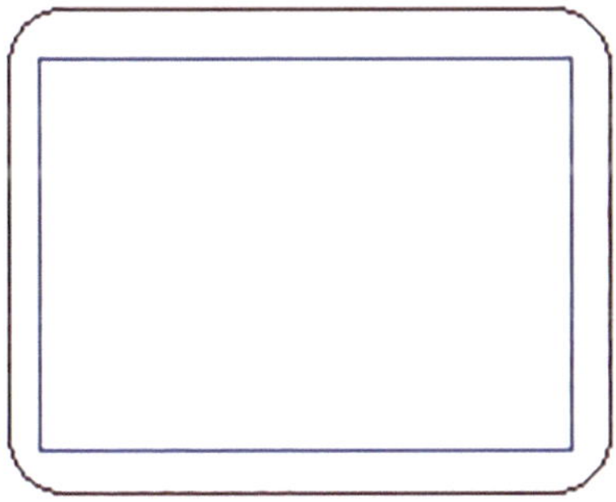

Figure 6.3: Normalized Device Coordinate

Mapping the window in the world coordinate space to viewport in NDC space is called the Normalization Transformation, N. It involves scaling of x and y, thus it is also referred to as scaling transformation.

Table 6.1: Differences between Window and Viewport

Window	*Viewport.*
1. Window is defined in world coordinate system	1. Viewport is defined in device co-ordinate system
2. Window defines what is to be viewed	2. Viewport defines where it is to be viewed
3. When the window is moved, the display picture changes.	3. When the viewport is moved, the display picture remains same only the area of display changes.
4. Window can be defined with GWINDOW statement	4. Viewport can be defined using VPORT command.
5. The window can be defined to select part of the picture or whole picture to display.	5. The viewport can be defined to select the part of the device to display the picture or the whole device to display picture.

6.2 VIEWING TRANSFORMATION

In general finding device co-ordinate of a viewport from world co-ordinate of window is called as Viewing transformation or window to viewport transformation or windowing transformation. Window-to-Viewport mapping is the process of mapping or transforming a two-dimensional world-coordinate scene to device coordinates. Viewing Transformation (V) consist of two parts as

- Normalization Transformation (N)

- Workstation Transformation (W)
  Where,
- **Normalization Transformation:** maps World Co-ordinate Systems to Normalized Device Coordinate Systems (NDCS).
- **Workstation Transformation:** maps this Normalize Device Co-ordinate Systems to physical Device Co- ordinate Systems that is

2D Viewing V=N.W

6.3 VIEWING PIPELINE

We know that world coordinate system is used to define the position of objects or picture in the natural world. However, when the picture is displayed on the display device, it is measured in the physical device coordinate system (PDCS) corresponding to the display device. Therefore, it is necessary to match the coordinates of the points and lines that make up the image with the coordinates of the correct physical device co-ordinate on which the image of a picture is displayed. This mapping of co-ordinates is achieved with the use of co-ordinate transformation known as viewing Pipeline. The viewing transformation which maps picture co-ordinates in the WCS to display co-ordinates in PDCS is performed by the following transformations.

- Converting world co-ordinates to viewing co-ordinates.
- Normalizing viewing co-ordinates.
- Converting normalized viewing co-ordinates to device coordinates.

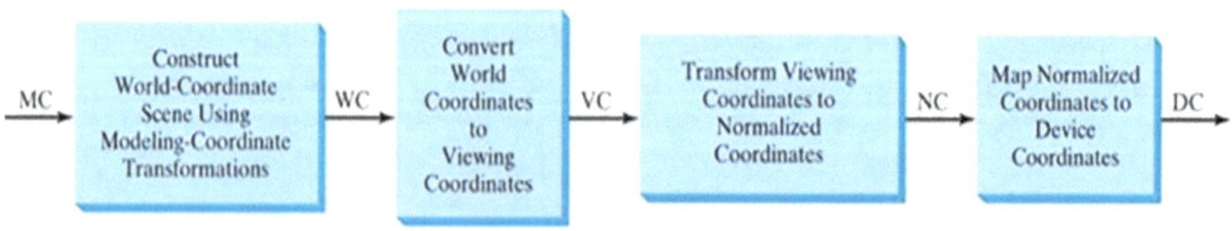

Figure 6.4: Two-Dimensional viewing transformation pipelines

The steps involved in viewing transformation:

1. Construct the scene in world co-ordinate using the output primitives and attributes.
2. Obtain a particular orientation for the window by setting a 2D viewing co-ordinate system in the world co-ordinate plane and define a window in the viewing co-ordinate system.

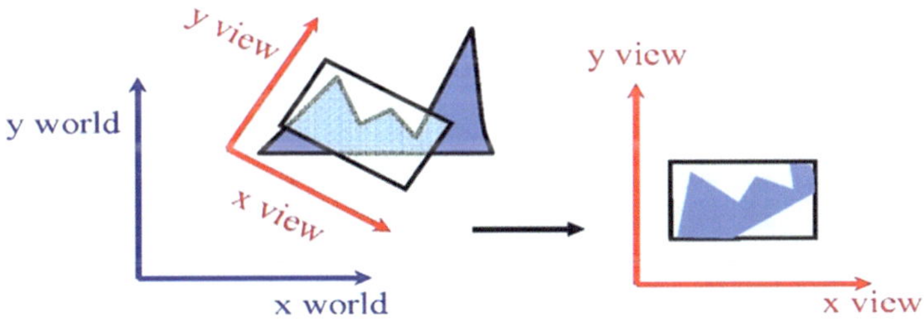

Figure 6.5: Error! No text of specified style in document.

3. Use viewing co-ordinates reference frame to provide a method for setting up arbitrary orientations for rectangular windows
4. Once the viewing reference frame is established, transform descriptions in world co-ordinates to viewing co-ordinates.
5. Define a view port in normalized co-ordinates and map the viewing co-ordinates description of the scene to normalized co-ordinates.

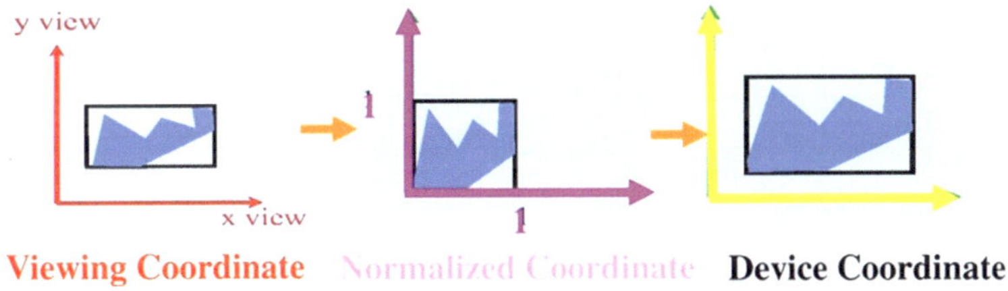

Figure 6.6: Normalized co-ordinates with viewing co-ordinates

6. Clip all the parts of the picture which lie outside the viewport.

We can perform it using some mathematical calculations.

Mapping of window co-ordinate to viewport is called window to viewport transformation. We do this using transformation that maintains relative position of window co-ordinate into viewport. That means centre co-ordinate in window must be remain at centre position viewport. The mapping achieved is proportional. Let (*xw*, *yw*) a point on Window (*xv*, *yv*) as a corresponding points on before we find relative position by equation, for x coordinate, as follow

$$\frac{xv - xv_{min}}{xv_{max} - xv_{min}} = \frac{xw - xw_{min}}{xw_{max} - xw_{min}}$$

$$xv - xv_{min} = xv_{max} - xv_{min} \frac{xw - xw_{min}}{xw_{max} - xw_{min}}$$

$$xv = xv_{min} + (xv_{max} - xv_{min})\frac{xw - xw_{min}}{xw_{max} - xw_{min}}$$

$$xv = xv_{min} + \left(xw - xw_{min}\right)\frac{xv_{max} - xv_{min}}{xw_{max} - xw_{min}}$$

If $$S_x = \frac{xv_{max} - xv_{min}}{xw_{max} - xw_{min}} \text{ then}$$

$$xv = xv_{min} + \left(xw - xw_{min}\right)s_x \qquad (1)$$

Similarly for y coordinate,

$$\frac{yv - yv_{min}}{yv_{max} - yv_{min}} = \frac{yw - yw_{min}}{yw_{max} - yw_{min}}$$

$$yv - yv_{min} = yv_{max} - yv_{min}\frac{yw - yw_{min}}{yw_{max} - yw_{min}}$$

$$yv = yv_{min} + \left(yw - yw_{min}\right)\frac{yv_{max} - yv_{min}}{yw_{max} - yw_{min}}$$

If $$s_y = \frac{yv_{max} - yv_{min}}{yw_{max} - yw_{min}} \text{ then}$$

$$yv = yv_{min} + \left(yw - yw_{min}\right)s_y$$

Where, S_x is scaling factor of x coordinate and S_y is scaling factor of y coordinate. Since the eight coordinate values that define the window and the viewport are just constant, we can express these two formulas for computing (xv, yv) from (xw, yw) in terms of translate-scale-translate transformation N.

$$\begin{bmatrix} xv \\ yv \\ 1 \end{bmatrix} = N\begin{bmatrix} xw \\ yw \\ 1 \end{bmatrix}$$

Where

$$N = \begin{bmatrix} 1 & 0 & xv_{min} \\ 0 & 1 & yv_{min} \\ 0 & 0 & 1 \end{bmatrix}\begin{bmatrix} s_x & 0 & 0 \\ 0 & s_y & 0 \\ 0 & 0 & 1 \end{bmatrix}\begin{bmatrix} 1 & 0 & -xw_{min} \\ 0 & 1 & -yw_{min} \\ 0 & 0 & 1 \end{bmatrix}$$

Then its composite transformation matrix is

$$N = \begin{bmatrix} s_x & 0 & -s_x xw_{min} + xv_{min} \\ 0 & s_y & -s_y yw_{min} + yv_{min} \\ 0 & 0 & 1 \end{bmatrix}$$

Example 6.1

Find the normalization transformation that maps a window whose lower left corner is at (1, 1) and upper right corner is at (3, 5) onto:

I. Viewport which is the entire normalized device screen.

II. A viewport whose lower left corner is at (0, 0) and upper right corner is at (1/2, 1/2).

Solution

(I) Given for window is $xw_{min} = 1$, $xw_{max} = 3$, $yw_{min} = 1$, $yw_{max} = 5$

For viewport is $xv_{min} = 0$, $xv_{max} = 1$, $yv_{min} = 0$, $yv_{max} = 1$

$$s_x = \frac{xv_{max} - xv_{min}}{xw_{max} - xw_{min}} = \frac{1-0}{3-1} = \frac{1}{2}$$

$$s_y = \frac{yv_{max} - yv_{min}}{yw_{max} - yw_{min}} = \frac{1-0}{5-1} = \frac{1}{4}$$

Now

$$N = \begin{bmatrix} s_x & 0 & -s_x xw_{min} + xv_{min} \\ 0 & s_y & -s_y yw_{min} + yv_{min} \\ 0 & 0 & 1 \end{bmatrix}$$

$$N = \begin{bmatrix} \frac{1}{2} & 0 & -\frac{1}{2}.1+0 \\ 0 & \frac{1}{4} & -\frac{1}{4}.1+0 \\ 0 & 0 & 1 \end{bmatrix} = \begin{bmatrix} \frac{1}{2} & 0 & -\frac{1}{2} \\ 0 & \frac{1}{4} & -\frac{1}{4} \\ 0 & 0 & 1 \end{bmatrix}$$

(II) Given for window is $xw_{min} = 1$, $xw_{max} = 3$, $yw_{min} = 1$, $yw_{max} = 5$

For viewport is $xv_{min} = 0$, $xv_{max} = \frac{1}{2}$, $yv_{min} = 0$, $yv_{max} = \frac{1}{2}$

$$S_x = \frac{xv_{max} - xv_{min}}{xw_{max} - xw_{min}} = \frac{\frac{1}{2} - 0}{3 - 1} = \frac{1}{4}$$

$$S_y = \frac{yv_{max} - yv_{min}}{yw_{max} - yw_{min}} = \frac{\frac{1}{2} - 0}{5 - 1} = \frac{1}{8}$$

Now

$$N = \begin{bmatrix} s_x & 0 & -s_x xw_{min} + xv_{min} \\ 0 & s_y & -s_y yw_{min} + yv_{min} \\ 0 & 0 & 1 \end{bmatrix}$$

$$N = \begin{bmatrix} \frac{1}{4} & 0 & -\frac{1}{4}.1 + 0 \\ 0 & \frac{1}{8} & -\frac{1}{8}.1 + 0 \\ 0 & 0 & 1 \end{bmatrix} = \begin{bmatrix} \frac{1}{4} & 0 & -\frac{1}{4} \\ 0 & \frac{1}{8} & -\frac{1}{8} \\ 0 & 0 & 1 \end{bmatrix}$$

Example 6.2

Let's assume, for window, XWmin = 20, XWmax = 80, YWmin = 40, YWmax = 80 and for viewport, XVmin = 30, XVmax = 60, YVmin = 40, YVmax = 60. Now a point (XW, YW) be (30, 80) on the window. Calculate the point on viewport that is (XV, YV).

Solution

First of all, calculate scaling factor of x coordinate S_x and scaling factor of y coordinate S_y using above mentioned formula.

S_x = (60 - 30) / (80 - 20) = 30 / 60

S_y = (60 - 40) / (80 - 40) = 20 / 40

So, now calculate the point on viewport (XV, YV).

XV = 30 + (30 - 20) * (30 / 60) = 35

YV = 40 + (80 - 40) * (20 / 40) = 60

So, the point on window (XW, YW) = (30, 80) will be (XV, YV) = (35, 60) on viewport.

6.4 INTRODUCTION OF CLIPPING

Any procedure that identifies those portions of a picture that are either inside or outside of a specified region of space is referred to as a clipping algorithm, or simply clipping. The region against which an object is to clip is called a clip window. Some applications of clipping are

- Drawing and painting operations that allow parts of a picture to be selected for copying, moving, erasing, or duplicating.
- Extracting part of a defined scene for viewing.
- Identifying visible surfaces in three-dimensional views.
- Antialiasing line segments or object boundaries.
- Creating objects using solid-modeling procedures.
- Displaying a multi window environment.

6.5 TYPES OF CLIPPING

There are number of clipping algorithm are used. Some of them are point clipping algorithm, line clipping algorithm, polygon clipping algorithm, curve clipping algorithm and text clipping algorithm.

6.5.1 Point Clipping

In point clipping we eliminate those points which are outside the clipping window and draw points which are inside the clipping window. Here we consider clipping window is rectangular boundary with edge (XWmin, XWmax, YWmin, and YWmax) and they can either world-coordinate window boundaries or viewport boundaries.

So for finding whether a point is inside or outside the clipping window we use following inequality: A point p = (X, Y) is saved for display, if the following inequalities are satisfied,

$$XWmin \le X \le XWmax$$

$$YWmin \le Y \le YWmax$$

If above both inequality is satisfied then the point is inside otherwise the point is outside the clipping window.

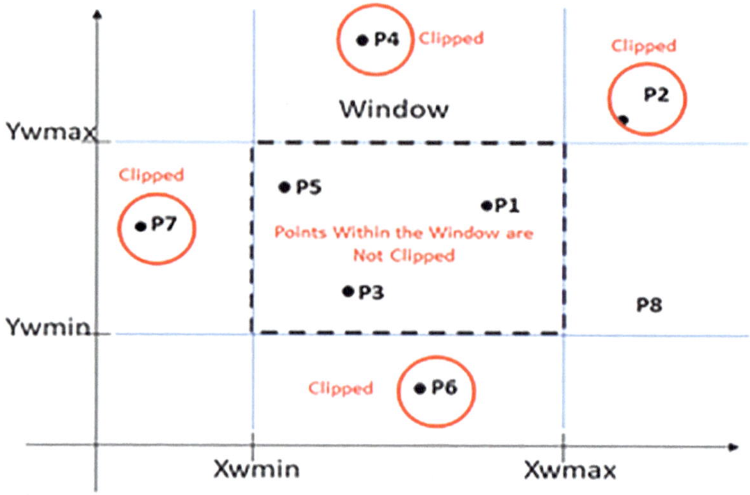

Figure 6.7: Point clipping

In the following figure points P1, P3 and P5 are inside a window and P2, P4, P6 and P7 are outside of the window.

6.5.2 Line Clipping

Given a set of lines and a rectangular area of window, the task is to remove lines which are outside the area of window and clip the lines which are partially inside the area. A line clipping procedure involves several parts.

- **Completely inside the window:** we can test a given line segment to determine whether it lies completely inside the clipping window.
- **Completely outside the window:** If it does not, we try to determine whether it lies completely outside the window.
- **Partially inside the window:** Finally, we must perform intersection calculations with one or more clipping boundaries. We process lines through the "inside - outside" tests by checking the line end points

Let us consider the following figure. A line with both end points inside all clipping boundaries such as the line from P1 to P2 is saved. A line with both end points outside any one of the clip boundaries (line P3 P4 and line P9 P10) is outside the window. All other lines cross one or more clipping boundaries and require calculation of multiple intersection points.

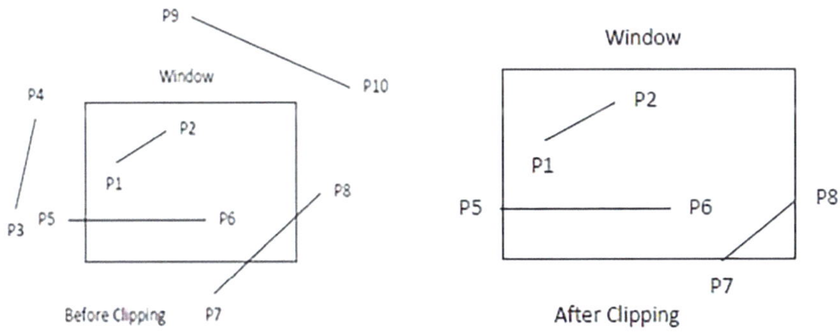

Figure 6.8: Line clipping

To minimize calculations, clipping algorithms are used that can efficiently identify outside lines and reduce intersection calculations. The line clipping algorithms are different types some of them are Cohen Sutherland line clipping algorithm, Midpoint Subdivision line clipping algorithm and Liang-Barsky line clipping algorithm.

6.5.2.1 Midpoint Subdivision Line Clipping Algorithm

For clipping any partially visible line we use this algorithm. It is based on the bisection method. The line is divided at its midpoint into two shorter line segments using the endpoint values.

Working of Algorithm

Midpoint sub-division line clipping algorithm find out the midpoint of a line segment and subdivide it into two equal parts. Then all possible cases are applied on line i.e. visible, invisible or partially visible. If line is visible then algorithm will display the line, if it is invisible then that segment of line is discarded. If line is partially visible then same sub-division process is continue till line segment become totally visible. This algorithm uses a binary search for the intersection point by always dividing the line at its mid point.

Midpoint Subdivision Line Clipping Algorithm

Step 1. Scan two end points for the line P1(x1, y1) and P2(x2, y2)

Step 2. Scan corners for the window as (XWmin, YWmin) and (XWmax, YWmax)

Step 3. Assign the region codes for endpoints P1 and P2 by initializing code with 0000.

- Bit 1 - if (x < XWmin) then bit 1 = 0 else bit 1 = 1.

- Bit 2 - if (x > XWmax) then bit 2 = 0 else bit 2 =1
- Bit 3 - if (y < YWmin) then bit 3 = 0 else bit 3 =1
- Bit 4 - if (y > YWmax) then bit 4 = 0 else bit 4 =1

Step 4. Check for visibility of line P1, P2

i. If region codes for both end points are zero then the line is visible, draw it and jump to step 6.

ii. If region codes for end points are not zero and the logical ANDing operation of them is also not zero then the line is invisible, reject it and jump to step 6.

iii. If region codes for end points does not satisfies the condition in 4(i) and 4(ii) then line is partly visible.

Step 5. Divide the partially visible line segments at mid-point (x_m, y_m) where

$x_m = \frac{(x_1 + x_2)}{2}$ and $y_m = \frac{(y_1 + y_2)}{2}$ and repeat steps 3 through step 5 for both subdivided line segments until you get completely visible and completely line segments.

Step 6. Exit

Example 6.3

Using Midpoint subdivision line clipping algorithm illustrate a clipping of a line segment joining two end points P1 (120, 5) and P2 (180, 30) by considering clipping window with left corner at (100, 10) and upper right comer at (160.40).

Solution:

At first considering the line P1 P2

We have P1 (120, 5) and P2 (180, 30)

$X_1 = 120,\ Y = 5,\ X_2 = 180,\ Y_2 = 30$

$XW_{min} = 100,\ XW_{max} = 160,\ YW_{min} = 10,\ YW_{max} = 40$

Assigning code for P1

If x < XWmin then bit 1 is set = 0.
If x > XWmax then bit 2 is set= 0.
If y < YWmin then bit 3 is set= 1.
If y > YWmax then bit 4 is set= 0.

Therefore Code for –P1 = 0100

Assigning code for P1

If x < XWmin then bit 1 is set = 0.

If x > XWmax then bit 2 is set= 1.
If y < YWmin then bit 3 is set= 1.
If y > YWmax then bit 4 is set= 0.
Therefore Code for –P2 = 0010

Since the code of P1 and P2 is nonzero then P1 P2 is not totally visible and, Code –P1 AND code P2 = 0, Hence the line P1P2 is not totally invisible, therefore find the midpoint of a line segment.

$$P_m = \frac{(P_1 + P_2)}{2} = \left(\frac{120+180}{2}, \frac{5+30}{2}\right) = (150, 17.5)$$

Assigning code for P_m
If X_m < XWmin then bit 1 is set = 0.
If X_m > XWmax then bit 2 is set= 0.
If Y_m < YWmin then bit 3 is set= 0.
If Y_m > YWmax then bit 4 is set= 0.

P_1	Code P_1	P_2	Code P_2	P_m	Code P_m	Comment
120, 5	0100	180, 30	0010	150, 17.5	0000	Continue with P1 Pm
120, 5	0100	150, 17.5	0000	135, 11.25	0000	Continue with P1 Pm
120, 5	0100	135,11.25	0000	127.5, 8.125	0100	Continue with Pm P2
127.5, 8.125	0100	135, 11.25	0000	131.25, 9.6875	0000	Succeeds

As the y coordinate of Pm almost equal to 10 we take the point as target point. So the intersection point has been found at (132, 10).

For the second intersection point

P_1	Code P_1	P_2	Code P_2	P_m	Code P_m	Comment
120, 5	0100	180,30	0010	150,17.5	0000	Continue with Pm P2
150, 17.5	0000	180,30	0010	165,23.75	0010	Continue with P1 Pm
150, 17.5	0000	165,23.75	0010	157.5,20.62	0000	Continue with Pm P2
157.5, 20.62	0000	165,23.75	0010	161.25,22.185	0010	Continue with P1 Pm
157.5, 20.62	0000	161.25,22.18	0010	159.37,21.4	0000	succeeds

As the x coordinate of Pm almost equal to 160 we take the point as target point. So the intersection point has been found at (160, 22). Hence the visible portion of the line P1 P2 is (132, 10) to (160, 22)

6.5.2.2 Cohen Sutherland Line Clipping Algorithm

One of the most important lines clipping algorithm is Cohen Sutherland algorithm, which can be explain in following points.

A. Region and Region Code

The Cohen Sutherland algorithm is divides the 2-D space into nine regions. Out of 9 only the middle part (viewport) is visible. Each region has a unique four bit region code. Region codes indicate the position of the regions with respect to the window.

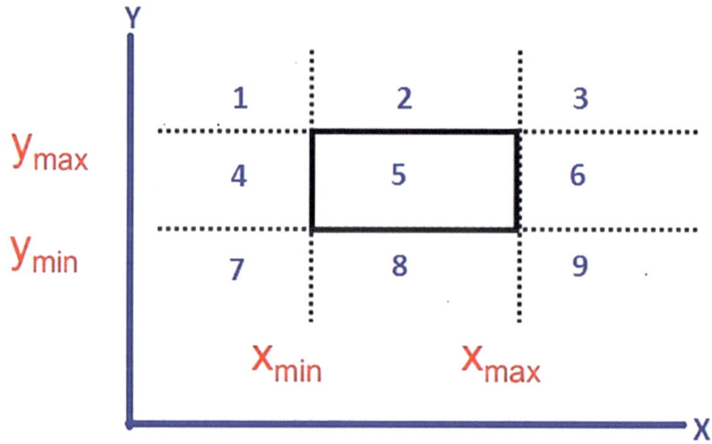

Figure 6.9: Region for Cohen Sutherland line algorithm

Every line endpoint in a picture is assigned a four digit binary code, called a region code that identifies the location of the point. Each bit position in the region code is used to indicate one of the 4 relative coordinate positions of the point with respect to the clip window; to the left, right, top or bottom. Bit values in a region code determined by comparing the coordinate values (x, y) endpoints to the clipping boundaries as

- If x < XWmin then bit 1 is set.
- If x > XWmax then bit 2 is set.
- If y < YWmin then bit 3 is set.
- If y > YWmax then bit 4 is set

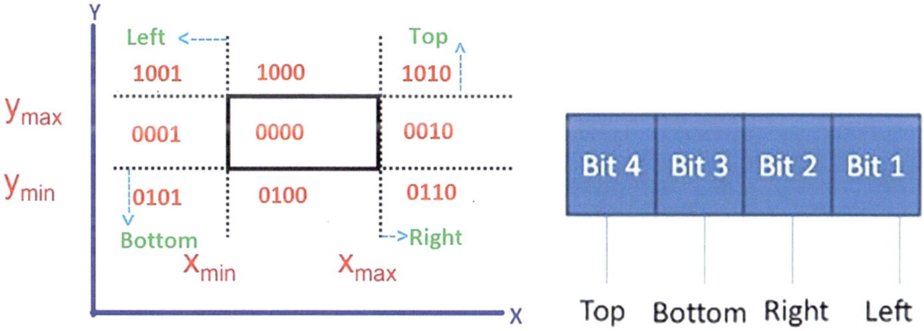

Figure 6.10: Region Code for Cohen Sutherland line algorithm

Where XWmin, XWmax, YWmin, YWmax are coordinates of the window. The value 1 in any bit position indicates that the point is in that relative position; otherwise the bit position is set to 0. If a point in within the clipping rectangle, the region code is 0000; a point that is below and to the left of the rectangle has a region code of 0101.

B. Rules for Rules for the visibility of the line

1. If both the end points have bit code zero (0000) the line is visible (inside).
2. If at least one of the end point is non zero and
   (a) The logical ANDing is zero (0000) then the line is partially visible.
   (b) If the logical ANDing is non-zero then line is not visible (outside).

C. Cohen-Sutherland Line Clipping Algorithm

Step 1. Assign a region code for two endpoints of given line.
Step 2. Scan corners for the window as (XWmin, YWmin) and (XWmax, YWmax).
Step 3. If both endpoints have a region code 0000 then given line is completely inside that is it is visible.
Step 4. If region codes for endpoints are not zero and the logical ANDing of them is also not zero then the line is invisible, reject it.
Step 5. If region codes for endpoints are not zero and the logical ANDing of them is also zero then the line is Partially Visible so
  Step 5.1. Choose an endpoint of the line that Partially Visible
  Step 5.2. Find the intersection point of the rectangular boundary (based on region code).
  Step 5.3. Replace endpoint with the intersection point and update the region code.
  Step 5.4. Repeat step 3 until we find a clipped line either completely inside (accepted) or completely outside (rejected).
Step 6. Repeat step 1 for other lines

D. Intersection Points Calculation with Clipping Window Boundary

Intersection points with the window boundaries are calculated using the line-equation parameters. Consider a line with the end-points (x1, y1) and (x2, y2). The m is the slope of the line in question and can be calculated as

$$m = \frac{(y_2 - y_1)}{(x_2 - x_1)}$$

Case I. If bit 1 position is 1 line intersects with left boundary of rectangle window

$$y = y_1 + m(x - x_1)$$

Where x = XWmin and XWmin is the minimum value of x-co-ordinate of window

Case II. If bit 2 position is 1 line intersect with right boundary

$$y = y_1 + m(x - x_1)$$

Where x = XWmax and XWmax is maximum value of x-co-ordinate of the window

Case III. If bit 3 position is 1 line intersects with bottom boundary

$$x = x_1 + \frac{(y - y_1)}{m}$$

Where y = YWmin and YWmin is the min value of y-co-ordinate of the window

Case IV. If bit 4 position is 1 line intersects with the top boundary

$$x = x_1 + \frac{(y - y_1)}{m}$$

Where y = YWmax and YWmax is the max value of y-co-ordinate of the window

Advantages of Cohen Sutherland line Algorithm

- It calculates end points very quickly and rejects and accepts lines quickly.
- It can clip pictures much large than screen size.

Disadvantages of Cohen Sutherland Line Algorithm

- Clipping window region can be rectangular in shape only and no other polygonal shaped window is allowed.
- Edges of rectangular shaped clipping window has to be parallel to the x axis and y axis.

Example 6.4

Apply the Cohen Sutherland line clipping algorithm to clip the line segment with coordinates (30, 60) and (60, 25) against the window with (XWmin, YWmin) = (10, 10) and (XWmax, YWmax) = (50, 50).

Solution

Let the endpoint of a line segment A (30, 60) and B (60, 25). Now we have the region code A (0010) and B (0010)

- If x < XWmin then bit 1 is set. That is If 30 < 10 then 0 is set.
- If x > XWmax then bit 2 is set. That is If 30 > 50 then 0 is set.
- If y < YWmin then bit 3 is set. That is If 60 < 10 then 0 is set.
- If y > YWmax then bit 4 is set. That is If 60 > 50 then 1 is set.

Therefore region code is (1000) for the line segment whose endpoint is A (30, 60).

- If x < XWmin then bit 1 is set. That is If 60 < 10 then 0 is set.
- If x > XWmax then bit 2 is set. That is If 60 > 50 then 1 is set
- If y < YWmin then bit 3 is set. That is If 25 < 10 then 0 is set.
- If y > YWmax then bit 4 is set. That is If 25 > 50 then 0 is set

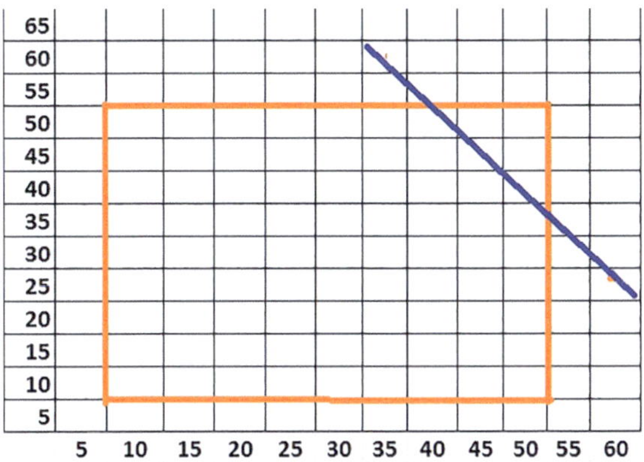

Figure 6.11: Rasterization of Example 6.4

Therefore region code is (0010) for the line segment whose endpoint is B (60, 25). Since region codes for both endpoints of line segment are non zero so compute the logical ANDing

1000 AND 0010= 0000 which means line is partially inside of the window. So First, Find the slop of line AB from the equation:

$$m = \frac{(y_2 - y_1)}{(x_2 - x_1)}$$

$$m = \frac{(25 - 60)}{(60 - 30)} = -\frac{35}{30} = -1.16$$

Then, we find the coordinate of intersection point from line AA′. The boundary line A A′ is horizontal, so YWmax = y = 50 and calculate x value from this i.e. (in this 1000, bit 4 is 1 line intersects with the top boundary)

$$x = x_1 + \frac{(y - y_1)}{m}$$

$$x = 30 + \frac{(50 - 60)}{-1.16}$$

$$= 30 + \frac{-10}{-1.16} = 30 + 8.6 = 38.6$$

The coordinate of intersection point is A′ is (38.6, 50). We find the coordinate of intersection point form line BB′. The boundary line BB is vertical, so XWmax = x= 50 and calculate y value from this: (in this 0010 if bit 2 is 1 line intersect with right boundary)

$$y = y_1 + m(x - x_1)$$

$$y = 25 + (-1.16)(50 - 60)$$

$$y = 25 + 11.6 = 36.6y = 25 + 11.6 = 36.6$$

Therefore, the coordinate of the point of intersection of a line segment is B′ (50, 36.6).

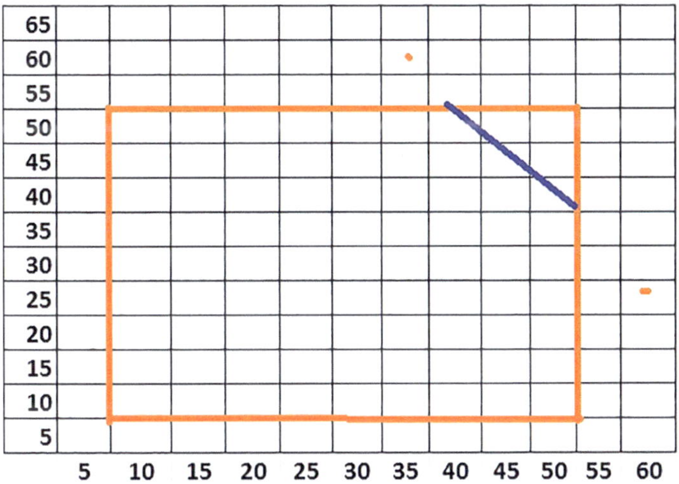

Figure 6.12: Rasterization of example 6.4 after clipping

Example 6.5

Window is defined A (20, 20), B (90, 20), C (90, 70), D (20, 70). Find visible portion of line1: P1 (10, 30), P2 (80, 90) and Line2: Q1 (20, 10), Q2 (70, 60) using Cohen Sutherland line clipping algorithm.

Solution

Given is XWmin=20, XWmax=90, YWmin=20, YWmax=70

Clip bit code for line P1P2 are P1 (0001) and P2 (1000) and the logical ANDing that is 0001 AND 1000= 0000 which means line is partially inside of the window.

Clip bit code for line Q1Q2are Q1 (0101) and Q2 (0000) and the logical ANDing that is 0101 AND 0000 = 0000 which means line is partially inside of the window. So first find the slop of line P1P2 from the equation:

$$m = \frac{(y_2 - y_1)}{(x_2 - x_1)}$$

$$m = \frac{(90 - 30)}{(80 - 10)} = \frac{60}{70} = 0.8$$

(a) Then fined the coordinate of intersection point from line P1P1′. The boundary line P1P1′ is vertical, so XWmin = x =20 and find y from this equation:

$$y = y_1 + m(x - x_1)$$

$$y = 30 + 0.8(20 - 10) = 30 + 8 = 38$$

The coordinate of intersection point P1 is (20, 38).

(b) Then fined the coordinate of intersection point from line P2P2′. The boundary line P2P2′ is horizontal , so YWmax = y =70 and find x from this equation:

$$x = x_1 + \frac{(y - y_1)}{m}$$

$$x = 80 + \frac{(70 - 90)}{0.8} = 80 + \frac{-20}{0.8} = 80 - 25 = 55$$

The coordinate of intersection point P2 is (55, 70).
Now fined the slop of second line Q1Q2

$$x = \frac{(y_2 - y_1)}{(x_2 - x_1)} = \frac{(60 - 10)}{(70 - 20)} = \frac{(50)}{(50)} = 1$$

Then fined the coordinate of intersection point from line Q1Q1′, the boundary line Q1Q1 is horizontal, so YWmin=y=20 and calculate x value from this:

$$x = x_1 + \frac{(y - y_1)}{m} = 20 + \frac{(20 - 10)}{1} = 20 + 10 = 30$$

Therefore, the coordinate of a point of intersection is Q1′ (30, 20).

Example 6.6

Rectangular area of windows are XWmin=4, YWmin=4, XWmax=10, YWmax=8. A set of lines Line 1: A (5, 5), B (7, 7), Line 2: C (7, 9), D (11, 4) and Line 3: E (1, 5), F (3, 2). Apply the Cohen Sutherland algorithm to clip the line.

Solution:

Given is XWmin=4, YWmin=4, XWmax=10, YWmax=8

Clip bit code AB

$$\begin{array}{ll} & 0001 \\ AND & 0101 \\ & 0001\,reject(outside) \end{array}$$

Clip bit code CD

$$\begin{array}{rl} & 0000 \\ AND & 0000 \\ & 0000\,accept(inside) \end{array}$$

Clip bit code EF

$$\begin{array}{rl} & 1000 \\ AND & 0110 \\ & 0000\,partially\,inside(clipping) \end{array}$$

Now find slop for line EF as follow:

$$m = \frac{(y_2 - y_1)}{(x_2 - x_1)} = \frac{(4-9)}{(11-7)} = \frac{(-5)}{(4)} = -1.25$$

We find the coordinate of intersection point from line EE′. The boundary line EE′ is horizontal, so YWmax=y=8 and find x as follow:

$$x = x_1 + \frac{(y - y_1)}{m} = 7 + \frac{(8-9)}{-1.25} = 7 + \frac{-1}{-1.25} = 7 + 0.8 = 7.8$$

The coordinate of intersection point is E′ (7.8, 8).

We find the coordinate of intersection point form line FF′, the boundary line FF′ is vertical, so XWmax=x=10 and find y as follow:

$$y = y_1 + m(x - x_1) = 4 + (-1.25)(10 - 11)$$
$$= 4 + (-1.25)(-1) = 5.25$$

The coordinate of intersection point is F′ (10, 5.25)

6.5.2.3 Liang-Barsky Line Clipping Algorithm

The Liang-Barsky algorithm is a line clipping algorithm. This algorithm is more efficient than Cohen–Sutherland line clipping algorithm and can be extended to 3-Dimensional clipping. This algorithm is considered to be the faster parametric line-clipping algorithm. The following concepts are used in this clipping:

1. The parametric equation of the line.
2. The inequalities describing the range of the clipping window which is used to determine the intersections between the line and the clip window.

The parametric equation of a line can be given by,

$$x = x_1 + t\Delta x$$

$$y = y_1 + t\Delta x$$

Where, $0 \leq t \leq 1$, $\Delta x = x_2 - x_1$, $\Delta y = y_2 - y_1$

if $t = 0$ then $x = x_{1,}\ y = y_1$ (starting point)

if $t = 1$ then $x = x_{2,}\ y = y_2$ (starting point)

From point clipping we know; to find weather given point is inside or outside the clipping window we use following inequality.

$xw_{min} \leq x \leq xw_{max},$ $yw_{min} \leq y \leq yw_{max}$

So we can write point clipping conditions in parametric form as

$xw_{min} \leq x_1 + t\Delta x \leq xw_{max},$ $yw_{min} \leq y_1 + t\Delta y \leq yw_{max}$

The above 4 inequalities can be written as

$$tp_k \leq q_k$$

Where k = 1, 2, 3, 4 (correspond to the left, right, bottom, and top boundaries, respectively) and the p and q are defined as,

$p_1 = -\Delta x$, $q_1 = x_1 - xw_{min}$,	$t = q_1/p_1$,	(Left Boundary)
$p_2 = \Delta x$, $q_2 = xw_{max} - x_1$,	$t = q_2/p_2$,	(Right Boundary)
$p_3 = -\Delta y$, $q_3 = y_1 - yw_{min}$,	$t = q_3/p_3$,	(Bottom Boundary)
$p_4 = -\Delta y$, $q_4 = yw_{max} - y_1$,	$t = q_4/p_4$,	(Top Boundary)

We can say that

- When the line is parallel to a view window boundary, the p_k value for that boundary is zero.
- When $p_k < 0$, line goes from the outside to inside (entering).
- When $p_k > 0$, line goes from inside to outside (exiting).
- When $p_k = 0$, and $q_k < 0$, then line is trivially invisible because it is outside view window.
- When $p_k = 0$ and $q_k > 0$ then the line is inside the corresponding window boundary.

Using the following conditions, the position of line can be determined:

- $p_k = 0$ parallel to the clipping boundaries
- $p_k = 0$ and $q_k < 0$, completely outside the boundary
- $p_k = 0$ and $q_k \geq 0$, inside the parallel clipping boundary
- $p_k = 0$, line proceeds from outside to inside
- $p_k = 0$, line proceeds from inside to outside

Using p_k and q_k (k = 1, 2, 3, and 4), find if the line can be rejected or intersection parameters (t1 and t2) must be adjusted.

- if $p_k < 0$ *update t1 as max*$[0, q_k/p_k]$ where $k = 1:4$
- if $p_k > 0$ *update t2 as max*$[1, q_k/p_k]$ where $k = 1:4$

After the update
If $t_1 > t_2$, reject the line.
If $t_1 > 0$, calculate new values of x_1, y_1
If $t_2 < 0$ calculate new values of x_2, y_2

Liang-Barsky Line Clipping Algorithm

Step 1. Set line intersection parameters t_entry (t1) = 0.0 and t_leaving (t2) = 1.0

Step 2. Obtain the p_k value and the q_k value for k =1: 4 as given in Table 6.2.

Table 6.2: Edge and K value for line clipping

Edge & K value	*p*	*q*	*t*
Left & k=1	$p_1 = -dx$	$q_1 = x_0 - xw_{min}$	$t = q_1/p_1$
Right & k=2	$p_2 = dx$	$q_2 = xw_{minx} - x_0$	$t = q_2/p_2$
Bottom & k=3	$p_3 = -dy$	$q_3 = y_0 - tyw_{min}$	$t = q_3/p_3$
Top & k=4	$p_4 = dy$	$q_4 = yw_{minx} - y_0$	$t = q_4/p_4$

Step 3. If $p_k = 0$, the line is parallel to the corresponding clipping boundary.

(a) If $p_k = 0$ and $q_k < 0$, the line is completely outside the boundary.
(b) If $p_k = 0$ and $q_k \geq 0$, the line is inside the parallel clipping boundary.

Step 4. Using p_k and q_k (k = 1, 2, 3, and 4), find if the line can be rejected or intersection parameters (t1 and t2) must be adjusted.

(a) if $p_k < 0$, *update t1 as max*$[0, q_k/p_k]$ where k = 1:4
(b) if $p_k > 0$, *update t2 as max*$[1, q_k/p_k]$ where k = 1:4

Step 5. After the update

i. If $t1 > t2$, reject the line.
ii. If $t1 > 0$, calculate new values $x0_{new}$, $y0_{new}$ that is
   If ($t_{entry} > 0.0$) calculate new x_0, y_0 by using
   $x0_{new} = x_0 + t_{entry} * dx$, and $y0_{new} = y_0 + t_{entry} * dy$
iii. $t2 < 0$, calculate new values $x1_{new}$, $y1_{new}$ that is
   If ($t_{leaving} < 1.0$) calculate new x_1, y_1
   $x1_{new} = x_0 + t_{leaving} * dx$, and $y1_{new} = y_0 + t_{leaving} * dy$

Step 6. Draw clipped line with the points $(x0_{new}, y0_{new})$ and $(x1_{new}, y1_{new})$.

Step 7. Stop

Example 6.7

If XWmin = 70, XWmax = 230, YWmin = 60, YWmax = 150 and endpoint of a line are P0 (30, 20) and P1 (280, 160). Apply the Liang-Barsky Line Clipping Algorithm to clip the line.

Solution

$dx = x_1 - x_0 = 280 - 30 = 250$
$dy = y_1 - y_0 = 160 - 20 = 140$
$dx = 250, dy = 140$
Initially t_{entry} (t1) = 0.0 and $t_{leaving}$ (t2) = 1.0

A. Left Edge Check

$p = -dx = -250$
$q = x_0 - xw_{min} = 30 - 70 = -40$
$t = q/p = -40/-250 = 0.16$
if $p < 0 = -250 < 0$ *TRUE* then update t1 and
if $t > t1 = 0.16 > 0$ *TRUE*
THEN set t1 = t => $t1 = 0.16$
Therefore t1 = 0.16, and t2 = 1.0

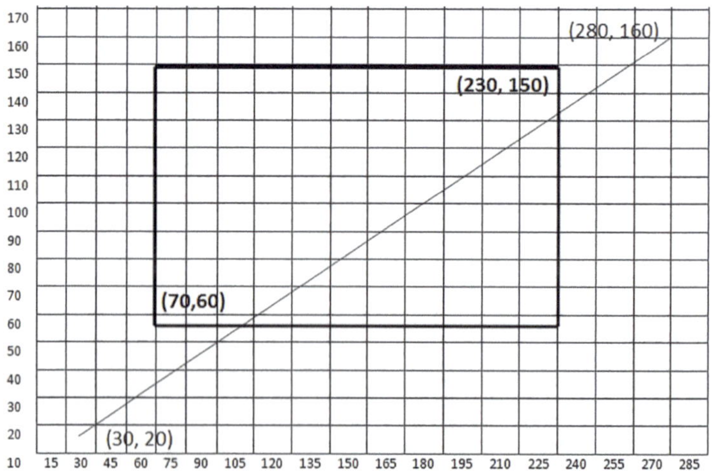

Figure 6.13: Rasterization of Example 6

B. Right Edge Check

$p = dx = 250$
$q = xw_{max} - x_0 = 230 - 30 = 200$

t = q/p = 200/250 = 0.8
if p < 0 = 250 < 0 FALSE then update t2 and
if t < *t*2 = 0.8 < 1 TRUE
THEN set t2 = t => t2 = 0.8
Therefore t1 = 0.16, and t2 = 0.8

C. Bottom Edge Check

p = –dy = –140
$q = y_0 - yw_{min}$ = 20 – 60 = –40
t = q/p = –40/–140 = 0.2857
if p < 0 = –140 < 0 *TRUE then update t1 and*
if t > t1 = 0.2857 > 0.16 *TRUE*
THEN set t1 = t => *t*1 = 0.2857
Therefore t1=0.2857,and t2=1.0

D. Top Edge Check

p = –dy = –140
$q = yw_{max} - y_0$ = 150 – 20 = 130
t = q/p = 130/140 = 0.928
if p < 0 = 140 < 0 *FALSE then update t2 and*
if t < t2 = 0.928 < 0.8 *FALSE*
THEN no change in t2
Therefore t1 = 0.2857, and t2 = 0.8

Now we have t1 = 0.2857, and t2 = 0.8, dx = 250, dy = 140

if (t_{entry} > 0.0) calculate new x_0 , y_0

Since (t_{entry} > 0.0) = 0.2857 > 0.0 *TRUE so*

$$x0_{new} = x_0 + t_{entry} * dx$$
$$= 30 + 0.2857 * 250 = 30 + 71.425 = 101.425$$
$$y0_{new} = y_0 + t_{entry} * dy$$
$$= 20 + 0.2857 * 140 = 20 + 39.998 = 59.998$$

Similarly

if ($t_{leaving}$ < 1.0) calculate new x_1, y_1

Since ($t_{leaving}$ < 1.0) = 0.8 < 1.0 *TRUE* so

$$x1_{new} = x_0 + t_{leaving} * dx$$
$$= 30 + 0.8 * 250 = 30 + 200 = 230$$
$$y1_{new} = y_0 + t_{leaving} * dy$$
$$= 20 + 0.8 * 140 = 20 + 112 = 132$$

So $x0_{new}$ = 101.425, $y0_{new}$ = 59.998, $x1_{new}$ = 230, $y1_{new}$ = 132

Draw clipped line with the points P0′ ($x0_{new}$ = 101.425, $y0_{new}$ = 59.998), and P1′ ($x1_{new}$ = 230, $y1_{new}$ = 132).

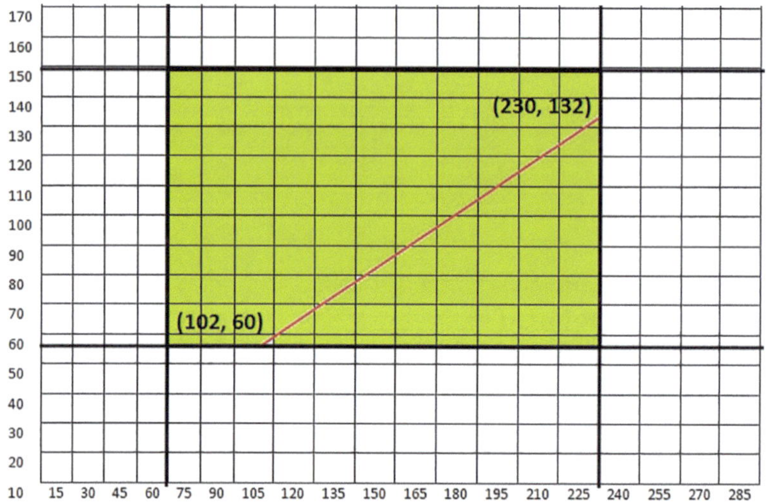

Figure 6.14: Clipped line

Advantages of Liang-Barsky Line Clipping

- More efficient.
- Only requires one division to update $t1$ and $t2$.
- Window intersections of line are calculated just once.

6.5.3 Polygon Clipping

To clip polygon, we need to modify the line clipping procedure because this approach would produce a series of unconnected line segments as shown in figure

What we really want to display as a bounded area after clipping. For polygon clipping, we require an algorithm that will generate one or more closed areas that are then scan converted for the appropriate areas fill. The

output of a polygon clipping should be sequence of vertices that define the clipped polygon boundary.

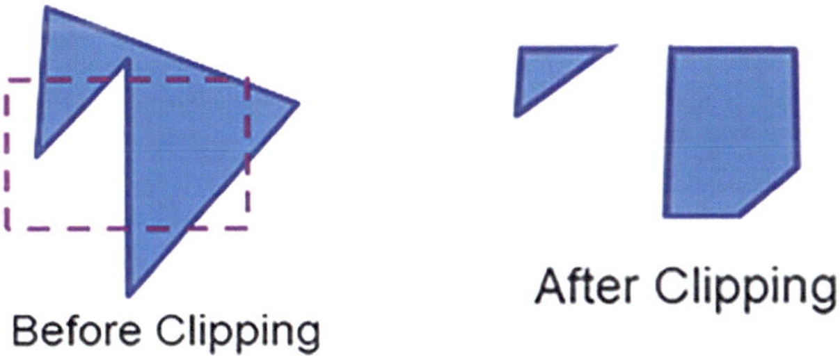

Figure 6.15: Polygon clipping

6.5.3.1 Sutherland-Hodgeman Polygon Clipping Algorithm

For polygon clipping we use a Sutherland –Hodgeman algorithm.

Working of Sutherland –Hodgeman Algorithm

The basic idea behind this algorithm is to compare the polygon to each window boundary one by one to obtain the clipped area. That is each vertex of the polygon is compare against the window boundary, those vertex which are within the window edge are saved, so that they can be used for clipping against the next boundary and the vertices outside the window edge rejected. This technique was developed by Sutherland Hodgeman. Let (V1, V2... VN) be the vertex list of the Polygon to be clipped and E is the edge of positively oriented, convex clipping window.

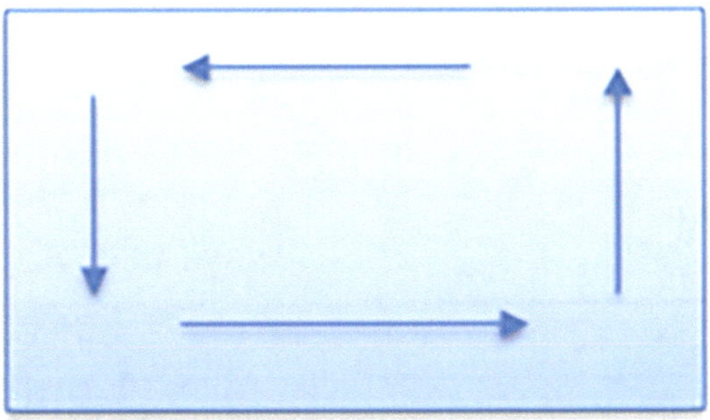

We clip each edge of the polygon in turn against each window edge E, forming a new polygon whose vertices are determined as follows:

A. **Inside:** If both V1 and V2 are to the right of window edge vertex then V2 is placed on the output vertex list.

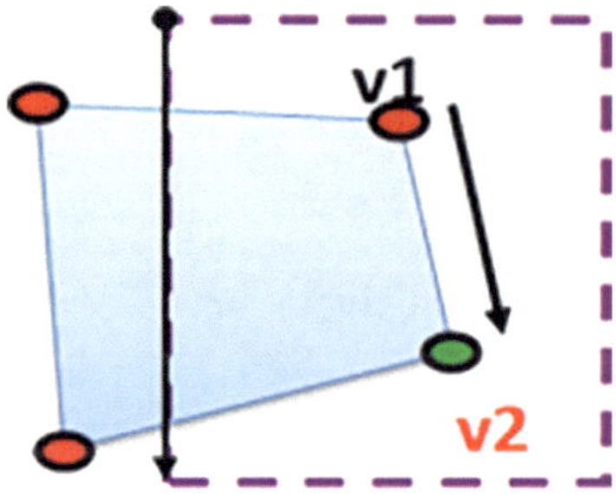

in → in
save ending vertex **v2**
Inside
(1 output)

B. **Entering:** If V1 is to the left of window edge and V2 is to the right of window edge vertex then intersection (I) of V1 V2 with edge E and V2 are placed on the output vertex list.

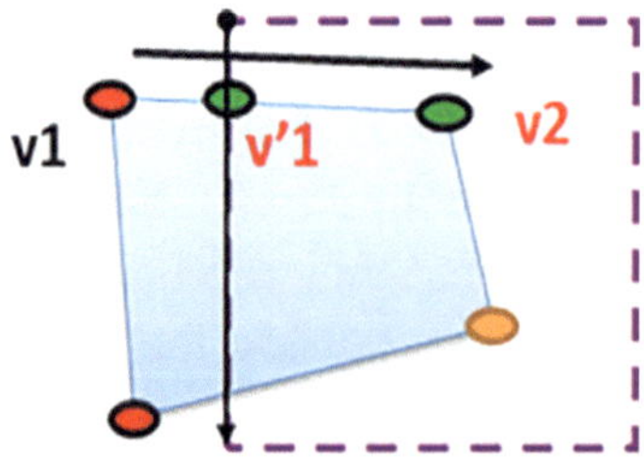

out → in
save new **v'1** clip vertex
and ending vertex v2
Entering
(2 outputs)

C. **Leaving:** If V1 is to the right of window edge and V2 is to the left of window edge vertex then only intersection (I) of V1 V2 with edge E is placed on the output vertex list.

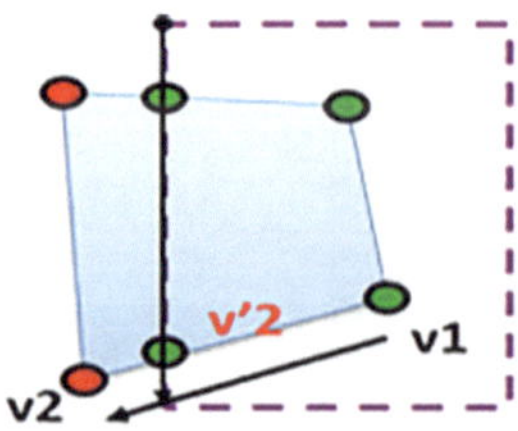

in → out
save new **v'2** clip vertex
Leaving
(1 output)

D. **Outside:** If both V1 and V2 are to the left of window edge nothing is placed on the output vertex list.

Sutherland-Hodgeman Polygon Clipping Algorithm

Step 1. Read co-ordinates of all vertices of the polygon.

Step 2. Read co-ordinates of the clipping window.

Step 3. Consider the left edge of window.

Step 4. Compare vertices of each of polygon, individually with the clipping plane.

Step 5. Save the resulting intersections and vertices in the new list of vertices according to four possible relationships between the edge and the clipping boundary.

Step 6. Repeat the steps (4) and (5) for remaining edges of clipping window. Each time resultant list of vertices is successively passed to process next edge of clipping window.

Step 7. Stop.

Example 6.8

Clip a polygon ABCDE against window PQRS. The co-ordinate of polygon are A (120, 180), B (220, 120), C (150, 100), D (100, 30) and E (20, 110). Co-ordinate of the window are P(200 ,50), Q(50, 150), R(200 ,150) and S(50 ,50) .

Solution

Step 1. Plot the point

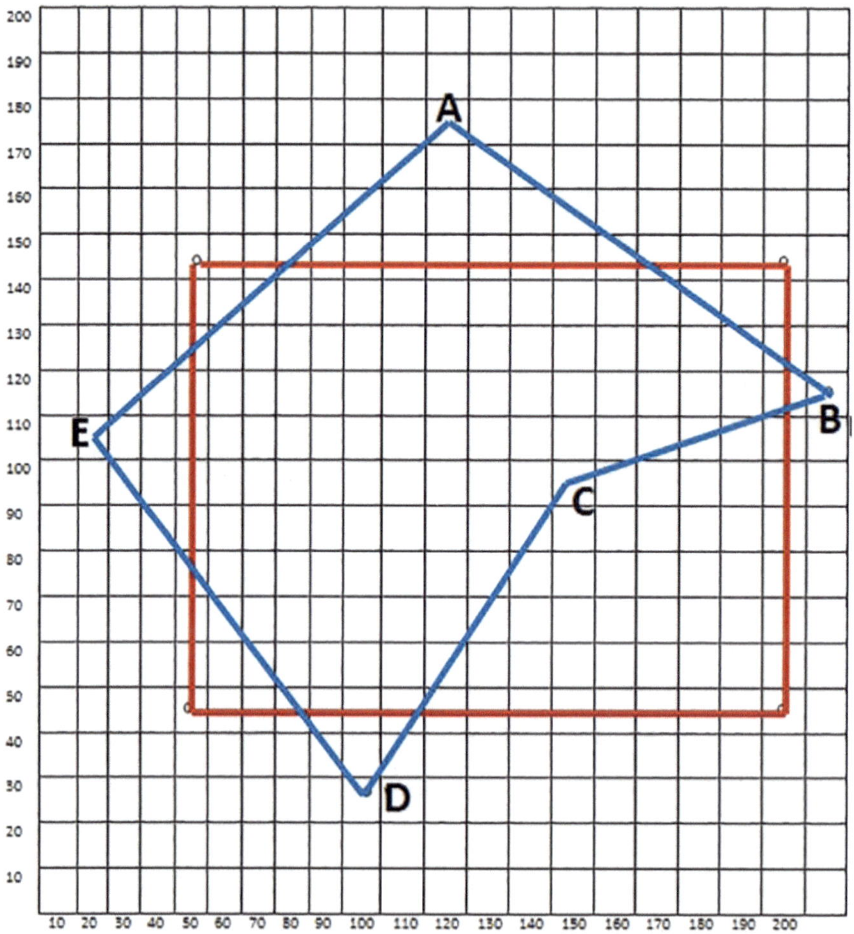

Step 2. Clipping against left edge of the windows using left clipper

Vertex	*case*	*Output*
AB	in-in	B
BC	in-in	C
CD	in-in	D
DE	in-out	E′
EA	out-in	A′ and A

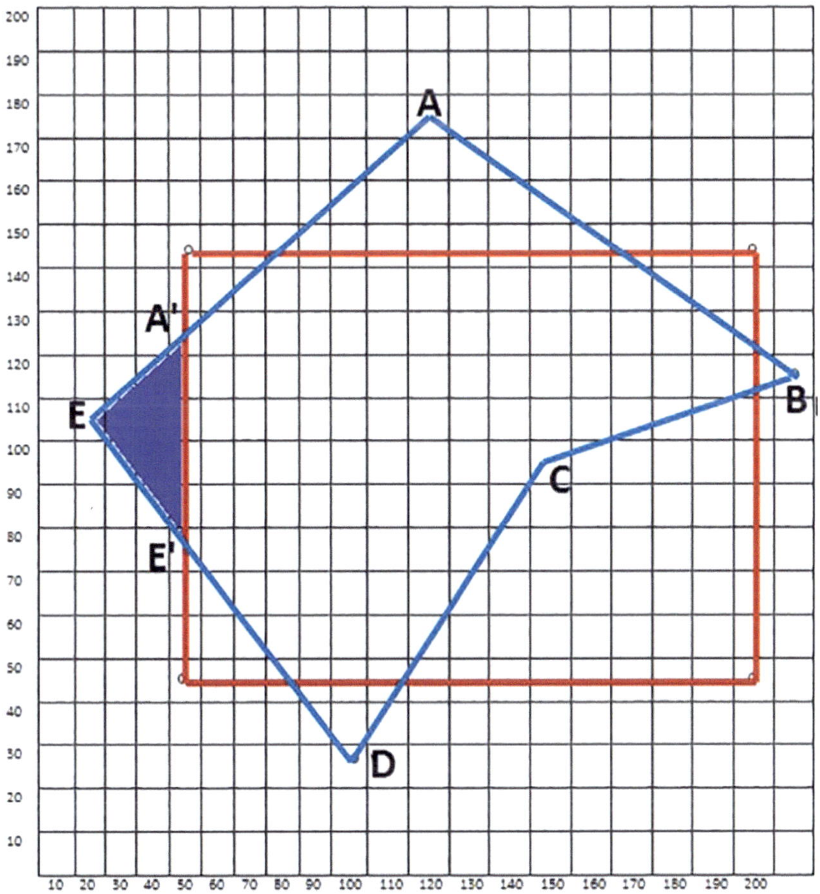

Step 3. Right clipper

Vertex	*case*	*Output*
AB	in-out	B′
BC	out-in	C′ and C
CD	in-in	D
DE′	in-in	E′
E′A′	in-in	A′
A′A	in-in	A

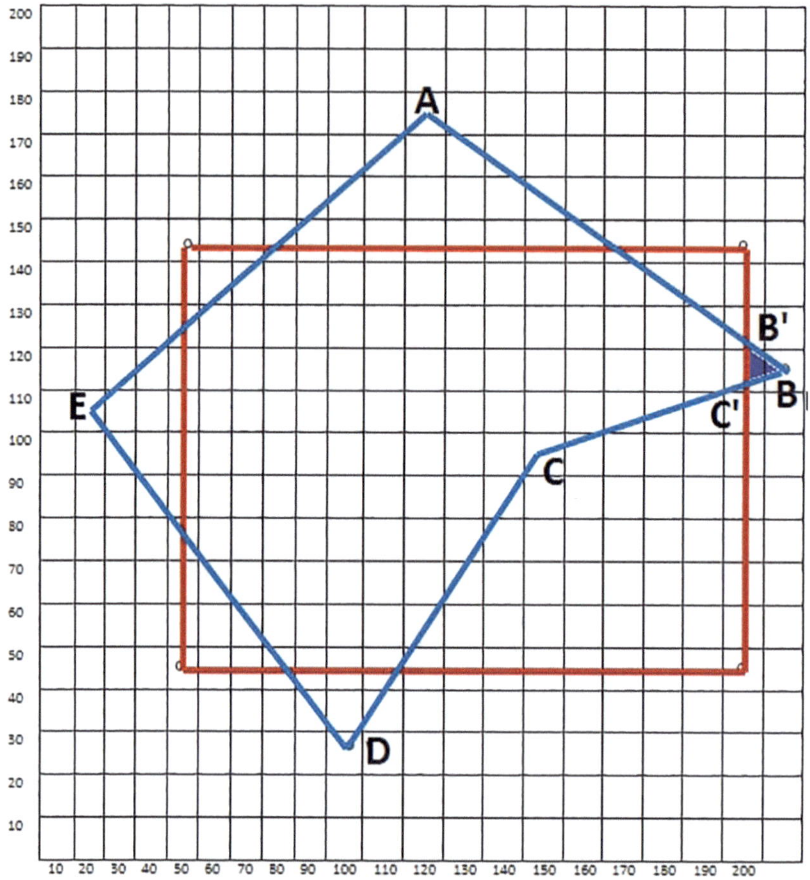

Step 4. Bottom clipper

Vertex	*case*	*Output*
AB′	in-in	B′
B′C′	in-in	C′
C′C	in-in	C
CD	in-out	D′
DE′	out-in	D″ and E′
E′A′	in-in	A′
A′A	in-in	A

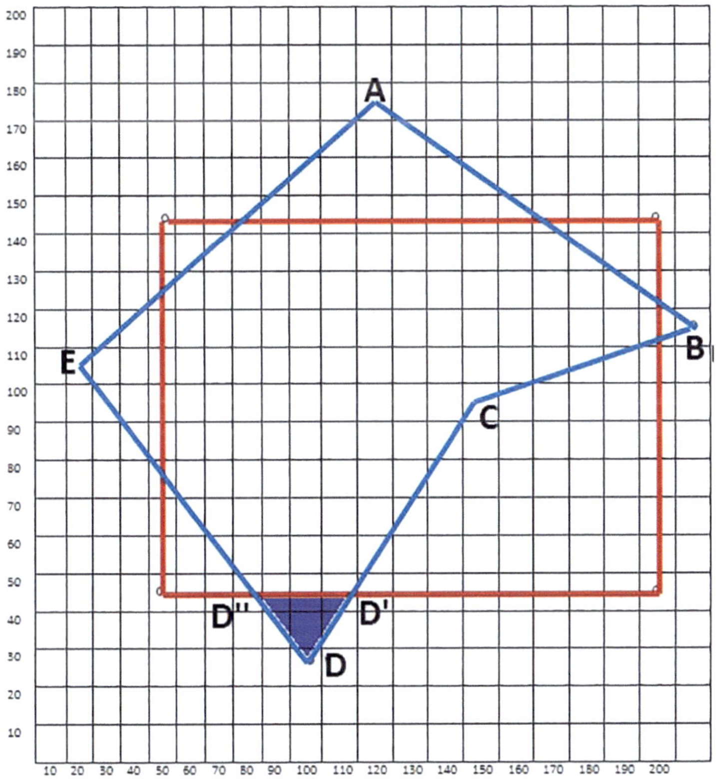

Step 5. Top clipper

Vertex	case	Output
AB′	out-in	B″ and B′
B′C′	in-in	C′
C′C	in-in	C
CD′	in-in	D′
D′D″	in-in	D″
D″E′	in-in	E′
E′A′	in-in	A′
A′A	in-out	A″

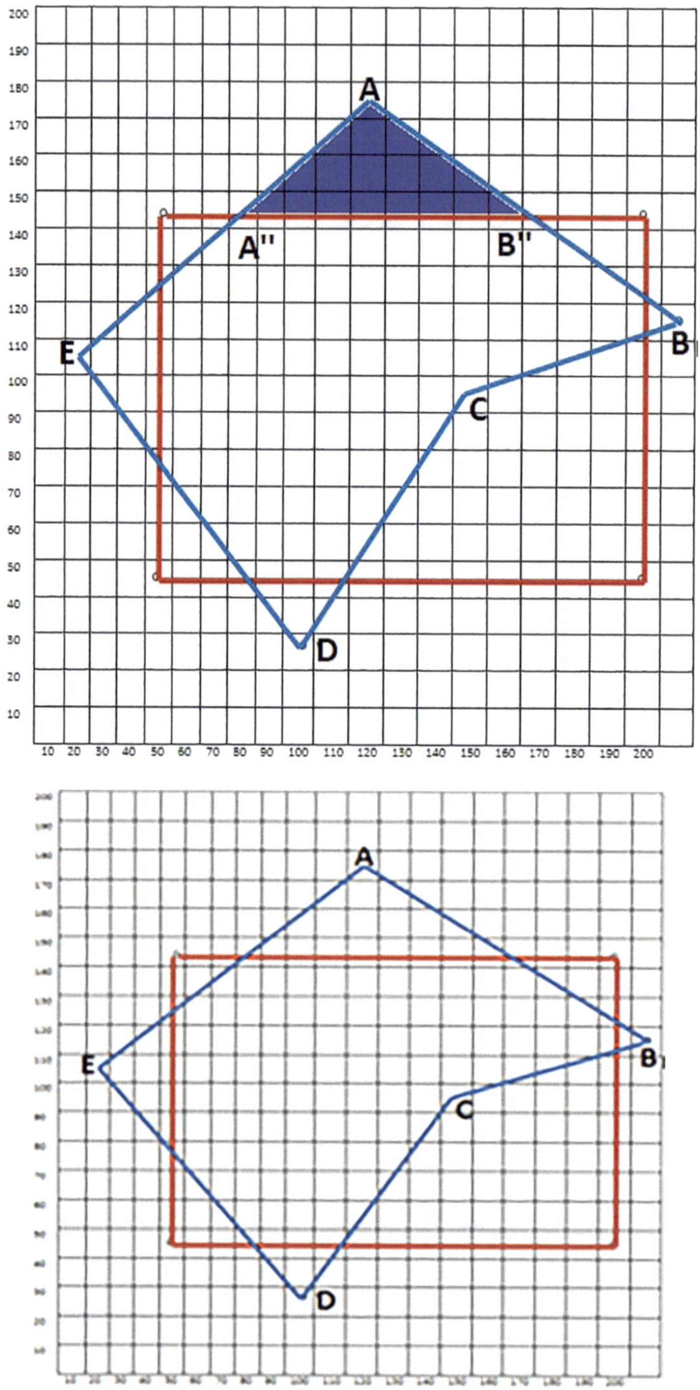

Figure 6.16(a): Before Clapping

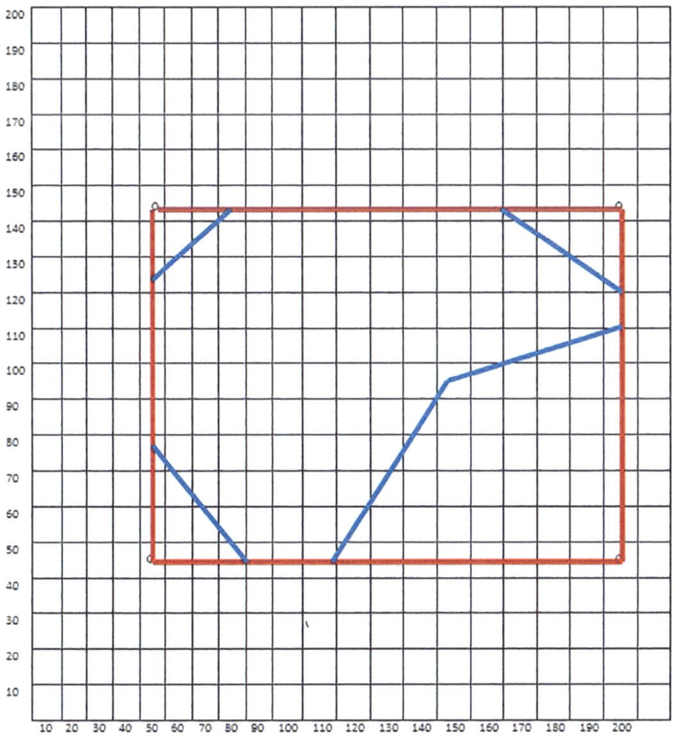

Figure 6.16(b): After Clipping

Advantages of Sutherland –Hodgeman algorithm

- Any desired shape/object can be achieved. Any small part of an object can be selected.

Disadvantages of Sutherland –Hodgeman algorithm

- Complexity for algorithm Complex shape polygon clipping is not easily achieved.

6.5.4 Curve Clipping

Curve clipping procedures will involve non-linear equations however this requires more processing than for object with linear boundaries. The bounding rectangle for a circle or other curved object can be used first to test for overlap with a rectangle clip window. If the bounding rectangle for the objects is completely inside the window we save the object. If the boundary rectangle for the object is determined to be completely outside the window, we discard the object. This procedure can be applied when clipping a curved object against a general polygon clip region. On the first pass we can clip the bounding rectangle of the clip region. If the region overlaps, we will need to store the simulations line-curve equation to obtain the clip intersection points.

6.5.5 Text Clipping

Various techniques are used to provide text clipping in a computer graphics. It depends on the methods used to generate characters and the requirements of a particular application. There are three methods for text clipping which are listed below –

- All or none string clipping
- All or none character clipping
- Text clipping

The Figure 6.17 shows all or none string clipping –

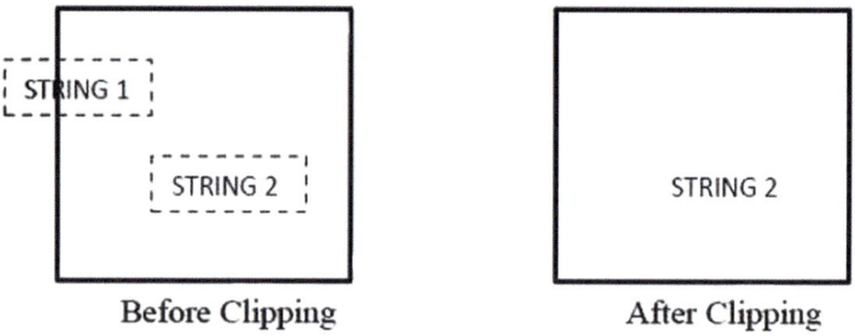

Figure 6.17: All or None String Clipping

In all or none string clipping method, either we keep the entire string or we reject entire string based on the clipping window. As shown in the above figure, STRING2 is entirely inside the clipping window so we keep it and STRING1 being only partially inside the window, we reject.

The Figure 6.18 shows all or none character clipping –

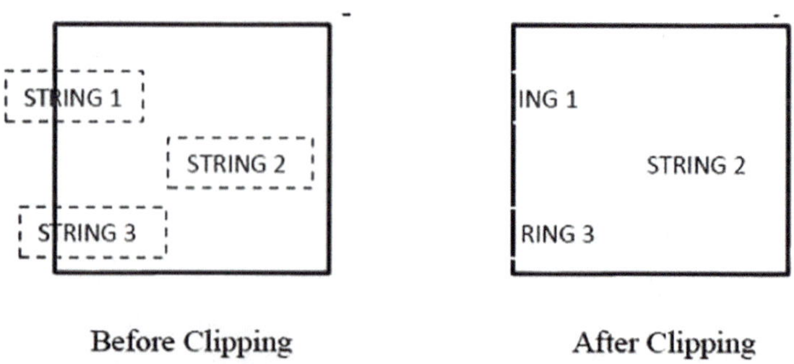

Figure 6.18: All or None Character Clipping

This clipping method is based on characters rather than entire string. In this method if the string is entirely inside the clipping window, then we keep it. If it is partially outside the window, then:

- You reject only the portion of the string being outside
- If the character is on the boundary of the clipping window, then we discard that entire character and keep the rest string. The Figure 6.19 shows text clipping –

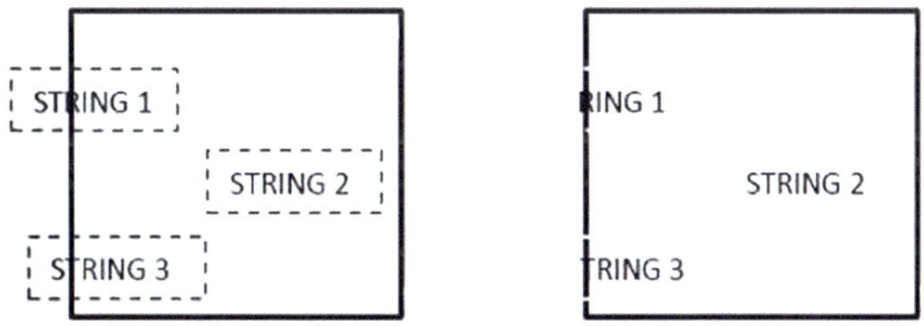

Before Clipping After Clipping

Figure 6.19: Text Clipping

This clipping method is based on characters rather than the entire string. In this method if the string is entirely inside the clipping window, then we keep it. If it is partially outside the window, then:

- You reject only the portion of string being outside.
- If the character is on the boundary of the clipping window, then we discard only that portion of character that is outside of the clipping window.

OBJECTIVE QUESTIONS

1. In the Cohen-Sutherland clipping algorithm using region codes, a line is already clipped if the
   (a) Codes of the endpoint are same
   (b) Logical AND of the endpoint code is not 0000
   (c) Logical AND of the endpoint code is 0000
   (d) Both (a) and (b)
2. The method of selecting and enlarging a portion of a drawing is called
   (a) Viewing (b) View port
   (c) Windowing (d) Clipping

3. The technique of not showing that part of the drawing which one is not interested is called
   (a) Windowing (b) Clipping
   (c) Viewing (d) View port
4. If the edges of the rectangular window are parallel to the coordinate axes, then such a window is called
   (a) Rectangular window (b) Standard window
   (c) Parallel window (d) Regular window
5. When an entire image is to be confined into a box, then that box in the screen space is called a
   (a) Window (b) View port
   (c) Both of these (d) None of the above
6. Consider a rectangular window whose lower left corner is at (-3, 1) and upper right corner is at (2, 6). What is the 4-bit area code for the endpoint of the line PQ having co-ordinates (-4, 2) and (-1, 8)?
   (a) P → 0001, Q → 0001 (b) P → 1010, Q → 1001
   (c) P → 0001, Q → 1000 (d) P → 0000, Q → 0110
7. A line clipping algorithm is presented by a
   (a) Cohen-Sutherland algorithm
   (b) Midpoint subdivision algorithm
   (c) Cyrus-Beck algorithm
   (d) All of above
8. Polygon clipping algorithm is presented by
   (a) Cohen-Sutherland algorithm
   (b) Cyrus-Beck algorithm
   (c) Cohen-Hodgeman algorithm
   (d) None of the above
9. Rearrange steps involved in two dimensional viewing transformations.
   I. Map normalized viewport to device Co-ordinates
   II. Convert world co-ordinate to viewing co-ordinates I
   III. Construct world – co-ordinate scene using modeling coordinate transformation
   IV. Map viewing co-ordinates to normalized viewing co-ordinates using window-viewport specification
   (a) II → III → IV → I (b) III → II → I → IV
   (c) I → II→ IV → III (d) III → II → IV → I

10. A rectangle is bound by the lines x = 0; y = 0; x = 5 and y = 3. The line segment joining (-1, 0) and (4, 5), if clipped against this window will connect the points _______.
    (a) (0, 1) and (3, 3)
    (b) (0, 1) and (2, 3)
    (c) (0, 1) and (4, 5)
    (d) (0, 1) and (3, 5)

11. Perform window to viewport transformation for the point (20, 15). Assume that (XWmin YWmin) is (0, 0); (XWmax, YWmax) is (100, 100); (XVmin, YVmin) is (5, 5) and (XVmax, YVmax) is (20, 20). The value of x and y in the viewport is
    (a) x = 4, y = 4
    (b) x = 3, y = 3
    (c) x = 8, y = 7.25
    (d) x = 3, y = 4

12. Which of the following algorithms is not used for line clipping?
    (b) Cohen-Sutherland algorithm
    (c) Southerland-Hodgeman algorithm
    (d) Liang-Barsky algorithm
    (d) Nicholl-Lee-Nicholl algorithm

13. Find the normalization transformation that maps a window whose lower left corner is at (1, 1) and upper right corner is at (3, 5) onto a viewport that is the entire normalized device screen.

    (a) $\begin{bmatrix} \frac{1}{2} & 0 & -\frac{1}{2} \\ 0 & \frac{1}{4} & -\frac{1}{4} \\ 0 & 0 & 1 \end{bmatrix}$

    (b) $\begin{bmatrix} \frac{1}{2} & 0 & \frac{1}{2} \\ 0 & -\frac{1}{4} & \frac{1}{4} \\ 1 & 1 & 1 \end{bmatrix}$

    (c) $\begin{bmatrix} \frac{1}{2} & 0 & -\frac{1}{2} \\ 0 & \frac{1}{4} & \frac{1}{4} \\ 0 & 0 & 1 \end{bmatrix}$

    (d) $\begin{bmatrix} \frac{1}{2} & 0 & \frac{1}{2} \\ 0 & \frac{1}{4} & -\frac{1}{4} \\ 0 & 0 & 1 \end{bmatrix}$

14. In Sutherland-Hodgeman algorithm for polygon clipping, assume P (present point) lies inside the window and S (previous point) lies outside the window. Then, while processing through that window boundary, we should
    (a) Store the intersection point of line PS (S′) only
    (b) Store the point P only
    (c) Store the points P and S′
    (d) Store the points S and S′

15. Applications of clipping include
    (a) Selecting a specific information
    (b) Antialiasing
    (c) Copying, moving, deleting a portion of picture
    (d) All of the above

ANSWERS

1. (d)	4. (d)	7. (d)	10. (b)	13. (a)
2. (c)	5. (b)	8. (c)	11. (c)	14. (c)
3. (b)	6. (c)	9. (d)	12. (b)	15. (d)

EXERCISES

1. Explain the two-dimensional viewing transformation pipeline with example?
2. Define the terms window, viewport and windowing transformation in the context of two-dimensional viewing with suitable diagrams.
3. Which are the steps involved in window to viewport coordinate transformation in 2D?
4. What do you understand by term "clipping and windowing"?
5. What is window to view point coordinate transformation? What are the issues related to multiple windowing.
6. Explain the difference between a window and a viewport.
7. Find a normalization transformation from the window whose lower left corner is at (0, 0) and upper right corner is at (4, 3) onto the normalized device screen so that aspect ratios are preserved.
8. Explain the window to viewport coordinate transformation and also derive the scaling factors during the transformation.
9. Derive an equation for window to viewport transformation by specifying the sequence of basic transformations involved.
10. Explain the concept of point clipping in two-dimensional.
11. Briefly explain the steps involved in clipping a line using Midpoint Subdivision algorithm.
12. Explain the Cohen Sutherland line clipping algorithm with suitable examples.
13. How does Cohen Sutherland algorithm determine whether a line is visible, invisible or a candidate for clipping based on the region codes assigned to the end points of the line?
14. What is the significance of 4-bit region code is Cohen-Sutherland algorithm?

15. Using Midpoint subdivision line clipping algorithm illustrate a clipping of a line segment joining two end points A(-1,5) and B(3,8) by considering clipping window with left corner at(-3,1) and upper right comer at(2.6).
16. Write Cohen-Sutherland line clipping algorithm. Apply it for calculating the saved portion of a line from (2, 7) to (8, 12) in a window (XWmin = YWmin = 5 and XWmax = YWmax = 10).
17. Given a clipping window A (-20,-20), B (40,-20), C (40, 30) and D (-20, 30). Using Cohen Sutherland line clipping algorithm, find the visible portion of the line segment joining the points P (-30, 20) and Q (60,-10).
18. Clip the line PQ having coordinates P (4, 1), and Q (6, 4) against the clipping window having vertices A (3, 2), B (7, 2), C (7, 6), and D (3, 6) using Cohen Sutherland Line Clipping Algorithm.
19. Write Liang and Barsky line clipping algorithm. Apply it for calculating the saved portion of line from (2, 7) to (8, 12) in a window (XWmin = YWmin = 5 and XWmax = YWmax = 10).
20. Apply the Liang-Barsky to clip the line segment from A(3,7) to B(8,10) against the regular rectangular window P(1,2) , Q(9,2) , R(9,8) and S(1,8).
21. Explain Liang Brasky line clipping algorithm. Apply the algorithm to clip the line with coordinate (30, 60) and (60, 20) against window (XWmin, YWmin) = (10, 10) and (XWmax, YWmax) = (50, 50).
22. Compare Cohen-Sutherland line clipping algorithm and Liang-Barsky line clipping algorithm.
23. What is polygon clipping? Explain Sutherland-Hodgeman polygon clipping algorithm with the help of an example.
24. Explain the Sutherland-Hodgeman algorithm for polygon clipping with an example.
25. Justify that the Sutherland-Hodgeman algorithm is not suitable for clipping when the clipping polygon is a concave window.
26. Develop a text-clipping algorithm that clips individual characters assuming that the characters are defined in a pixel grid of a specified size.

7

Three-Dimensional Transformation

In computer graphics, 3D transformation is an expansion of 2D transformation involving the z-axis coordinates. The coordinates of a point in 3D transformation are represented by (x, y, z), and the homogeneous coordinate is expressed as [x y z w]. In 3D transformation, the value of w will always be 1. Computer graphics encompasses all aspects of graphical images and can be classified into 2D, 3D, 5D, and animated graphics. 3D graphics generates images from non-representational data of an object which are projected onto a 2D plane. These models are then converted into graphical images when displayed on a computer screen or printed. They are realistic renderings of surfaces, illumination sources, and more. This chapter focuses mainly on the creation of 3D images. Computer-generated images have various applications such as simulation and training, medical imaging, special effects in movies, and so on.

7.1 INTRODUCTION OF 3D TRANSFORMATION

When we translate, rotate, and scale objects in the three-dimensional plane then, it is called Three-Dimensional (3D) Transformation. A three-dimensional plane consists of x, y, and z-axis. Just as in two-dimensional any three-dimensional transformation can be represented by

$$[X'] = [T]\,[X]$$

Where

[X′] Represents transformed object coordinates $\begin{bmatrix} x' \\ y' \\ z' \\ 1 \end{bmatrix}$

[X] Represents the original object coordinate $\begin{bmatrix} x \\ y \\ z \\ 1 \end{bmatrix}$

[T] The 4 × 4 transformation matrix

7.2 BASIC TRANSFORMATION

Geometric transformations and object modeling in three dimensions are extended from two-dimensional methods by including considerations for the z-coordinate. Therefore 3D transformations are three types: translation, scaling, and rotation.

7.2.1 Translation Transformation

In a three-dimensional homogeneous coordinate representation, a point or an object is translated from position P = (x, y, z) to position P′ = (x′, y′, z) with the matrix operation.

$$P' = TP$$

This may be written as

$$\begin{bmatrix} x' \\ y' \\ z' \\ 1 \end{bmatrix} = \begin{bmatrix} 1 & 0 & 0 & t_x \\ 0 & 1 & 0 & t_y \\ 0 & 0 & 1 & t_z \\ 0 & 0 & 0 & 1 \end{bmatrix} \begin{bmatrix} x \\ y \\ z \\ 1 \end{bmatrix} \qquad ...(1)$$

Parameters t_x, t_y and t_z specifying translation distances for the coordinate directions x, y and z are assigned any real values. The matrix representation in equation (1) is equivalent to the three equations.

$$x' = x + t_x$$

$$y' = y + t_y$$

$$z' = z + t_z$$

7.2.2 Scaling Transformation

The matrix expression for the scaling transformation of a position P = (x, y, z) relative to the coordinate origin can be written as

$$P' = SP$$

This may be written as

$$\begin{bmatrix} x' \\ y' \\ z' \\ 1 \end{bmatrix} = \begin{bmatrix} s_x & 0 & 0 & 0 \\ 0 & s_y & 0 & 0 \\ 0 & 0 & s_z & 0 \\ 0 & 0 & 0 & 1 \end{bmatrix} \begin{bmatrix} x \\ y \\ z \\ 1 \end{bmatrix} \qquad .... (2)$$

Where scaling parameters S_x, S_y and S_z are assigned any position values. The matrix representation in equation (2) is equivalent to the three equations

$$x' = xS_x$$
$$y' = yS_y$$
$$z' = zS_x$$

7.2.3 Rotation Transformation

To generate a rotation transformation for an object, we must designate an axis of rotation (about which the object is to be rotated) and the (angle of rotation) amount of angular rotation unlike the two-dimensional application, where all transformations are carried out in the XY plane; a three-dimensional rotation can be specified around any line in space. Three-dimensional rotations can be performed in the following way.

- Rotation about the Z-axis is defined by the XY Plan.
- Rotation about the X-axis is defined by the ZY Plan.
- Rotation about the Y-axis is defined by the ZX Plan.

Case I. Rotation about Z-axis is defined by the XY Plan

Let us assume, the initial coordinates of an object = (x, y, z), the Initial angle from origin = α. The Rotation angle = θ, and the new coordinates after Rotation = (x′, y′, z′).

$$x = r \cos \alpha$$
$$y = r \sin \alpha$$
$$z = z$$

Rotated point is

$$x' = r \cos(\alpha + \theta)$$
$$y' = r \sin(\alpha + \theta)$$
$$z' = z$$

This may be written as

$$x' = r(\cos\alpha \cos\theta - \sin\alpha \sin\theta)$$

$$y' = r(\sin\alpha \cos\theta + \cos\alpha \sin\theta)$$

$$z' = z$$

$$x' = r \cos\alpha \cos\theta - r \sin\alpha \sin\theta$$

$$y' = r \sin\alpha \cos\theta + r \cos\alpha \sin\theta$$

$$z' = z$$

By using the x and y values we get

$$x' = x \cos \theta - y \sin\theta$$
$$y' = y \cos \theta - x \sin\theta$$
$$z' = z$$

Now arranging the values

$$x' = x\cos\theta - y\sin\theta$$
$$y' = x\sin\theta - y\cos\theta$$
$$z' = z$$

Now we have the following equations for x, y, z coordinates

$$x' = x\cos\theta - y\sin\theta$$
$$y' = x\sin\theta + y\cos\theta$$
$$z' = z \qquad \text{---(3)}$$

Parameter θ specifies the rotation angle in homogenous coordinate form. In the three dimensional z – axis rotation equations are expressed as:

$$P' = R_z(\theta)P$$

This can be written in matrix form as:

$$\begin{bmatrix} x' \\ y' \\ z' \\ 1 \end{bmatrix} = \begin{bmatrix} \cos\theta & -\sin\theta & 0 & 0 \\ \sin\theta & \cos\theta & 0 & 0 \\ 0 & 0 & 0 & 0 \\ 0 & 0 & 0 & 1 \end{bmatrix} \begin{bmatrix} x \\ y \\ z \\ 1 \end{bmatrix}$$

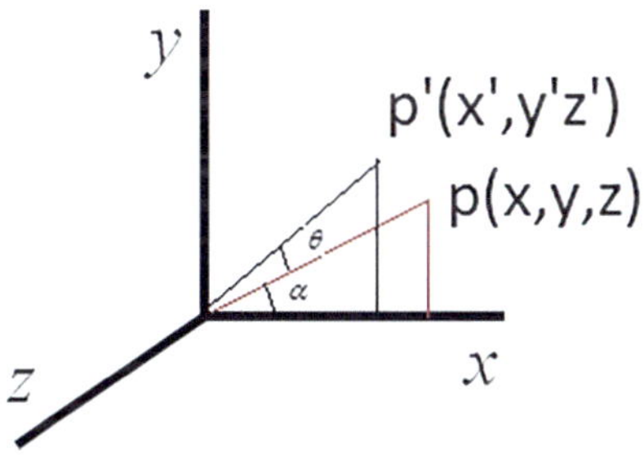

Figure 7.1: Rotations about a Z-axis

Case II. Rotation about X-axis is defined by the ZY Plan

Transformation equation for rotation about the other two coordinate axes can be obtained with a cyclic permutation of the coordinate parameters x, y, z in equation (3), that is we use the replacements $x \to y \to z \to x$.

$$x' = x\cos\theta - y\sin\theta$$

$$y' = x\sin\theta + y\cos\theta$$

$$z' = z$$

Then above equation may be written as

$$y' = y\cos\theta - z\sin\theta$$

$z' = y \sin\theta + z\cos\theta$

$x' = x$

By arranging the values

$x' = x$

$y' = y\cos\theta - z\sin\theta$

$z' = y \sin\theta + z\cos\theta$ (4)

Parameter θ specifies the rotation angle in homogenous coordinate form. In the three dimensional x – axis rotation equations are expressed as:

$$P' = R_x(\theta)P$$

This can be written in matrix form as:

$$\begin{bmatrix} x' \\ y' \\ z' \\ 1 \end{bmatrix} = \begin{bmatrix} 1 & 0 & 0 & 0 \\ 0 & \cos\theta & -\sin\theta & 0 \\ 0 & \sin\theta & \cos\theta & 0 \\ 0 & 0 & 0 & 1 \end{bmatrix} \begin{bmatrix} x \\ y \\ z \\ 1 \end{bmatrix}$$

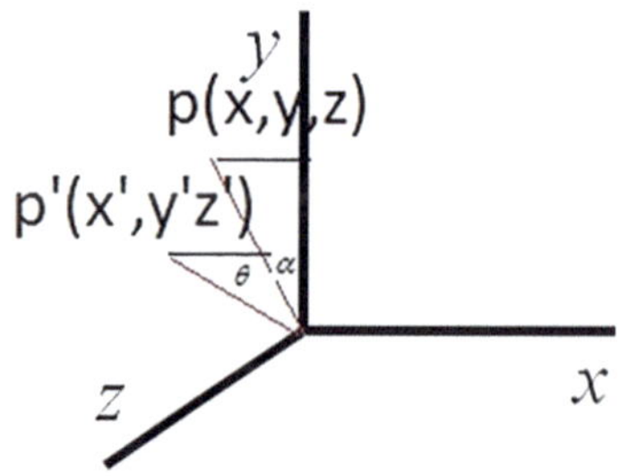

Figure 7.2: Rotations about a X-axis

Case III. Rotation about Y-axis is defined by the ZX Plan

Now again using the cyclic permutation of the coordinate parameters x, y, z in equation (4), that is we use the replacement $x \to y \to z \to x$.

$$x' = x$$
$$y' = x \cos\theta - z \sin\theta$$
$$z' = y \sin\theta + z \cos\theta$$

Then above equation may be written as

$$y' = y$$
$$z' = z \cos\theta - x \sin\theta$$
$$x' = z \sin\theta + x \cos\theta$$

By arranging the values

$$x' = x \cos\theta + z \sin\theta$$

$$y' = y$$
$$z' = -x \sin \theta + z \cos \theta \qquad \text{---(5)}$$

Parameter θ specifies the rotation angle in homogenous coordinate form. In the three dimensional y – axis rotation equations are expressed as:

$$P' = R_y(\theta)P$$

This can be written in matrix form as:

$$\begin{bmatrix} x' \\ y' \\ z' \\ 1 \end{bmatrix} = \begin{bmatrix} \cos\theta & 0 & \sin\theta & 0 \\ 0 & 1 & 0 & 0 \\ -\sin\theta & 0 & \cos\theta & 0 \\ 0 & 0 & 0 & 1 \end{bmatrix} \begin{bmatrix} x \\ y \\ z \\ 1 \end{bmatrix}$$

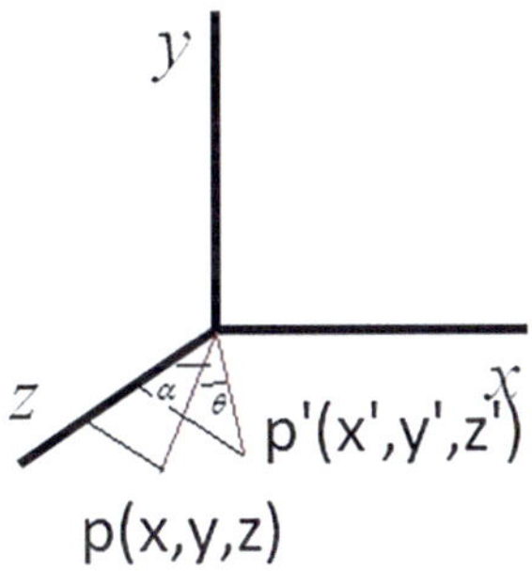

Figure 7.3: Rotations about a -axis

Example 7.1

Tetrahedron with vertex A (2, 4, 5), B (4, 2, 0), C (2, 6, 0), and D (1, 3, 0) is rotated about y-axis in anticlockwise direction to an angle of 30 degree, and then is scaled in X and Y direction to a factor of 2. Find Transformer co-ordinate of tetrahedron.

Solution

We have A (2, 4, 5), B (4, 2, 0), C (2, 6, 0), and D (1, 3, 0) coordinate of a tetrahedron and direction to a angle of 30 degree among y axis.

So

$$\begin{bmatrix} A1' & B1' & C1' & D1' \\ A2' & B2' & C2' & D2' \\ A3' & B3' & C3' & D3' \\ 1 & 1 & 1 & 1 \end{bmatrix} = \begin{bmatrix} \cos\theta & 0 & \sin\theta & 0 \\ 0 & 1 & 0 & 0 \\ -\sin\theta & 0 & \cos\theta & 0 \\ 0 & 0 & 0 & 1 \end{bmatrix} \begin{bmatrix} A1 & B1 & C1 & D1 \\ A2 & B2 & C2 & D2 \\ A3 & B3 & C3 & D3 \\ 1 & 1 & 1 & 1 \end{bmatrix}$$

$$\begin{bmatrix} A1 & B1 & C1 & D1 \\ A2 & B2 & C2 & D2 \\ A3 & B3 & C3 & D3 \\ 1 & 1 & 1 & 1 \end{bmatrix} = \begin{bmatrix} \cos 30^\circ & 0 & \sin 30^\circ & 0 \\ 0 & 1 & 0 & 0 \\ -\sin 30^\circ & 0 & \cos 30^\circ & 0 \\ 0 & 0 & 0 & 1 \end{bmatrix} \begin{bmatrix} 2 & 4 & 2 & 1 \\ 4 & 2 & 6 & 3 \\ 5 & 0 & 0 & 0 \\ 1 & 1 & 1 & 1 \end{bmatrix}$$

$$\begin{bmatrix} A1' & B1' & C1' & D1' \\ A2' & B2' & C2' & D2' \\ A3' & B3' & C3' & D3' \\ 1 & 1 & 1 & 1 \end{bmatrix} = \begin{bmatrix} \sqrt{3}/2 & 0 & 1/2 & 0 \\ 0 & 1 & 0 & 0 \\ -1/2 & 0 & \sqrt{3}/2 & 0 \\ 0 & 0 & 0 & 1 \end{bmatrix} \begin{bmatrix} 2 & 4 & 2 & 1 \\ 4 & 2 & 6 & 3 \\ 5 & 0 & 0 & 0 \\ 1 & 1 & 1 & 1 \end{bmatrix}$$

$$\begin{bmatrix} A1' & B1' & C1' & D1' \\ A2' & B2' & C2' & D2' \\ A3' & B3' & C3' & D3' \\ 1 & 1 & 1 & 1 \end{bmatrix} = \begin{bmatrix} \sqrt{3}+\frac{5}{2} & 2\sqrt{3} & \sqrt{3} & \frac{\sqrt{3}}{2} \\ 4 & 2 & 6 & 3 \\ -1+\frac{5\sqrt{3}}{2} & -2 & -1 & -\frac{1}{2} \\ 1 & 1 & 1 & 1 \end{bmatrix}$$

Rotated tetrahedron coordinate are A′ $\left(\sqrt{3}+\frac{5}{2}, 4, -1+\frac{5\sqrt{3}}{2} \atop 1\right)$, B′ $\left(2\sqrt{3}, 2, -2\right)$, C′ $\left(\sqrt{3}, 6, -1\right)$ and D′ $\left(\frac{\sqrt{3}}{2}, 3, -\frac{1}{2}\right)$. Now, the tetrahedron is scaled in x and y direction by factor 2. So

$$\begin{bmatrix} s_x & 0 & 0 & 0 \\ 0 & s_y & 0 & 0 \\ 0 & 0 & s_z & 0 \\ 0 & 0 & 0 & 1 \end{bmatrix} = \begin{bmatrix} 2 & 0 & 0 & 0 \\ 0 & 2 & 0 & 0 \\ 0 & 0 & 0 & 0 \\ 0 & 0 & 0 & 1 \end{bmatrix}$$

$$\begin{bmatrix} A1'' & B1'' & C1'' & D1'' \\ A2'' & B2'' & C2'' & D2'' \\ A3'' & B3'' & C3'' & D3'' \\ 1 & 1 & 1 & 1 \end{bmatrix} \begin{bmatrix} 2 & 0 & 0 & 0 \\ 0 & 2 & 0 & 0 \\ 0 & 0 & 0 & 0 \\ 0 & 0 & 0 & 1 \end{bmatrix} \begin{bmatrix} \sqrt{3}+\frac{5}{2} & 2\sqrt{3} & \sqrt{3} & \frac{\sqrt{3}}{2} \\ 4 & 2 & 6 & 3 \\ -1+\frac{5\sqrt{3}}{2} & -2 & -1 & -\frac{1}{2} \\ 1 & 1 & 1 & 1 \end{bmatrix}$$

$$\begin{bmatrix} A1'' & B1'' & C1'' & D1'' \\ A2'' & B2'' & C2'' & D2'' \\ A3'' & B3'' & C3'' & D3'' \\ 1 & 1 & 1 & 1 \end{bmatrix} = \begin{bmatrix} 2\sqrt{3}+5 & 4\sqrt{3} & 2\sqrt{3} & \sqrt{3} \\ 8 & 4 & 12 & 6 \\ 0 & 0 & 0 & 0 \\ 1 & 1 & 1 & 1 \end{bmatrix}$$

Hence Transformer co-ordinate of tetrahedron are A″ $\left(2\sqrt{3}+5,\ 8,\ 0\right)$, B″ $\left(4\sqrt{3}, 4, 0\right)$, C″ $\left(2\sqrt{3}, 12, 0\right)$, and D″ $\left(\sqrt{3}, 6, 0\right)$.

7.3 REFLECTION TRANSFORMATION

The Reflection is a mirror image of the original object. We can differentiate 2D and 3D reflection by adding Z-axis. The Z-axis shows the depth of the surface. In the Reflection process, the size of the object does not change. We can represent Reflection by using the three ways-

- Reflection along with X-Y Plane
- Reflection along with X-Z Plane
- Reflection along with Y-Z Plane

Case I. Reflection along with X-Y Plane

In the x-y plane reflection, the value of z is negative. Consider, a point P(x, y, z) which is in 3D space is made to reflect along X-Y direction after reflection P(x, y, z) becomes P′(x′, y′, z′).

$$\begin{bmatrix} x' \\ y' \\ z' \\ 1 \end{bmatrix} = \begin{bmatrix} 1 & 0 & 0 & 0 \\ 0 & 1 & 0 & 0 \\ 0 & 0 & -1 & 0 \\ 0 & 0 & 0 & 1 \end{bmatrix} \begin{bmatrix} x \\ y \\ z \\ 1 \end{bmatrix}$$

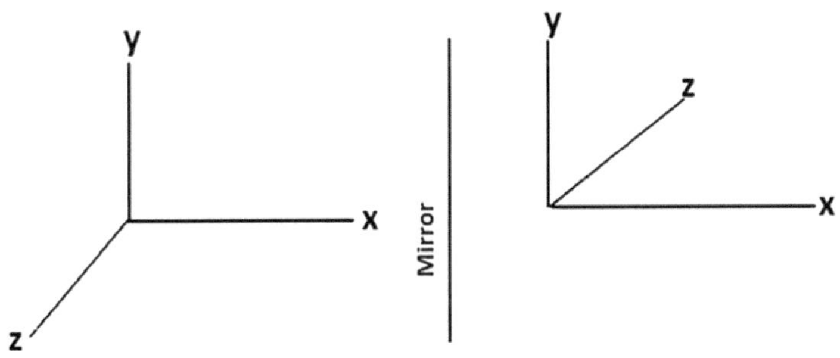

Figure 7.4: Reflection along X-Y plane

Example 7.2

Given a 3D triangle with coordinate points A (5, 2, 7), B (6, 4, 9), C (3, 1, 8). Apply the reflection on the XY plane and find out the new coordinates of the object.

Solution

We have

$$\begin{bmatrix} A1' & B1' & C1' \\ A2' & B2' & C2' \\ A3' & B3' & C3' \\ 1 & 1 & 1 \end{bmatrix} = \begin{bmatrix} 1 & 0 & 0 & 0 \\ 0 & 1 & 0 & 0 \\ 0 & 0 & -1 & 0 \\ 0 & 0 & 0 & 1 \end{bmatrix} \begin{bmatrix} A1 & B1 & C1 \\ A2 & B2 & C2 \\ A3 & B3 & C3 \\ 1 & 1 & 1 \end{bmatrix}$$

$$\begin{bmatrix} A1' & B1' & C1' \\ A2' & B2' & C2' \\ A3' & B3' & C3' \\ 1 & 1 & 1 \end{bmatrix} = \begin{bmatrix} 1 & 0 & 0 & 0 \\ 0 & 1 & 0 & 0 \\ 0 & 0 & -1 & 0 \\ 0 & 0 & 0 & 1 \end{bmatrix} \begin{bmatrix} 5 & 6 & 3 \\ 2 & 4 & 1 \\ 7 & 9 & 8 \\ 1 & 1 & 1 \end{bmatrix}$$

$$\begin{bmatrix} A1' & B1' & C1' \\ A2' & B2' & C2' \\ A3' & B3' & C3' \\ 1 & 1 & 1 \end{bmatrix} = \begin{bmatrix} 5 & 6 & 3 \\ 2 & 4 & 1 \\ -7 & -9 & -8 \\ 1 & 1 & 1 \end{bmatrix}$$

Thus, New coordinates of the triangle after reflection = A′ (5, 2, -7), B′ (6, 4, -9), C′ (3, 1, --8).

Case II. Reflection along with X-Z Plane

In the x-z plane reflection the value of y is negative. Consider, a point P(x, y, z) which is in 3D space is made to reflect along X-Z direction after reflection P(x, y, z) becomes P′(x′, y′, z′).

$$\begin{bmatrix} x' \\ y' \\ z' \\ 1 \end{bmatrix} = \begin{bmatrix} 1 & 0 & 0 & 0 \\ 0 & -1 & 0 & 0 \\ 0 & 0 & 1 & 0 \\ 0 & 0 & 0 & 1 \end{bmatrix} \begin{bmatrix} x \\ y \\ z \\ 1 \end{bmatrix}$$

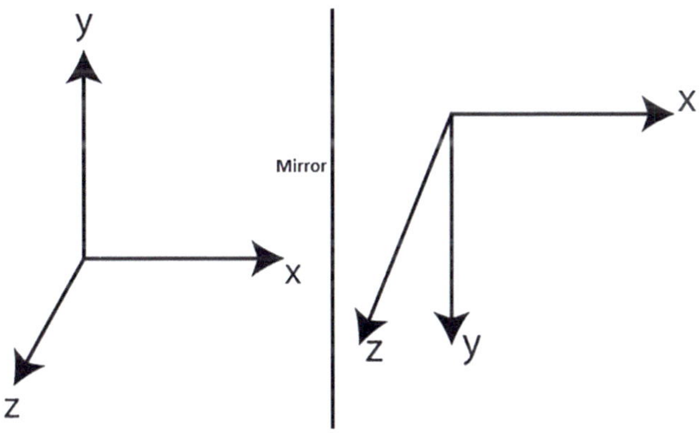

Figure 7.5: Reflection along X-Z plane

Example 7.3

Given a 3D triangle with coordinate points A (3, 4, 7), B (6, 4, 8), C (5, 6, 9). Apply the reflection on the XZ plane and find out the new coordinates of the object.

Solution

We have

$$\begin{bmatrix} A1' & B1' & C1' \\ A2' & B2' & C2' \\ A3' & B3' & C3' \\ 1 & 1 & 1 \end{bmatrix} = \begin{bmatrix} 1 & 0 & 0 & 0 \\ 0 & -1 & 0 & 0 \\ 0 & 0 & 1 & 0 \\ 0 & 0 & 0 & 1 \end{bmatrix} \begin{bmatrix} A1 & B1 & C1 \\ A2 & B2 & C2 \\ A3 & B3 & C3 \\ 1 & 1 & 1 \end{bmatrix}$$

$$\begin{bmatrix} A1' & B1' & C1' \\ A2' & B2' & C2' \\ A3' & B3' & C3' \\ 1 & 1 & 1 \end{bmatrix} = \begin{bmatrix} 1 & 0 & 0 & 0 \\ 0 & -1 & 0 & 0 \\ 0 & 0 & 1 & 0 \\ 0 & 0 & 0 & 1 \end{bmatrix} \begin{bmatrix} 3 & 6 & 5 \\ 4 & 4 & 6 \\ 7 & 8 & 9 \\ 1 & 1 & 1 \end{bmatrix}$$

$$\begin{bmatrix} A1' & B1' & C1' \\ A2' & B2' & C2' \\ A3' & B3' & C3' \\ 1 & 1 & 1 \end{bmatrix} = \begin{bmatrix} 3 & 6 & 5 \\ -4 & -4 & -6 \\ 7 & 8 & 9 \\ 1 & 1 & 1 \end{bmatrix}$$

Thus, New coordinates of the triangle after reflection = A′ (3, -4, 7), B′ (6, -4, 8), C′ (5, -6, 9).

Case III. Reflection along with Y-Z Plane

In the y-z plane reflection the value of x is negative. Consider, a point P(x, y, z) which is in 3D space is made to reflect along Y-Z direction after reflection P(x, y, z) becomes P′(x′, y′, z′).

$$\begin{bmatrix} x' \\ y' \\ z' \\ 1 \end{bmatrix} = \begin{bmatrix} -1 & 0 & 0 & 0 \\ 0 & 1 & 0 & 0 \\ 0 & 0 & 1 & 0 \\ 0 & 0 & 0 & 1 \end{bmatrix} \begin{bmatrix} x \\ y \\ z \\ 1 \end{bmatrix}$$

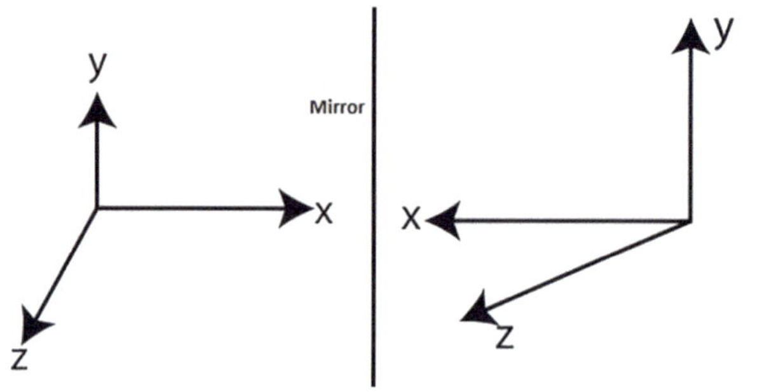

Figure 7.6: Reflection along Y-Z plane

Example 7.4

Given a 3D triangle with coordinate points A (1, 5, 9), B (4, 8, 7), C (2, 6, 3). Apply the reflection on the Y-Z plane and find out the new coordinates of the object.

Solution

We have

$$\begin{bmatrix} A1' & B1' & C1' \\ A2' & B2' & C2' \\ A3' & B3' & C3' \\ 1 & 1 & 1 \end{bmatrix} = \begin{bmatrix} -1 & 0 & 0 & 0 \\ 0 & 1 & 0 & 0 \\ 0 & 0 & 1 & 0 \\ 0 & 0 & 0 & 1 \end{bmatrix} \begin{bmatrix} A1 & B1 & C1 \\ A2 & B2 & C2 \\ A3 & B3 & C3 \\ 1 & 1 & 1 \end{bmatrix}$$

$$\begin{bmatrix} A1' & B1' & C1' \\ A2' & B2' & C2' \\ A3' & B3' & C3' \\ 1 & 1 & 1 \end{bmatrix} = \begin{bmatrix} -1 & 0 & 0 & 0 \\ 0 & 1 & 0 & 0 \\ 0 & 0 & 1 & 0 \\ 0 & 0 & 0 & 1 \end{bmatrix} \begin{bmatrix} 1 & 4 & 2 \\ 5 & 8 & 6 \\ 9 & 7 & 3 \\ 1 & 1 & 1 \end{bmatrix}$$

$$\begin{bmatrix} A1' & B1' & C1' \\ A2' & B2' & C2' \\ A3' & B3' & C3' \\ 1 & 1 & 1 \end{bmatrix} = \begin{bmatrix} -1 & -4 & -2 \\ 5 & 8 & 6 \\ 9 & 7 & 3 \\ 1 & 1 & 1 \end{bmatrix}$$

Thus, New coordinates of the triangle after reflection = A′ (-1, 5, 9), B′ (-4, 8, 7), C′ (-2, 6, 3).

7.4 SHEAR TRANSFORMATION

Shearing transformation is the same as we see in 2D space, but here we have to deal with the x, y, and z axes whereas in 2D we deal with the only x and y axes. Shearing is the process of slanting an object in 3D space either in x, y, or in the z-direction. Shearing changes (or deformed) the shape of the object. Shearing transformation are following types.

- Shearing in X-direction.
- Shearing in y-direction
- Shearing in z-direction.

Case I. Shearing in x-direction.

Here the coordinate of X remain unchanged while the coordinate of Y and Z are changed. Shearing is done through the Shearing Transformation matrix, which is represented as follows.

$$sh_x = \begin{bmatrix} 1 & sh_y & sh_z & 0 \\ 0 & 1 & 0 & 0 \\ 0 & 0 & 1 & 0 \\ 0 & 0 & 0 & 1 \end{bmatrix}$$

Consider a point P(x, y, z) in 3D space over which we perform the shearing transformation in the X-direction and it becomes P′(x′, y′, z′)

$$\begin{bmatrix} x' & y' & z' & 1 \end{bmatrix} = \begin{bmatrix} x & y & z & 1 \end{bmatrix} \begin{bmatrix} 1 & sh_y & sh_z & 0 \\ 0 & 1 & 0 & 0 \\ 0 & 0 & 1 & 0 \\ 0 & 0 & 0 & 1 \end{bmatrix}$$

Case II. Shearing in y-direction

Here the coordinate of Y remain unchanged while the coordinate of X and Z are changed. Shearing is done through the Shearing Transformation matrix, which is represented as follows

$$= \begin{bmatrix} 1 & 0 & 0 & 0 \\ sh_x & 1 & sh_z & 0 \\ 0 & 0 & 1 & 0 \\ 0 & 0 & 0 & 1 \end{bmatrix}$$

Consider a point P(x, y, z) in 3D space over which we perform the shearing transformation in the y-direction and it becomes P′(x′, y′, z′)

$$\begin{bmatrix} x' & y' & z' & 1 \end{bmatrix} = \begin{bmatrix} x & y & z & 1 \end{bmatrix} \begin{bmatrix} 1 & 0 & 0 & 0 \\ sh_x & 1 & sh_z & 0 \\ 0 & 0 & 1 & 0 \\ 0 & 0 & 0 & 1 \end{bmatrix}$$

Case III. Shearing in z-direction

Here the coordinate of Z remain unchanged while the coordinate of X and Y are changed. Shearing is done through the Shearing Transformation matrix, which is represented as follows for the shearing in Z-direction.

$$sh_z = \begin{bmatrix} 1 & 0 & 0 & 0 \\ 0 & 1 & 0 & 0 \\ sh_x & sh_y & 1 & 0 \\ 0 & 0 & 0 & 1 \end{bmatrix}$$

Consider a point P(x, y, z) in 3D space over which we perform the shearing transformation in the z-direction and it becomes P′(x′, y′, z′).

$$\begin{bmatrix} x' & y' & z' & 1 \end{bmatrix} = \begin{bmatrix} x & y & z & 1 \end{bmatrix} \begin{bmatrix} 1 & 0 & 0 & 0 \\ 0 & 1 & 0 & 0 \\ sh_x & sh_y & 1 & 0 \\ 0 & 0 & 0 & 1 \end{bmatrix}$$

Example 7.5

Given coordinate of a cuboid is A (0, 0, 4), B (0, 4, 2), C (2, 4, 0) ,D (2, 2, 4), E(2, 0, 0) , F(0, 0, 2), G(2, 0, 2), and H(0, 0, 0) . Apply shear parameter 2 on X-axis, 2 on Y-axis and find out the new coordinates of the object along Z-direction.

Solution

Given value is

$$\begin{bmatrix} A1 & B1 & C1 & D1 & E1 & F1 & G1 & H1 \\ A2 & B2 & C2 & D2 & E2 & F2 & G2 & H3 \\ A3 & B3 & C3 & D3 & E3 & F3 & G3 & H \\ 1 & 1 & 1 & 1 & 1 & 1 & 1 & 1 \end{bmatrix} = \begin{bmatrix} 0 & 0 & 2 & 2 & 2 & 0 & 2 & 0 \\ 0 & 4 & 4 & 2 & 0 & 0 & 0 & 0 \\ 4 & 2 & 0 & 4 & 0 & 2 & 2 & 0 \\ 1 & 1 & 1 & 1 & 1 & 1 & 1 & 1 \end{bmatrix}$$

and shearing parameter $sh_x = 2$, $sh_y = 3$

Therefore shearing in z-axis is calculated as

$$\begin{bmatrix} A1' & B1' & C1' & D1' & E1' & F1' & G1' & H1' \\ A2' & B2' & C2' & D2' & E2' & F2' & G2' & H2' \\ A3' & B3' & C3' & D3' & E3' & F3' & G3' & H3' \\ 1 & 1 & 1 & 1 & 1 & 1 & 1 & 1 \end{bmatrix} =$$

$$\begin{bmatrix} 1 & 0 & sh_x & 0 \\ 0 & 1 & sh_y & 0 \\ 0 & 0 & 1 & 0 \\ 0 & 0 & 0 & 1 \end{bmatrix} \begin{bmatrix} A1 & B1 & C1 & D1 & E1 & F1 & G1 & H1 \\ A2 & B2 & C2 & D2 & E2 & F2 & G2 & H2 \\ A3 & B3 & C3 & D3 & E3 & F3 & G3 & H3 \\ 1 & 1 & 1 & 1 & 1 & 1 & 1 & 1 \end{bmatrix}$$

$$\begin{bmatrix} A1' & B1' & C1' & D1' & E1' & F1' & G1' & H1' \\ A2' & B2' & C2' & D2' & E2' & F2' & G2' & H2' \\ A3' & B3' & C3' & D3' & E3' & F3' & G3' & H3' \\ 1 & 1 & 1 & 1 & 1 & 1 & 1 & 1 \end{bmatrix} =$$

$$\begin{bmatrix} 1 & 0 & 2 & 0 \\ 0 & 1 & 3 & 0 \\ 0 & 0 & 1 & 0 \\ 0 & 0 & 0 & 1 \end{bmatrix} \begin{bmatrix} 0 & 0 & 2 & 2 & 2 & 0 & 2 & 0 \\ 0 & 4 & 4 & 2 & 0 & 0 & 0 & 0 \\ 4 & 2 & 0 & 4 & 0 & 2 & 2 & 0 \\ 1 & 1 & 1 & 1 & 1 & 1 & 1 & 1 \end{bmatrix}$$

$$\begin{bmatrix} A1' & B1' & C1' & D1' & E1' & F1' & G1' & H1' \\ A2' & B2' & C2' & D2' & E2' & F2' & G2' & H2' \\ A3' & B3' & C3' & D3' & E3' & F3' & G3' & H3' \\ 1 & 1 & 1 & 1 & 1 & 1 & 1 & 1 \end{bmatrix} = \begin{bmatrix} 8 & 8 & 2 & 10 & 2 & 4 & 6 & 0 \\ 12 & 10 & 4 & 14 & 0 & 6 & 6 & 0 \\ 4 & 2 & 0 & 4 & 0 & 2 & 2 & 0 \\ 1 & 1 & 1 & 1 & 1 & 1 & 1 & 1 \end{bmatrix}$$

Thus, New coordinates of the cubiod after shearing in z- axis = A (8, 12, 4), B (8, 10, 2), C (2, 4, 0), D (10, 14, 4), E (2, 0, 0), F (4, 6, 2), G (6, 6, 1), and H (0, 0, 0).

OBJECTIVE QUESTIONS

1. The size of a 3D homogeneous transformation matrix is
   (a) 2×2 (b) 3×3
   (c) 4×4 (d) 5×5
2. A 3D rotation matrix about the x-axis is given by

   (a) $\begin{bmatrix} \cos\theta & 0 & \sin\theta & 0 \\ 0 & 1 & 0 & 0 \\ -\sin\theta & 0 & \cos\theta & 0 \\ 0 & 0 & 0 & 1 \end{bmatrix}$ (b) $\begin{bmatrix} 1 & 0 & 0 & 0 \\ 0 & \cos\theta & -\sin\theta & 0 \\ 0 & \sin\theta & \cos\theta & 0 \\ 0 & 0 & 0 & 1 \end{bmatrix}$

   (c) $\begin{bmatrix} \cos\theta & -\sin\theta & 0 & 0 \\ \sin\theta & \cos\theta & 0 & 0 \\ 0 & 0 & 0 & 0 \\ 0 & 0 & 0 & 1 \end{bmatrix}$ (d) None of the above
3. In a scaling transformation matrix, scaling factors are placed along
   (a) Horizontal places (b) Vertical places
   (c) Random places (d) Diagonal places

4. Rotation about any arbitrary line in 3D space can be captured by performing a series of transformations to
   (a) Align the line with any of the principle axes
   (b) Bring one end of the line on origin
   (c) All of the above
   (d) None of the above

5. Reflection about any arbitrary plane in 3D space can be captured by performing a series of transformations to
   (a) Align the plane with any of the principle planes
   (b) Align normal to the plane with any of the principle axes
   (c) All of the above
   (d) None of the above

6. 3D rotation matrices are given about
   (a) One principle axes
   (b) Two principle axes
   (c) Three principle axes
   (d) None of the above

7. The transformation in which a object is changed relative to a stationary co-ordinate system is called as
   (a) Transformation
   (b) Geometric Transformation
   (c) Coordinate Transformation
   (d) Reflection

8. A The transformation in which an object is moved from one position to another in circular path around a specified pivot point is called
   (a) Translation
   (b) Scaling
   (c) Rotation
   (d) Reflection

9. What are the final coordinates after a translation of point P (10, 10, 10) into 3D space with translation factor T (10, 20, 5)?
   (a) (20, 30, 15)
   (b) (20, 20, 25)
   (c) (15, 30, 25)
   (d) (15, 20, 25)

10. Which is a correct matrix for 3D shearing about X-axis (for column-major matrix)?

   (a) $\begin{bmatrix} 1 & 0 & a & 0 \\ 0 & 1 & b & 0 \\ 0 & 0 & 1 & 0 \\ 0 & 0 & 0 & 1 \end{bmatrix}$

   (b) $\begin{bmatrix} 1 & a & 0 & 0 \\ 0 & 1 & 0 & 0 \\ 0 & b & 1 & 0 \\ 0 & 0 & 0 & 1 \end{bmatrix}$

   (c) $\begin{bmatrix} 1 & 0 & 0 & 0 \\ a & 1 & 0 & 0 \\ b & 0 & 1 & 0 \\ 0 & 0 & 0 & 1 \end{bmatrix}$

   (d) $\begin{bmatrix} 1 & 0 & 0 & a \\ 0 & 1 & 0 & b \\ 0 & 0 & 1 & 0 \\ 0 & 0 & 0 & 1 \end{bmatrix}$

11. Which is a correct matrix for 3D reflection about XZ-plane (for column-major matrix)?

(a) $\begin{bmatrix} -1 & 0 & 0 & 0 \\ 0 & 1 & 0 & 0 \\ 0 & 0 & 1 & 0 \\ 0 & 0 & 0 & 1 \end{bmatrix}$ (b) $\begin{bmatrix} 1 & 0 & 0 & 0 \\ 0 & -1 & 0 & 0 \\ 0 & 0 & 1 & 0 \\ 0 & 0 & 0 & 1 \end{bmatrix}$

(c) $\begin{bmatrix} 1 & 0 & 0 & 0 \\ 0 & 1 & 0 & 0 \\ 0 & 0 & -1 & 0 \\ 0 & 0 & 0 & 1 \end{bmatrix}$ (d) $\begin{bmatrix} 1 & 0 & 0 & 0 \\ 0 & 1 & 0 & 0 \\ 0 & 0 & 1 & 0 \\ 0 & 0 & 0 & -1 \end{bmatrix}$

12. Which is a correct equation for 3D scaling?

(a) $\begin{bmatrix} x' \\ y' \\ z' \\ 1 \end{bmatrix} = \begin{bmatrix} 1 & 0 & 0 & 0 \\ 0 & 0 & 0 & 0 \\ 0 & 0 & 0 & 0 \\ s_x & s_y & s_y & 1 \end{bmatrix} \begin{bmatrix} x \\ y \\ z \\ 1 \end{bmatrix}$ (b) $\begin{bmatrix} x' \\ y' \\ z' \\ 1 \end{bmatrix} = \begin{bmatrix} s_x & 0 & 0 & 0 \\ s_y & 0 & 0 & 0 \\ s_z & 0 & 0 & 0 \\ 0 & 0 & 0 & 1 \end{bmatrix} \begin{bmatrix} x \\ y \\ z \\ 1 \end{bmatrix}$

(c) $\begin{bmatrix} x' \\ y' \\ z' \\ 1 \end{bmatrix} = \begin{bmatrix} s_x & s_y & s_z & 0 \\ 0 & 0 & 0 & 0 \\ 0 & 0 & 0 & 0 \\ 0 & 0 & 0 & 1 \end{bmatrix} \begin{bmatrix} x \\ y \\ z \\ 1 \end{bmatrix}$ (d) $\begin{bmatrix} x' \\ y' \\ z' \\ 1 \end{bmatrix} = \begin{bmatrix} s_x & 0 & 0 & 0 \\ 0 & s_y & 0 & 0 \\ 0 & 0 & s_z & 0 \\ 0 & 0 & 0 & 1 \end{bmatrix} \begin{bmatrix} x \\ y \\ z \\ 1 \end{bmatrix}$

13. What are the final coordinates after rotation of the point P (5, 5, 5) 90 degree about Z-axis?

(a) (5, -5, -5) (b) (-5, 5, 5)

(c) (-5, -5, -5) (d) (5, -5, 5)

14. Arrange steps of general 3D rotations in the correct order:
   1 Apply inverse rotations to bring the rotation axis back to its original orientation.
   2 Apply the inverse translation to bring the rotation axis back to its original position.
   3 Rotate the object so that the axis of rotation coincides with one of the coordinate axes.
   4 Perform the specified rotation about that coordinate axis.
   5 Translate the object so that the rotation axis passes through the coordinate origin.
   (a) 3, 5, 4, 2, 1 (b) 3, 2, 4, 5, 1
   (c) 5, 3, 4, 1, 2 (d) 1, 2, 3, 4, 5
15. 3D reflection matrices are given about
   (a) One principle plane (b) Two principle planes
   (c) Three principle planes (d) None of the above

ANSWERS

1. (c)	4. (a)	7. (b)	10. (c)	13. (b)
2. (b)	5. (c)	8. (c)	11. (b)	14. (c)
3. (d)	6. (c)	9. (a)	12. (d)	15. (c)

EXERCISES

1. What is 3D transformation? Write the matrix of each transformation.
2. Differentiate between 2D and 3D transformation.
3. A cube of 6 mm side having one corner point at is translated by 3 mm in x direction and scaled twice in all directions. Find the final position of the cube.
4. A triangle ABC is defined as A (0, 0, 0), B (1, 2, 3), and C (3, 2, 1). Find the reflection of ABC about mirror surface $4x + 7y + 4z + 1 = 0$.
5. Perform the following transformations on a point P (2, 6, 7) using a homogeneous coordinate system.
   a. Translate by 4, 2, 1
   b. Translate by vector $2\hat{i} + 3\hat{j} - k$
6. A prism is marked by six vertices (8, 6, 0), (6, 6, 0), (6, 8,0), (8, 6, 4), (6, 6, 4), and (6, 8, 4). Find the reflection of this triangular prism about a mirror surface given by $2x + 6y + 3z = 6$.

7. Derive rotation about x-axis, y-axis, and z-axis matrices in 3D. Also, prove that for any rotation matrix: - $-R^{(-1)}(\theta) = R(-\theta)$.
8. Find the translation matrix for $t_x = 2,\ t_y = 2,\ t_z = 4$.
9. Obtain scaling matrix for $s_x = 2,\ s_y = 3$ and $s_z = 2$
10. Obtain rotation matrix for $\theta = 45^{\circ}$ along z axis.
11. Find the rotation matrix for $\theta = 30^{\circ}$ about x axis.
12. What do you mean by 3D Clipping? Discuss in details.
13. Write the 3D translation matrix for moving an object by -2 units, -4 units and -6 units' respectively in x, y and z directions.
14. Describe the steps involved in scaling a 3D object with respect to a fixed point (x_f, y_f, z_f). Derive the composite transformation matrix
15. What are the steps for general 3D rotation if the rotation axis is not parallel to any one of the principal axis. The rotation axis is defined by the points P1 (x1, y1, z1) and P2 (x2, y2, z2). Write down the composite matrix representation.
16. Explain basic 3D transformations.
17. Write Short note on
    a. 3D Rotation
    b. 3D Translation
    c. 3D Scaling.

8

Projection

In the real world, we see three-dimensional images that have height, width, and depth. However, when we display a 3D object on a 2D screen, it becomes a difficult task known as projection. This task is complicated because 3D objects have an extra dimension and we have limited display space. This means that 3D viewing operations are more complex than 2D viewing. In 2D, a simple mapping produces an image, whereas in 3D, there are many options depending on how the model is to be viewed, such as front, side, top, and back. There is also a mismatch between the 3D model and the 2D image. To overcome all these differences, we must use projection to map the 2D projection plane. There are various types of projection used to generate multiple views of a model. Therefore, projection is an important concept in the 3D viewing process In this chapter, you will learn about projection, its different types, and their advantages and disadvantages, along with figures to aid the understanding

8.1 INTRODUCTION OF PROJECTION

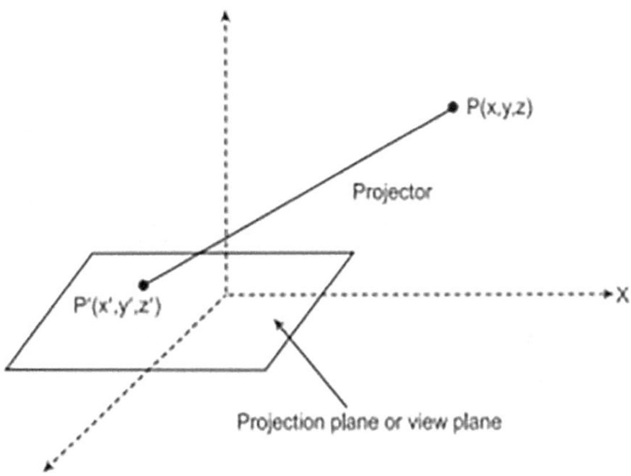

Figure 8.1: Projection

It is the process of converting a 3D object into a 2D object. It is also defined as mapping or transformation of the object in projection plane or view plane. The view plane is displayed surface. Projection can be defined as a mapping of point P (x, y, z) onto its image P′ (x′, y′, z′) in the projection plane or view plane which constitute the display surface.

The mapping is determined by a projection line called projector that passes through P and intersects the view plane. The intersection point is P′. The result of projecting an object is dependent on the spatial relationship among the projectors that project the points on the object and the spatial relationship between the projectors and the view plane.

8.2 TAXONOMY OF PROJECTION

The major two categories of projection are: a) Parallel projection b) Perspective projection. Figure 8.2 describes taxonomy of projections.

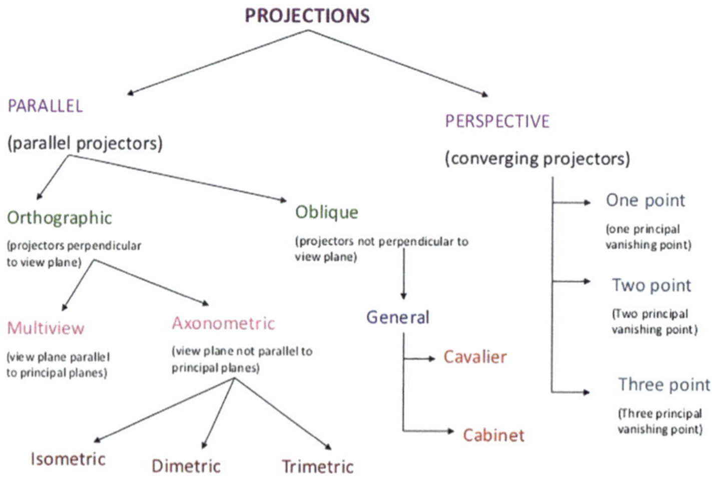

Figure 8.2: Taxonomy of projection

8.3 PARALLEL PROJECTION

When the centre of projection is situated at an infinite distance such that the projectors are parallel to each other, the type of projection is called Parallel Projection. The plane on which we are taking the projection is called as a view plane.

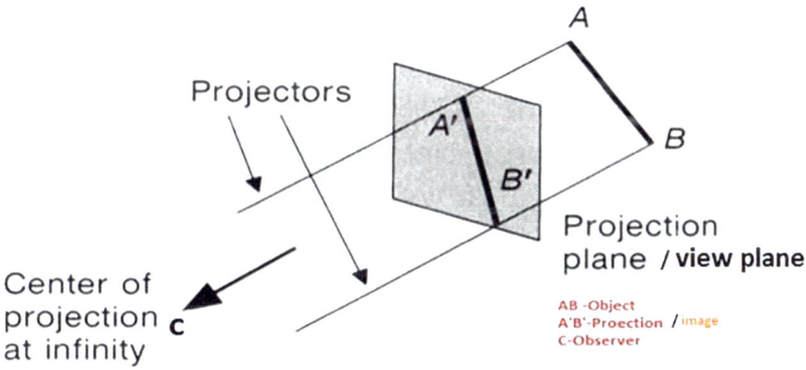

Figure 8.3: Parallel Projection

In Parallel Projection, image points are found at the intersection of the view plane with parallel projectors drawn from the object points in a fixed direction. In parallel projection, the view formed on the picture plane is of the same size and shape as that of the object. Parallel Projection may have the following characteristics:

1. Parallel projection can give the accurate view of object.
2. Parallel projection represents the object in a different way like telescope.
3. Parallel projection does not form realistic view of object.
4. In parallel projection, the distance of the object from the center of projection is infinite.
5. Projector in parallel projection is parallel.
6. Parallel projection can preserve the relative proportion of an object.
7. The lines of parallel projection are parallel.

Parallel projections are basically two type's orthographic parallel projection oblique parallel projection.

8.3.1 Orthographic Parallel Projection

A type of parallel projection in which the center of projection lies at infinity and the projectors are perpendicular to the view plane or at an angle of 90 degree to the picture plane is known as orthographic parallel projection. Hence only one principal face of the object will be seen on the picture plane. In orthographic projections, the direction of projection is perpendicular to the projection plane. So, true size and shape of a single face of an object is obtained.

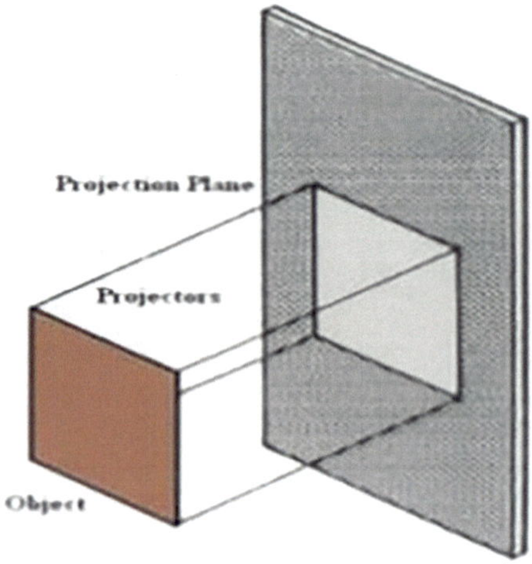

Figure 8.4: Orthographic Projection

Orthographic projections are most often used to produce the front, side, and top views of an object. It is commonly used in engineering drawing because it is good for accurate measurements. There are two different types of orthographic parallel projection multiview orthographic and axonometric orthographic.

8.3.1.1 Multiview Orthographic

Multiview is an orthographic projection in which view plane is parallel to the principal planes that is the direction of projection line is parallel to any principal axes. This produces the front, top and side views of mechanical drawings. Front, side, and rear orthographic projections are called elevations and a top orthographic projection is called a plane view. It always shows the true size and shape of a single plane face parallel to the projection plane.

Advantage and Disadvantage of Multiview Orthographic

1. Preserves both distances and angles.
2. Shapes preserved.
3. Can be used for measurements.
4. Building plans.
5. Manuals.
6. Cannot see what object really looks like because many surfaces hidden from view.
7. Often we add the isometric.

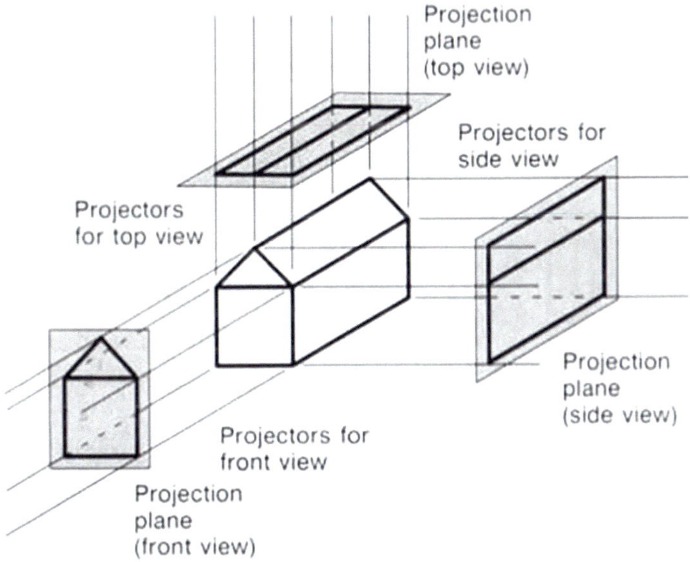

Figure 8.5: Multiview Orthographic

8.3.1.2 Axonometric Orthographic

In axonometric projection view plane is not parallel to the principle axis. That is when projection line are not making 90 degree angle with any principal axis. This is used to overcome the limitation of single orthographic projection which is unable to illustrate the general 3D shape of an object. The construction of an axonometric projection is done by using rotation and translation to manipulate the object such that at least three adjacent faces are shown. The result is then projected at infinity onto one of the coordinate planes from the center of projection.

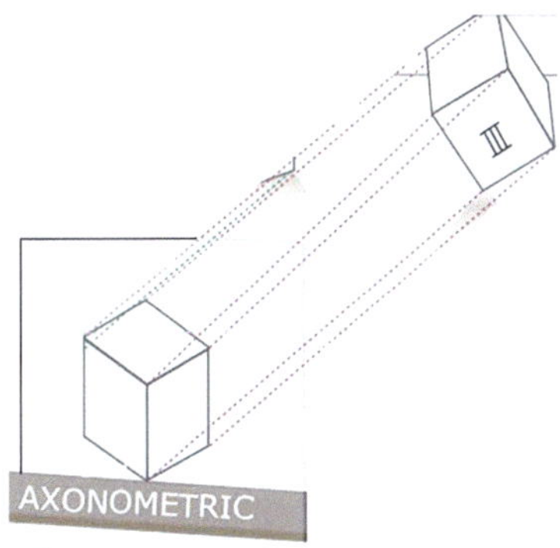

Figure 8.6: Axonometric Orthographic Projections

An axonometric projection shows its true shape only when a face is parallel to the projection plane. Axonometric projections are classified according to the angles made between the principal axes and the view plane.

Advantage and Disadvantage of Axonometric Orthographic

1. Lines are scaled (foreshortened) but can find scaling factors.
2. Lines preserved but angles are not.
3. Projection of a circle in a plane not parallel to the projection plane is an ellipse.
4. Can see three principal faces of a box-like object.
5. Some optical illusions possible.
6. Parallel lines appear to diverge.
7. It does not look real because far objects are scale the same as near objects.
8. Used in CAD applications.

Axonometric Projection is further divided into three types isometric, diametric and trimetric projection.

8.3.1.2.1. Isometric Projection

In isometric projection the direction of projection makes equal angle with all three principle axes. The 'iso' means 'equal' and 'metric projection' means 'a projection to reduced measure'. An isometric projection is generated by aligning the projection plane so that it intersects each coordinate axis in which the object is defined. All three principal axes are foreshortened equally so that relative proportions are maintained. All principal axes make an angle of 120 degrees. Normally one axis will be remaining vertical. That is angle a=b=c=120 degrees.

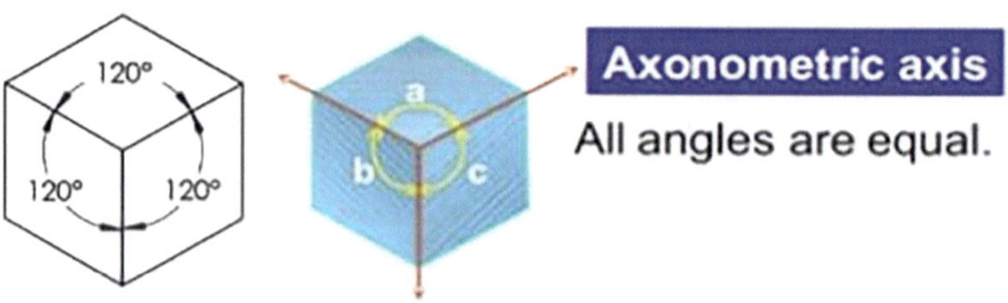

Figure 8.7: Isometric Projection

8.3.1.2.2. Diametric Projection

Two of the angles between the principal axes and the view plane are equal and therefore foreshortening along two axes will be the same. When two of the three angles are equal, the drawing is classified as a diametric projection.

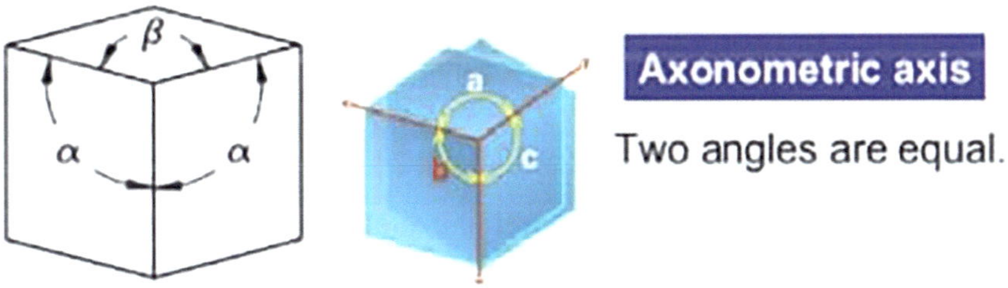

Figure 8.8: Diametric Projection

8.3.1.2.3. Trimetric Projection

The angles between the principal axes and the view plane are all different. This means that the foreshortening along each axis will be different.

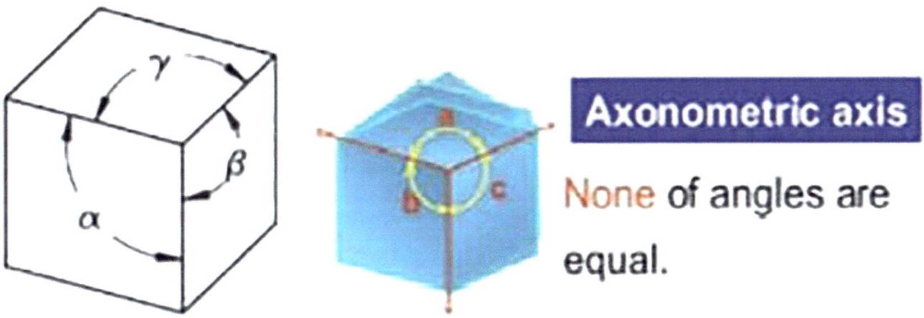

Figure 8.9: Trimetric Projection

8.3.2 Oblique Parallel Projection

If the direction of projection is not perpendicular to the projection plane, then it is called as oblique projection. The projectors are NOT perpendicular to the view plane. Usually the view plane is positioned parallel to the principal face of the object so that this face is projected without distortion. This allows direct measurements to be made of this face. The angle between the projectors and the view plane is chosen so as to best illustrate the third dimension, the oblique projection are further classified as the cavalier and cabinet projections.

8.3.2.1 Cavalier

The Cavalier projection makes 45° angle with the projection plane. The projection of a line perpendicular to the view plane has the same length as the line itself in Cavalier projection. In a cavalier projection, the foreshortening factors for all three principal directions are equal.

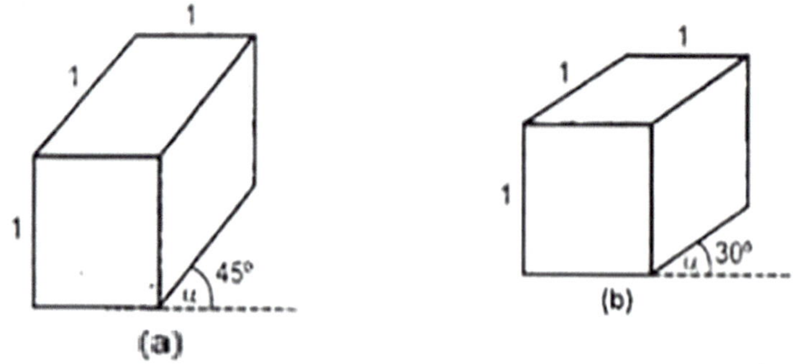

Figure 8.10: Cavalier Projection

8.3.2.2 Cabinet

The Cabinet projection makes 63.4° angle with the projection plane. In Cabinet projection, lines perpendiculars to the viewing surface are projected at 1/2 their actual length.

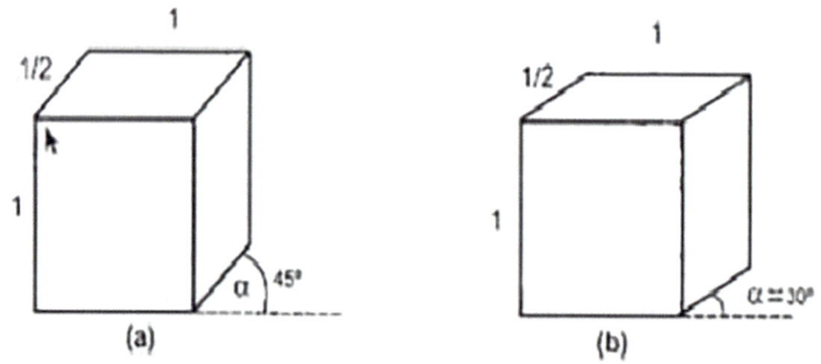

Figure 8.11: Cabinet Projection

8.4 PERSPECTIVE PROJECTION

In the perspective projection, the distance of the project plane from the center of projection is finite. The object size keeps changing in reverse order with distance. Perspective projection is used to determine the projector lines come together at a single point. The single point is also called "Project Reference Point (PRP)" or "Center of projection."

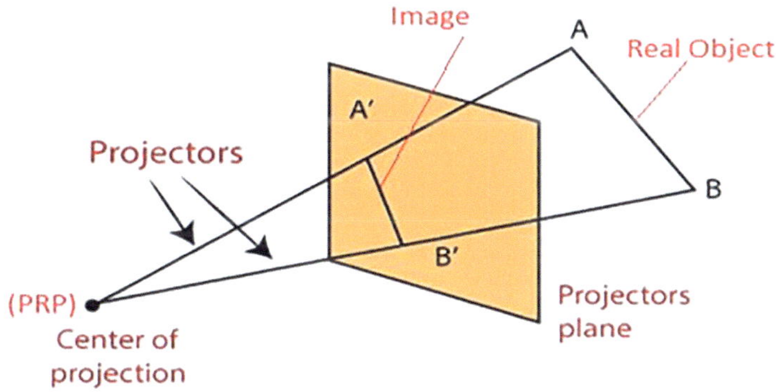

Figure 8.12: Perspective Projection

Characteristic of Perspective Projection

- The Distance between the object and projection center is finite.
- In this, it is difficult to define the actual size and shape of the object.
- It has the concept of vanishing points.
- It is realistic but tough to implement.

Vanishing Point

Vanishing point can be defined as a point in image plane where all parallel lines are interlinked. The Vanishing point is also called "Directing Point."

Use of Vanishing Point

- It is used in 3D games and graphics editing.
- It is also used to represent 3D objects.
- We can also include perspective in the background of an image.
- We can also insert the shadow effect in an image.

Perspective projections are classified according to the number of vanishing points in the projection one point, two point and three point perspective projections.

8.4.1 One Point Perspective Projection

One Point perspective contains only one vanishing point on the horizon line. That is when only one of the principal axes intersects the view plane. It is easy to draw. The One Point projection is mostly used to draw the images of roads, railway tracks, and buildings.

Example of one point vanishing:

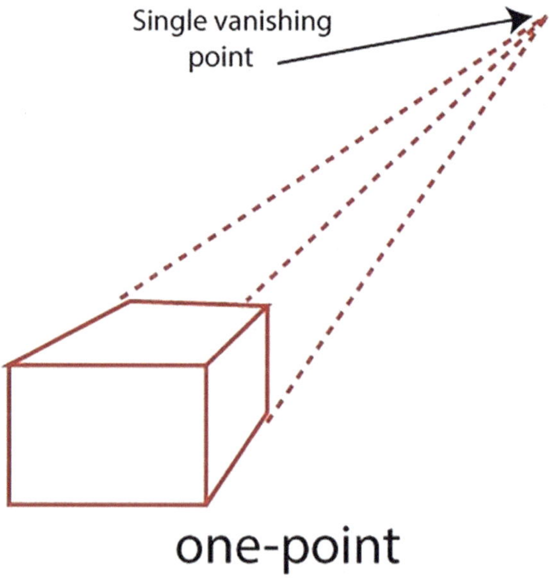

Figure 8.13: One Point Perspective Projections

8.4.2 Two Point Perspective Projection

It is also called "Angular Perspective." A Two Point perspective contains two vanishing points on the line. That is when exactly two of the principal axes intersect the view plane. The main use of Two Point projection is to draw the two corner roads.

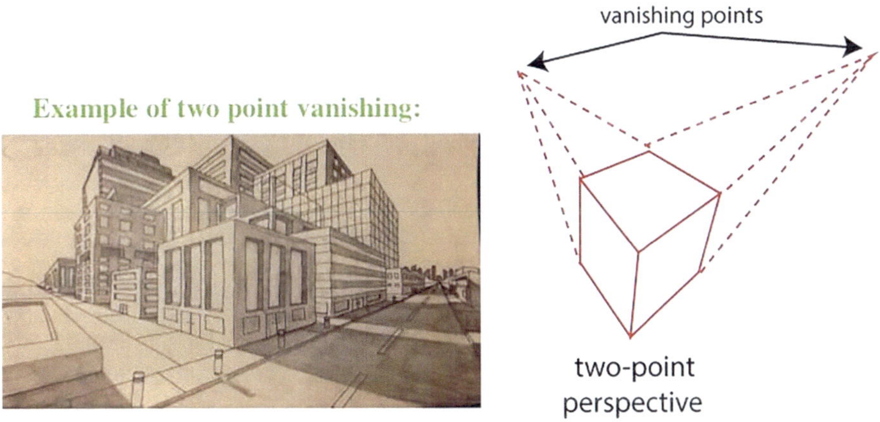

Figure 8.14: Two Point Perspective Projections

8.4.3 Three Point Perspective Projection

The Three-Point Perspective contains three vanishing points. Two points lie on the horizon line, and one above or below the line. That is when all three principal axes intersect the view plane. It is very difficult to draw. When we see an object from above, than the third point is below the ground. If we see at an object from below, then the third point is in the space above. It is mainly used in skyscraping.

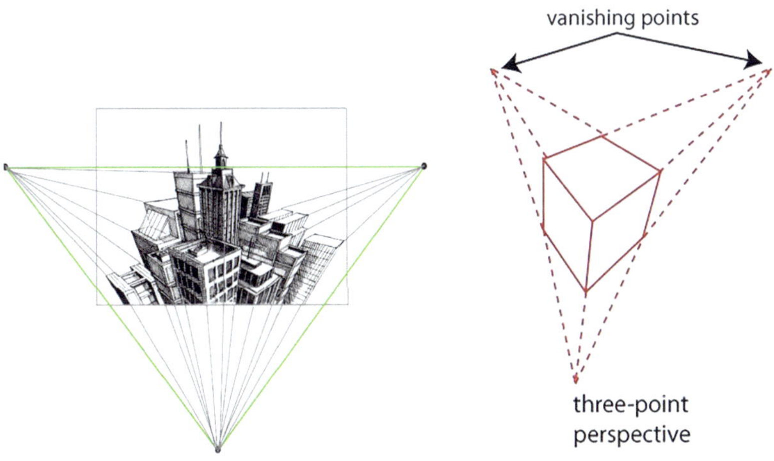

Figure 8.15: Three Point Perspective Projections

The Table 8.1 gives the differences between parallel projection and perspective projection.

Table 8.1: Differences between Parallel and Perspective Projection

Parameters	*Parallel Projection*	*Perspective Projection*
Representation of objects	It represents any given object in a different way- as we view it on a telescope.	It represents any given object in a three-dimensional manner.
Shape and Size of objects	It does not alter the shape or the size of the given object on a plane.	In this, the objects that stay far away appear to be smaller in size, while the ones near to viewer's eyes appear big in size.
Distance from Center of Projection	The distance of the given object is infinite from the center of the projection.	The distance of the given object is finite from the center of the projection.
Accuracy of View	It can provide a user with an accurate view of the given object.	It cannot provide a user with an accurate view of the given object. The shapes and sizes of the projection tend to differ from its origination.
Lines of Projection	The parallel projection lines are parallel to each other.	The perspective projection lines are not parallel to each other.
Projector	The projector is also parallel.	The projector is not at all parallel.
Types of Projection	There are basically two types of parallel projections: ♦ Oblique ♦ Orthographic	There are basically three types of perspective projections: ♦ One Point ♦ Two Point ♦ Three Point
Realistic View	Parallel Projection does not form a realistic view of the world and its objects.	Perspective Projection generates a very realistic view of the world and the objects present in it.

OBJECTIVE QUESTIONS

1. Subcategories of orthographic projection are
   (a) Isometric, Diametric, Trimetric
   (b) Cavalier, Cabinet, Isometric
   (c) Cavalier, Cabinet
   (d) Isometric, Cavalier, Trimetric
2. When the center of projection is located at a finite distance from the projection plane, this projection method is called
   (a) Orthographic projection
   (b) Perspective projection

(c) Parallel projection
(d) Planar geometric projection

3. Match the following:

List I	List II
(a) Cavalier Projection	(i) The direction of projection is chosen so that there is no foreshortening of lines perpendicular to the xy plane.
(b) Cabinet Projection	(ii) The direction of projection is chosen so that lines perpendicular to the xy planes are foreshortened by half their lengths.
(c) Isometric Projection	(iii) The direction of projection makes equal angles with the entire principal axis.
(d) Orthographic Projection	(iv) Projections are characterized by the fact that the direction of projection is perpendicular to the view plane.

Codes:

	(a)	(b)	(c)	(d)
A	(i)	(iii)	(iv)	(ii)
B	(ii)	(iii)	(i)	(iv)
C	(iv)	(ii)	(iii)	(i)
D	(i)	(ii)	(iii)	(iv)

(a) A
(b) B
(c) C
(d) D

4. Perspective projections are characterized by perspective foreshortening in which
   (a) The object appears bigger as its distance from the center of projection increases
   (b) The object appears smaller as its distance from the center of projection increases
   (c) The object appears unchanged as its distance from the center of projection changes
   (d) None of the above

5. In 3D perspective projection, the vanishing point can be thought of as
   (a) Finite distance
   (b) Infinity
   (c) Two times the distance of the object from the projection plane
   (d) Three times the distance of the object from the projection plane

6. 1-point perspective projection occurs when the projection plane is
   (a) Parallel to one of the principle axes
   (b) Inclined to one of the principle axes

(c) Perpendicular to one of the principle axes
(d) None of the above

7. In parallel projection, the center of projection is located at
(a) Finite distance
(b) Infinity
(c) Two times the distance of the object from the projection plane
(d) Four times the distance of the object from the projection plane

8. In orthographic parallel projection, the direction of projectors is
(a) Parallel to the plane of projection
(b) Inclined to the plane of projection
(c) Oblique to the plane of projection
(d) Perpendicular to the plane of projection

9. A multi-view projection method is
(a) Isometric (b) Diametric
(c) Trimetric (d) None of the above

10. Projection planes are not perpendicular to a principle axis and show multiple faces of an object at once; such a type of projection is called
(a) Orthographic projection (b) Oblique projection
(c) Parallel projection (d) Axonometric projection

11. In oblique projection, projectors are
(a) Parallel to the plane of projection
(b) Inclined to the plane of projection
(c) Perpendicular to the plane of projection
(d) None of the above

12. If a plane is parallel to the plane of projection, it appears
(a) True size (b) As a line or edge
(c) Foreshortened (d) As an oblique surface

13. In 3D Graphics, which of the following statements about perspective and parallel projection is/are true?
P:. In a perspective projection, the farthest an object is from the center of projection, the smaller it appears.
Q:. Parallel projection is equivalent to a perspective projection where the viewer is standing infinitely far away
R:. Perspective projections do not preserve straight lines.
(a) P and R only (b) P, Q and R
(c) Q and R only (d) P and Q only

14. Which of the following is not true in case of Oblique Projections?
(a) Parallel projection rays are not perpendicular to the viewing plane.
(b) Parallel lines in space appear parallel on the final projected image.

(c) Used exclusively for pictorial purposes rather than formal working drawings.
(d) Projectors are always perpendicular to the plane of projection.

15. In cavalier projection, the angle between the projector and the plane of projection is
(a) 30° (b) 45°
(c) 63.4° (d) 120°

ANSWERS

1. (a)	4. (b)	7. (b)	10. (d)	13. (d)
2. (b)	5. (b)	8. (d)	11. (b)	14. (d)
3. (d)	6. (c)	9. (d)	12. (a)	15. (b)

EXERCISES

1. What do you mean by Projection? Explain the types of Projection; differentiate between Parallel and Perspective Projection.
2. What do you understand by Parallel Projection? Also describe Orthogonal and Oblique Projection.
3. Explain Oblique Parallel Projection and Perspective Projection matrix.
4. Explain Parallel and Perspective Projection. Justify the depth cueing projection for 3D display method.
5. Find the general form of an Oblique Projection onto the xy plane.
6. Differentiate between Orthographic and Oblique Parallel projections.
7. Find the transformation for
   a. Cavalier with $\theta = 45$ degree
   b. Cabinet projection with $\theta = 30$ degree.
8. Define the terms
   a. Centre of projection
   b. Principal vanishing point
9. Write any six differences between Perspective Projection and Parallel Projection.
10. Distinguish between Cavalier and Cabinet Projection.
11. Draw the Isometric and Diametric projections of a unit cube onto the xy-plane.
12. Explain Perspective Projection transformation matrix. Also, describe anomalies of Perspective Projection.
13. Describe Perspective Projection and explain Perspective Foreshortening and Vanishing Points.

14. Find the Perspective Projection onto the view plane z=d where the center of projection is the origin (0, 0).
15. Define the terms
    a. Perspective foreshortening
    b. Center of projection
    c. Vanishing point
16. What do you mean by Projection? Discuss principal vanishing points for the standard Perspective transformation.
17. Describe the
    a. One principal vanishing point perspective
    b. Two principal vanishing point perspective
    c. Three principal vanishing point perspective

9

Hidden and Visible Surfaces

When viewing a 3-dimensional object, only the front surfaces and edges can be seen by the viewer. This means that the surfaces and edges at the rear end cannot be seen, and this is also true for an overlapping 2-dimensional object. These invisible surfaces and edges are referred to as hidden surfaces and hidden edges, respectively. The visibility of an object depends on the viewing parameters, such as rear view, side view, top view, and bottom view. When one object obstructs another, only the object in front is visible. In this chapter, we will learn how to determine which lines or surfaces of an object should be visible. This process is called hidden surfaces, hidden line elimination, or visible surface determination. There are two categories of hidden line or hidden surface algorithms: those that deal with object definitions directly and those that deal with object definitions through projected images. Object space methods, such as back face and Painter's algorithm, compare objects and parts of objects to each other to decide visibility. In contrast, image space methods, such as area subdivision, Z-buffer, and scan line, determine visibility point by point at each pixel position on the view plane. Although object space methods require less work in theory, image space methods are considered more efficient in practice because they can take advantage of consistency in the raster scan implementation.

9.1 INTRODUCTION OF HIDDEN AND VISIBLE SURFACES

A major part of rendering (making images more realistic) is the visible surface problem. That is, only display those surfaces which should be visible. When we view a picture containing non-transparent objects and surfaces, we cannot see those objects from views which are behind objects closer to the eye. We must remove these hidden surfaces to get a realistic screen image. The identification and removal of these surfaces is called the Hidden-surface problem. Techniques used for solving these problems are known as Visible Surface Detection or Hidden Surface Removal.

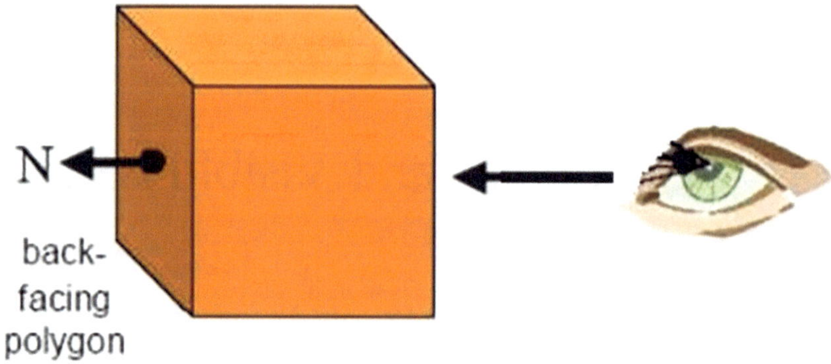

Figure 9.1: Hidden Surface Removals

9.2 CLASSIFICATION OF VISIBLE SURFACE

Visible surface detection can be classified into two types object space methods and image space methods.

9.2.1 Object Space Methods

In this method, different parts of objects are compared. Compare objects and parts of objects to each other within the scene definition to determine which surface is visible. It is implemented in the world coordinate system. Screen resolution is irrelevant here. These methods generally decide the visible surface. It is line-based rather than surface-based. Some examples of object space methods are Back Face algorithms, Depth Sorting (Painter's algorithm), BSP-tree methods, Octree methods, Ray-Casting methods, etc.

9.2.2 Image Space Methods

Visibility is decided point-by-point at each pixel position on the view plane. It is implemented in the device coordinate system. Screen resolutions are a major component. Here positions of various pixels are determined. It is used to locate the visible surface instead of a visible line. Each point is detected for its visibility. If a point is visible, then the pixel is on, otherwise off. So the object close to the viewer that is pierced (cross) by a projector through a pixel is determined. That pixel is drawn in the appropriate color. Some examples of image space methods are Z-buffer, A-buffer, Scan-Line method, and Area Subdivision methods so on. Table 9.1 shows the differences between Object Space Methods and Image Space Methods.

Table 9.1: Differences between Object Space Methods and Image Space Methods

S. no.	*Object-space Methods*	*Image-space Methods (Mostly used)*
1.	Image space is object based. It concentrates on geometrical relations among objects in the scene.	It is a pixel-based method. It is concerned with the final image, what is visible within each raster pixel.
2.	Here surface visibility is determined.	Here line visibility or point visibility is determined.
3.	It is performed at the precision with which each object is defined, No resolution is considered.	It is performed using the resolution of the display device.
4.	Calculations are not based on the resolution of the display so change of object can be easily adjusted.	Calculations are resolution base, so the change is difficult to adjust.
5.	Developed for vector system.	Developed for raster devices.
6.	Object-based algorithms operate on continuous object data.	These operate on object data.
7.	Vector display used for object method has large address space.	Raster systems used for image space methods have limited address space.
8.	Object precision is used for applications where speed is required.	They are suitable for applications where accuracy is required.
9.	It requires a lot of calculations if the image is to enlarge.	Image can be enlarged without losing accuracy.
10.	If the number of objects in the scene increases, computation time also increases.	In this method, complexity increase with the complexity of visible parts.

9.3 TYPES OF VISIBLE SURFACE DETECTION

Visible surface detection methods are so many; some of them are Back-Face Detection, Z-buffer method, A-buffer method, Scan-line method, Depth-sorting method, Area-subdivision method, etc.

9.3.1 Back-Face Detection

It is an object space method in which objects and parts of objects are compared to find out the visible surfaces. Let us consider a cube surface whose visibility needs to be decided. The idea is to check if the cube will be facing away from the viewer or not. If it does so, discard it for the current frame and move on to the next one.

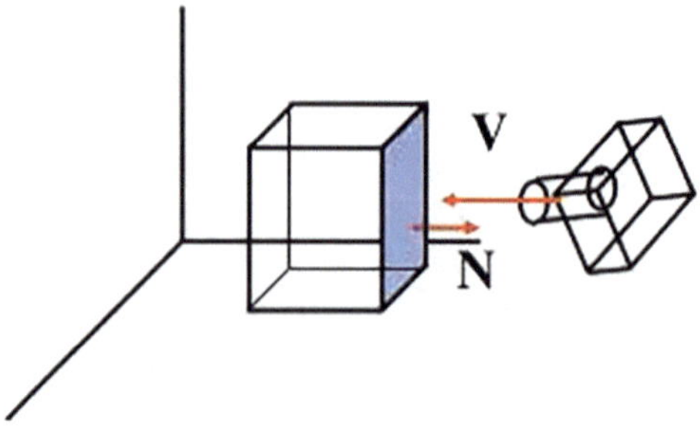

Figure 9.2: Front face

Each surface has a normal vector. If this normal vector is pointing in the direction of the center of projection, then it is a front face and can be seen by the viewer. If this normal vector is pointing away from the center of the projection, then it is a back face and cannot be seen by the viewer.

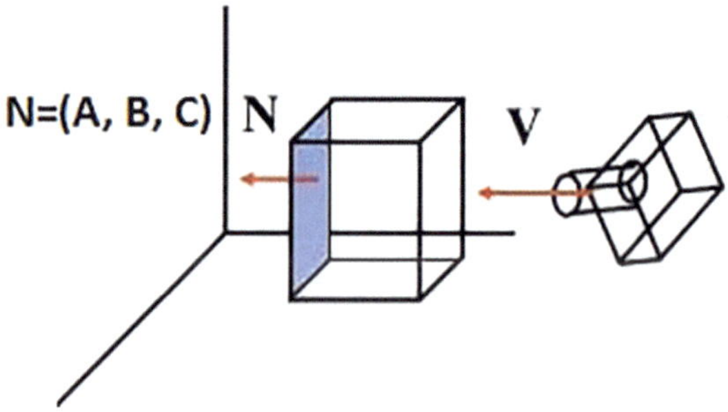

Figure 9.3: Back face

A point (x, y, z) is "inside" a polygon surface with plane parameters A, B, C, and D if:

$$A_x + B_y + C_z + D < 0$$

When an inside point is along the line of sight on a surface, the surface must be back face and therefore cannot be seen, that is if V N >0 then it is back face. Where N is the normal vector of the polygon and V is the view vector.

We know that $V.N = |V|.|N|\cos\theta$ so if the vector is in the same direction, that is $0 \leq \theta \leq \pi/2$, then it is in the back face and if the vector is in the opposite direction, that is $\pi/2 \leq \theta \leq \pi$, then it is in the front face.

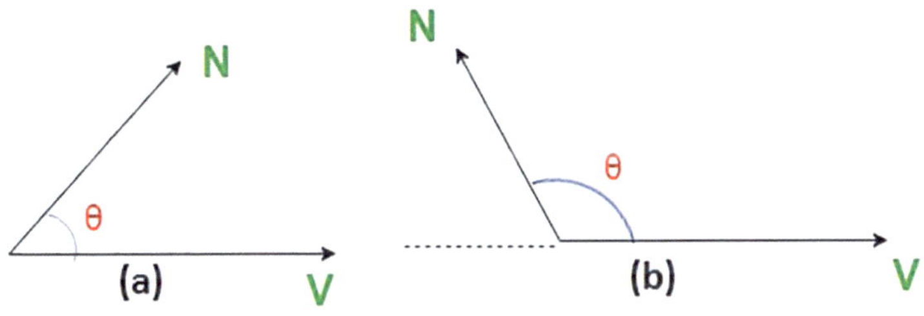

Figure 9.4: (a) $0 \leq \theta \leq \pi/2$, Back-face and (b) $\pi/2 \leq \theta \leq \pi$, Front-face

A polygon is a back face if $V_Z.N > 0$, that is viewer is looking down the negative Z-axis. Therefore, a polygon is back face if: $VN = V_Z.C$ since $V = (0, 0, V_z)$ and $N = (\underline{A}, B, C)$.

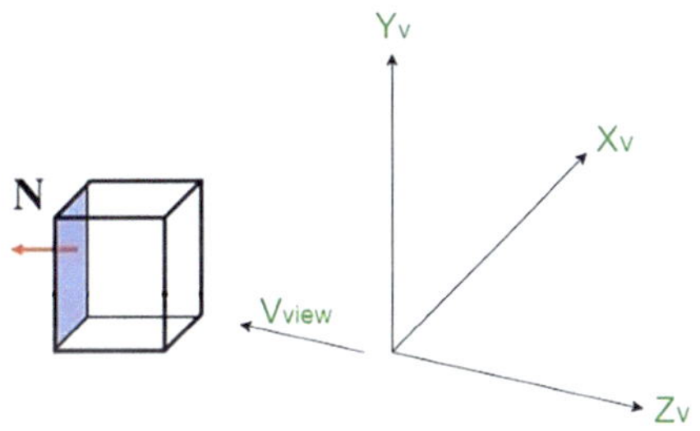

Figure 9.5: Back face detection

In a right-handed viewing system with viewing direction along the negative Z-axis, the polygon is a back face if $C \leq 0$. Thus, in general, we can label any polygon as a back face if its normal vector has a z component value that is $C \leq 0$. Now we can simply say that if the Z component of the polygon's normal is less than zero the surface cannot be seen.

Back Face Removed Algorithm

Repeat for all polygons in the scene.

Step 1. Do numbering of all polygons in a clockwise direction that is V1, V2, V3…Vn.

Step 2. Calculate normal vector N1 that is N1= (V2 - V1)*(V3 - V2).

Step 3. Consider projector P, it is a projection from any vertex calculated dot product Dot = N.P.

Step 4. Test and plot whether the surface is visible or not.
If Dot ≥ 0 then the surface is visible
Else
Not visible

Step 5. Stop

Advantages of Back-Face Detection Method

- It is a simple and straightforward method.
- It is a simple object space method.
- It reduces the size of databases, because no need to store all surfaces in the database, only the visible surface is stored.

Disadvantages of Back-Face Detection Method

- This method works fine for convex polyhedra, but not necessarily for concave polyhedra, that is, partially hidden faces will not be eliminated by Back-face removal.

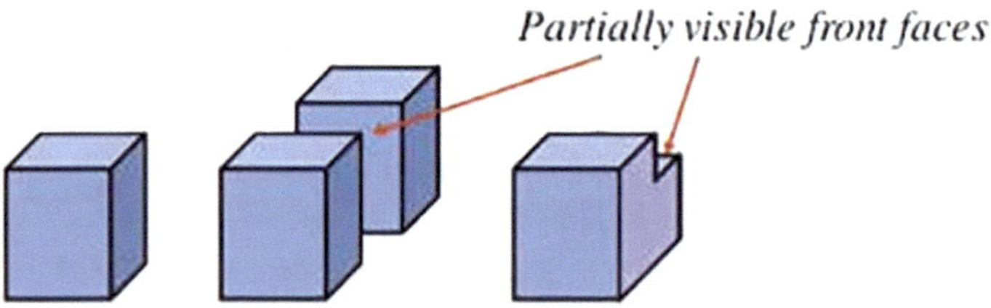

- It can only be used on solid objects modeled as polygon mesh.

Example 9.1

If N1 = (2, 1, 2), N2= (-3, 1 -2) and V= (-1, 0 -1) then determine whether it is back face or front face as given in Figure 9.6.

Solution

N1.V = (2, 1, 2) (-1, 0 -1) = -2.-2 = -4
Since, N1.V < 0 so N1 is a front facing Polygon.
N2.V = (-3, 1, -2) (-1, 0 -1) = 3+2= 5
Since N2.V > 0 so N2 is a back facing Polygon

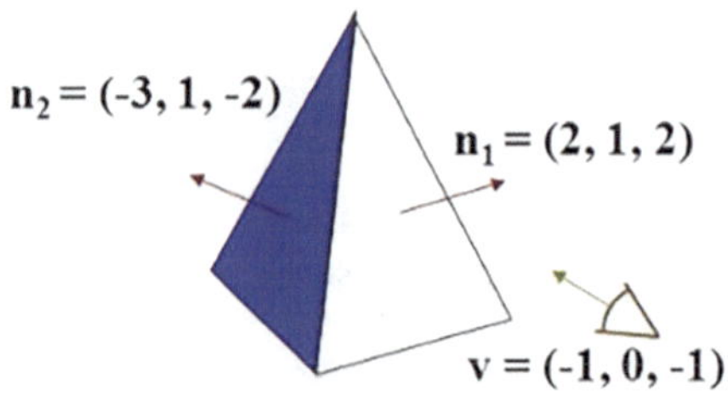

Figure 9.6: Example 9.1

9.3.2 Z-Buffer Algorithms

It is also called a Depth Buffer Algorithm and was developed by Cat Mull in 1974. It is an image-space approach. The basic idea is to test the Z-depth of each surface to determine the closest (visible) surface. In this method, each surface is processed separately one pixel position at a time across the surface. The depth values for a pixel are compared and the closest (smallest z) surface determines the colour to be displayed in the frame buffer. To override the closer polygons from the far ones, two buffers named depth buffer and frame buffer, are used.

Depth buffer is used to store depth values for each (x, y) position, as surfaces are processed ($0 \leq \text{depth} \leq 1$). The frame buffer is used to store the intensity value of colour value at each position (x, y). There are two cases in the Z-Buffer algorithm

i. When viewing direction is from + Z to –Z.
ii. When viewing direction is from –Z to +Z.

In the first scenario, a polygon with a lower z value is situated at the back, while the others are in the front. In the second scenario, polygons with higher z values are positioned at the back, while the others are in the front.

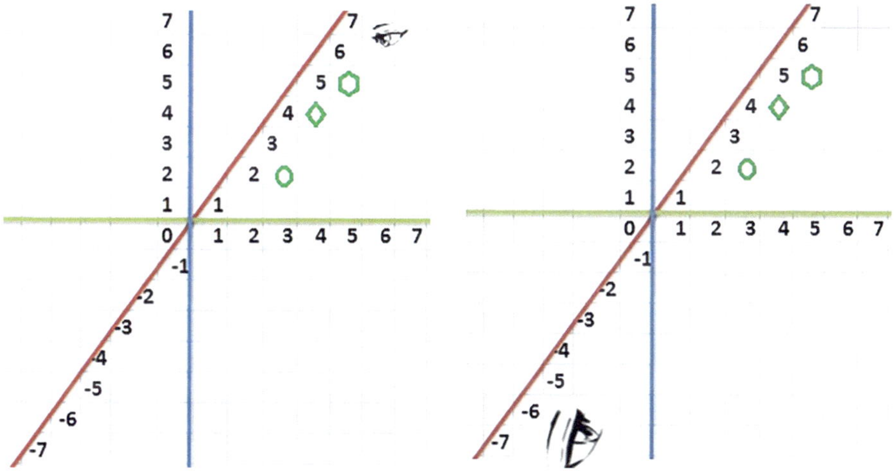

Figure 9.7: (a) Viewing Direction From + Z To –Z and (b) –Z to +Z.

Z-Buffer Algorithm (When view direction is from +Z to –Z direction)

Step 1. Larger value= closer (frontside)
Smaller Z value= farther (backside)

Step 2. Set the buffer values
depthbuffer (x, y) = 0
framebuffer (x, y) = background colour

Step 3. Process each polygon (One at a time)
For each projected (x, y) pixel position of a polygon
i. Calculate depth z
ii. If Z > depthbuffer (x, y) then
Step 4. Compute surface color
Set depthbuffer (x, y) = z
Step 5. framebuffer (x, y) = surfacecolor (x, y)
Step 6. Stop.

Z-Buffer Algorithm (When view direction is from –Z to +Z direction)

Step 1. Larger value = farther (backside)
Smaller Z value = closer (frontside)
Step 2. Set the buffer values
depthbuffer (x, y) = infinite
framebuffer (x, y) = background colour
Step 3. Process each polygon (One at a time)
For each projected (x, y) pixel position of a polygon
i. Calculate depth z.
ii. If Z < depthbuffer ((x, y) then
Step 4. Compute surface color
Set depthbuffer (x, y) = z
Step 5. framebuffer (x, y) = surfacecolor (x, y)
Step 6. Stop.

For all pixels on the screen, set depth [x, y] to 1.0 and intensity [x, y] to a background value. For each polygon in the scene, find all pixels (x, y) that lie within the boundaries of a polygon when projected onto the screen. For each of these pixels, calculate the depth z of the polygon at (x, y).

If z < depth [x, y], this polygon is closer to the observer than others already recorded for this pixel. In this case, set depth [x, y] to z and intensity [x, y] to a value corresponding to polygon's shading. If instead z > depth [x, y], the polygon already recorded at (x, y) lies closer to the observer than does this new polygon, and no action is taken. After all, polygons have been processed; the intensity array will contain the solution.

Advantages of Z-Buffer Algorithm

- It is easy to implement.
- It reduces the speed problem if implemented in hardware.
- It processes one object at a time.
- Accurate performance.

Disadvantages of Z-Buffer Algorithm

- It requires a large memory.
- It is time consuming process.
- This should only be utilized on a surface that is not transparent (opaque).

9.3.3 A- Buffer Algorithms

This method falls under the category of the image-space method. It extends the algorithm of the depth-buffer (or Z-Buffer) technique. This method is also known as anti-aliased or area-averaged or accumulation buffer. The depth buffer method can only be used for opaque objects but is not good for transparent objects. Each position in the A-buffer has two fields:

i. **Depth Field:** It stores a positive or negative real number
ii. **Intensity Field:** It stores surface-intensity information or a pointer value (a pointer to a linked list of surfaces that contribute to that pixel position).

If the value of depth ≥ 0 the number stored at that position is the depth of a single surface overlapping the corresponding pixel area. The 2nd field, that is, the intensity field then stores the RGB components of the surface color at that point and the percent of pixel coverage.

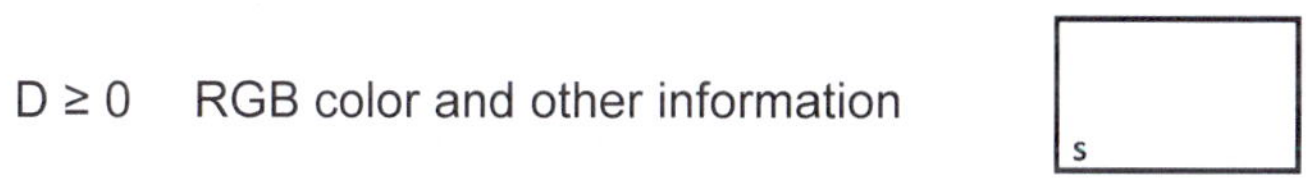

Figure 9.8: When a pixel overlaps by only one surface

If the value of depth is < 0, this indicates multiple-surface contributions to the pixel intensity. The 2nd field, i.e., the intensity field then stores a pointer to a linked list of surface data.

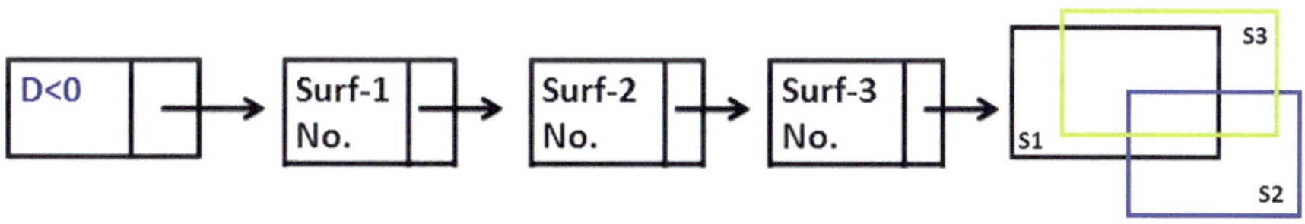

Figure 9.9: When a pixel overlaps by multiple surface

The surface buffer includes the following:

- RGB intensity components
- Opacity Parameter (percent of transparency)
- Depth
- Percent of area coverage
- Surface Identifier

- Pointer to the next surface

The algorithm proceeds just like the depth buffer algorithm. The depth and opacity values are used to determine the final colour of a pixel.

Advantages of A- Buffer Algorithms

- The surface intensity at each pixel position can be taken into consideration more than once.
- It also anti-aliased the object edges.
- In this, surfaces are divided into polygon mesh and clipped against the pixel boundaries.
- The intensity of pixel is determined by considering opacity parameter and percentage of overlaps of the overlapping surface.

Disadvantages of A-Buffer Algorithms

- This algorithm processes multiple objects at a time. The total number of polygons in a picture can be arbitrarily large.

Example 9.2

Consider the Figure 9.10 uses the Z-buffer and A-buffer algorithms to determine surface visibility.

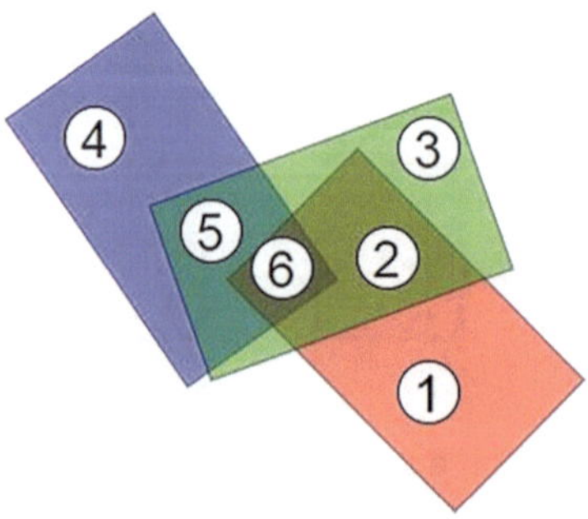

Figure 9.10: Multiple Surfaces

Solution

If we have used z-buffer then this method detects only one visible surface at each pixel position, which means it deals only with opaque surfaces.

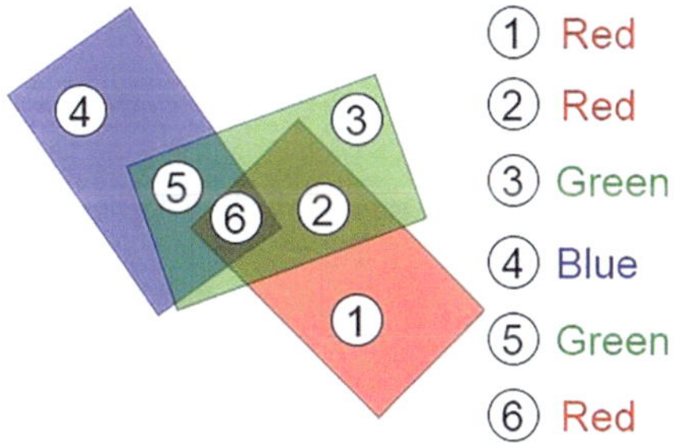

Figure 9.11: Multiple surfaces detected by Z-buffer algorithm

If we have used an A-buffer then this method detects multiple visible surfaces at each pixel position, which means it deals with opaque as well as transparent surfaces.

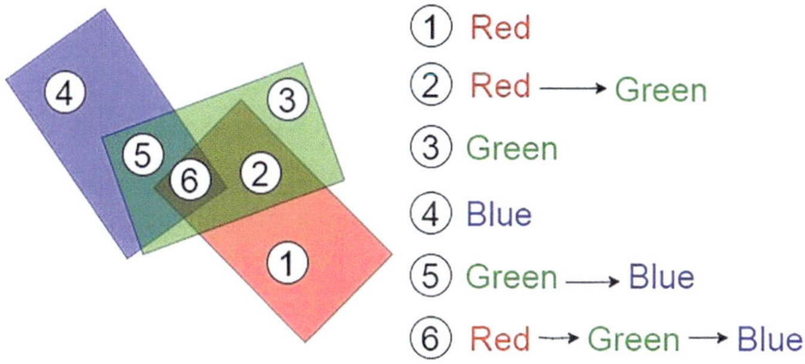

Figure 9.12: Multiple Surfaces detected by A-buffer algorithm

9.3.4 Scan-line Algorithms

It is an image-space method for identifying the visible surface. It is an extension of the scan-line algorithm for polygon fill. We have seen that, we can process only one surface at a time if we use the depth buffer method, but by scan-line method, we can process more than one surface at a time. This method has depth information for only a single scan- line. In order to require one scan-line of depth values, we must group and process all polygons intersecting a given scan-line at the same time before processing the next scan-line. For all polygons intersecting each scan-line

- Processed from left to right
- Depth calculations for each overlapping surface
- The intensity of the nearest position is entered into the refresh buffer.

In this method, as each scan-line is processed, all polygonal surfaces intersecting that line are examined to determine which one is visible. A cross to each scan-line, depth is calculated for each overlapping surface to determine which one is closest to the plane of view. When the visible surface is determined, the intensity value for that position is recorded in the image buffer. To facilitate the search for surfaces crossing a given scan-line, an active list of edges is formed. Only edges that cross the scan-line are stored by the active list. A flag is set to indicate whether the position along the scan-line is inside or outside the surface. At the left intersection, the surface flag is activated, while it is deactivated at the right intersection. Each of the scan-line is a process from left to right. The surface flag is turned on at the left intersection and turned off at the right intersection.

Data Structure used by Scan-Line Algorithm

Three important tables are maintained for this.

- Edge table (ET)
- Polygon table (PT)
- Active Edge Table (AET)

Edge Table

Create an Edge Table (ET) for all non-horizontal edges of all polygons projected on the view plane. Entries in the ET are sorted into bucket based on each edge's smaller y coordinates and within bucket are ordered by increasing the x coordinate. Edge Table contains the following fields: –

- The x-coordinate of the end with the smaller y-coordinate.
- The y-coordinate of the edge's other end.
- Δx used in stepping from one scan line to the next.
- ID indicating the polygon to which the edge belongs.
- Pointers into the surface facet table to connect edges to surfaces.

Table 9.2: Edge Table

X	Ymax	Dx	ID	→

Polygon Table

Polygon Table contains the following fields:

- Polygon ID
- The coefficients of the plane equation
- Shading or Color information for the Polygon
- An 'in-out' Boolean flag, initiated to false and used during Scan-line processing.

Table 9.3: Polygon Table

ID	Plane Coeffs.	Shading Info.	In/Out

Active Edge Table

This table contains all those edges of the polygon that are intersected (crossed) by the current scan-line and sorted in order of increasing x.

Table 9.4: Polygon table

Scanline	*Entries*			
Scanline 1	AB	BC	HE	FG

Flag for Each Surface

Indicate whether inside or outside of the surface. If the flag is at the leftmost boundary of a surface then the surface flag is at turned on or if the flag at the rightmost boundary of a surface then the surface flag is turned off.

Scan-line Algorithm (Visible Surface Determination)

Step 1. Initialize the desired data structure.

1.1 Create a Polygon Table (PT) having color, edge pointers, and coefficients.

1.2 Establish Edge Table (ET) contains information regarding, the endpoint of edges, pointer to polygon, and inverse slope.

1.3 Create Active Edge Table (AET) this will be sorted in increasing order of x.

1.4 Create a flag (F), it will have two values IN (TRUE) or OUT (FALSE). Initially, F is OUT.

Step 2. Perform the following steps for all scan lines.

2.1 Enter values in Active edge table (AET) in sorted order using y as value.

2.2 Scan until the flag F is IN using a background color.

2.3 When one polygon flag F is IN and this is for surface S1, enter color intensity as I1 into refresh buffer.

2.4 When two or more surface flags are IN, sort the surfaces according to depth and use intensity value Sn for nth surface. This surface will have least Z depth value.

2.5 Use the concept of coherence for remaining planes.

Step 3. Stop.

Advantages of Scan Line algorithm

- Any number of overlapping surfaces can be processed.
- Take advantage of the coherence principle.

Disadvantages of Scan Line algorithm

- It does not work for surfaces that cut through or cyclically overlap each other.

Example 9.3

Consider the scan-line with following figure. Determine the visible portions of surfaces for pixel positions along the line.

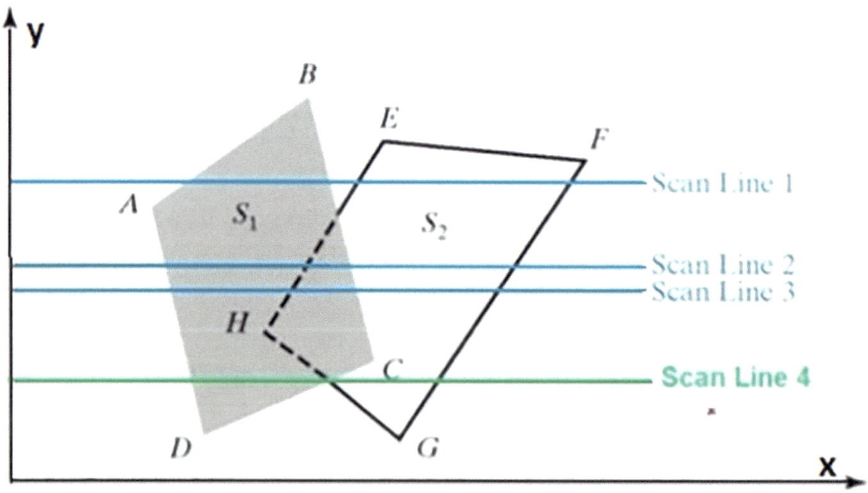

Figure 9.13: Surfaces along the Line

Solution

Figure 9.14 illustrates the scan-line method for locating visible portions of surfaces for pixel positions along the line

- Sorted edges are: AD, CD, GH, FG, BC, HE, AB, and EF.
- Polygon table has entries for ABCD and EFGH.
- Prepare an Active Edge Table (AET).

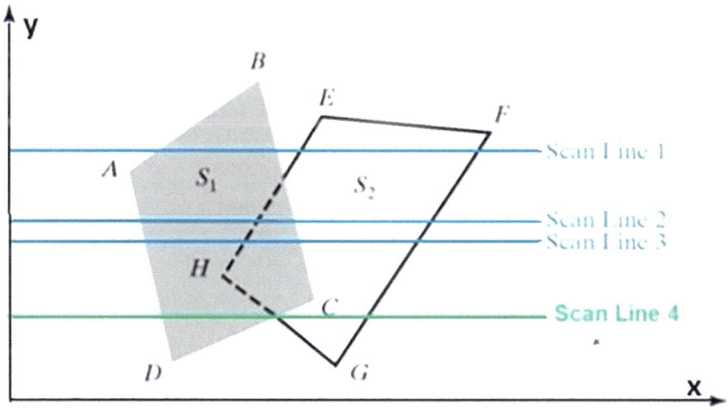

Figure 9.14: Illustrates the Scan-Line Method

Table 9.5: Active Edge Table (AET)

Scan line	*Entries*
1	AB, BC, HE, FG
2	AD, HE, BC, FG
3	AD, HE, BC, FG
4	AD, DC, GH, FG

Active List for Scan Line 1:

- **Active Edge List:**
  - AB, BC, EH, and FG.
  - Between AB and BC, only the flag for surface S1 is on.
    - Therefore no depth calculations are necessary.
    - Intensity for surface S1 is entered from the polygon table into the refresh buffer.
  - Similarly, between EH and FG, only the flag for S2 is on.
    - Therefore no depth calculations are necessary.
    - Intensity for surface S2 is entered into the frame buffer.

Active List for Scan Line 2

- **Active Edge List:**
  - AD, EH, BC, and FG.
  - Between AD and EH, only the flag for S1 is on.
    - Therefore no depth calculations are necessary.
    - Intensity for surface S1 is entered into the frame buffer.

- Between EH and BC, the flags for both surfaces are on.
- Depth calculation is needed.
- Depth of S1 is less therefore Intensities for S1 are loaded into the refresh buffer until boundary BC is encountered.

- Between BC and FG, only the flag for S2 is on.
    - ◊ Therefore no depth calculations are necessary.
    - ◊ Intensity for surface S2 is entered into the frame buffer.

Active List for Scan Line 3

- **Active Edge List:**
    - AD, EH, BC, and FG
    - Take advantage of coherence.
        - ◊ Pass from one scan line to next.
        - ◊ Scan line 3 has the same active list as scan line 2.
        - ◊ Unnecessary to make depth calculations, between EH and BC.
    - Active Edge list of scan line 2 and scan line 3 is same therefore take advantage of coherence.

9.3.5 Depth-Sorting Algorithms

A visible surface detection method that uses both image-space and object-space operations is called depth sort. The depth-sorting method is often also known as the Painter's method, because the painter first, paints more distance polygons and over it the next farther polygon, totally or partially obscuring them from view, and so on. So the basic problem is to find the priority ordering of the polygons in order to determine which polygons are to be painted first (scan converted). Basically, the following two operations are performed

- Surfaces are sorted in order of decreasing depth.
- Surfaces are scanned and converted in order, starting with the surface of greatest depth.

Depth-Sorting Algorithm Process

1. First, assume that we are viewing along the z direction.
2. All surfaces in the scene are ordered according to the smallest z value on each surface.
3. The surface S at the end of the list is then compared against all other surfaces to see if there are any depth overlaps.
4. If no overlaps occur then the surface is scan converted and the process is then repeated for the next surface in the list.

5. If depth overlap is detected at any point in the list, then need some additional comparisons to determine whether any of the surfaces should be reordered.

Test for Depth Overlap

Step 1. Compare S with all other polygons (P) to see if there is any depth overlap, that is $S \times Z_{min} \leq P \times Z_{max}$.

Step 2. If condition is true then perform the following test (Tests for each surface that overlaps with S).

2.1 The bounding rectangles in the x-y plane for the two surfaces do not overlap.

2.2 Surface S is completely behind the overlapping surface relative to the viewing position.

2.3 The overlapping surface is completely in front of S relative to the viewing position.

2.4 The boundary edge projections of the two surfaces onto the view plane do not overlap.

Step 3. If all the surfaces pass at least one of the tests, none of them is behind S, no reordering is then necessary and S is scan converted.

Step 4. If all tests fail then we swap the orders of the surfaces.

The Initial Tests for Depth-Overlapping

Compare S with all other polygons (P) to see if there is any depth overlap.

If $S \times Z_{min} \leq P \times Z_{max}$, then have depth overlap (as in below figures), Test-1 will perform

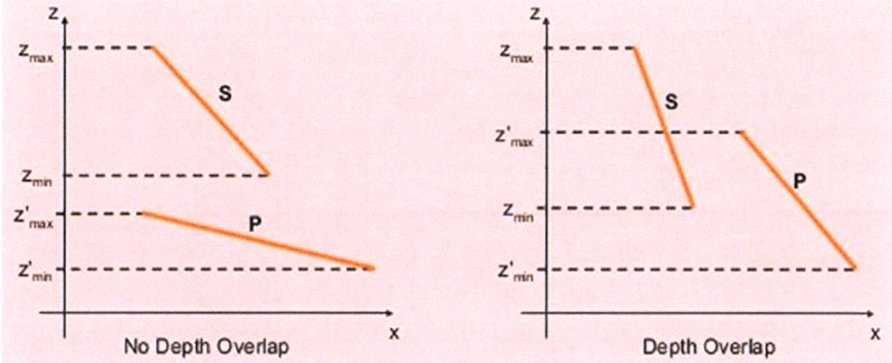

Figure 9.15: Depth Overlapping

Test 1. For Depth-Overlapping

Check to see if polygons overlap in x-y plane (use bounding rectangles). Depth overlap, check for x-y overlap

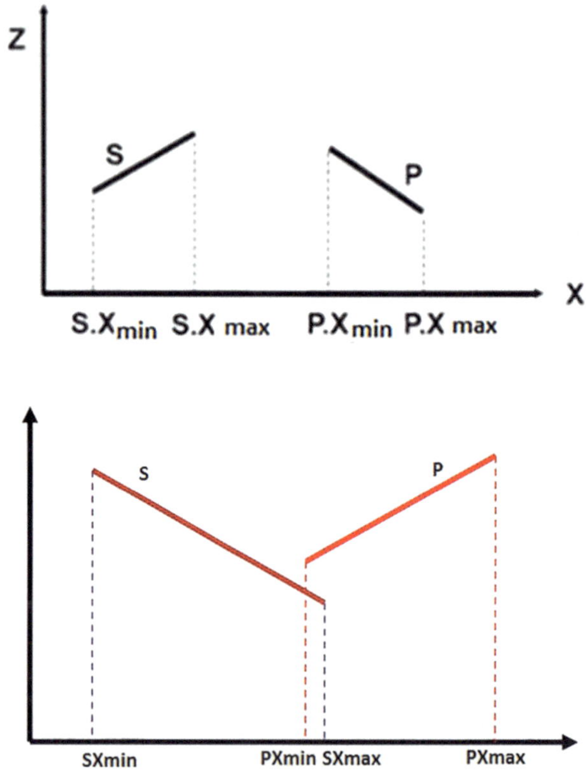

Figure 9.16: Overlap in X-Y Plane

Test 2. For Depth-Overlapping

If the test surface S is located "inside" the polygon P in relation to the view plane.

Suppose the plane equation for P is $A_x + B_y + C_z + D$. So to test for S outside of P, put all vertices of S into the plane equation for P and check that all vertices give a result that is > 0, that is $A_{x'} + B_{y'} + C_{z'} + D > 0$, where x', y', z' are S vertices . Choose Normal away from the view plane since define "inside" with respect to the view. We know that a point (x, y, z) is "outside" of a plane if we put that point into the plane equation and we get $A_{x'} + B_{y'} + C_{z'} + D > 0$.

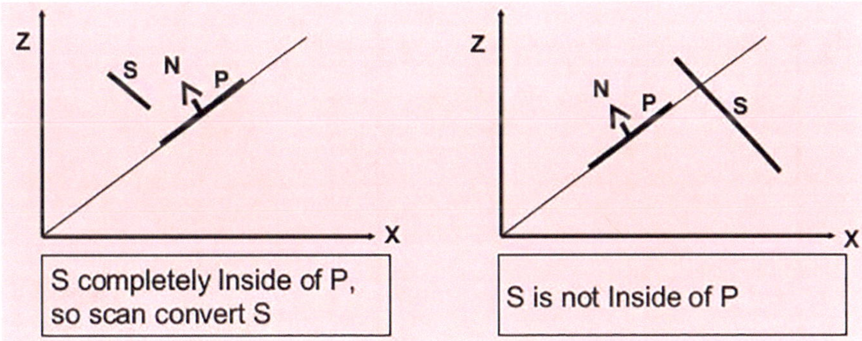

Figure 9.17: Tests of Inside and Outside Surface

Test 3. For Depth-Overlapping

If the test for S "inside" P fails, test to see if P is "outside" S (again with respect to the visual plane) (test 2). Compute plane equation of S and put in all vertices of P, if all vertices of P are inside of S then P is inside. Inside Test: $A_{x'} + B_{y'} + C_{z'} + D$ and it is zero, where x′, y′, z′ are coordinates of P vertices.

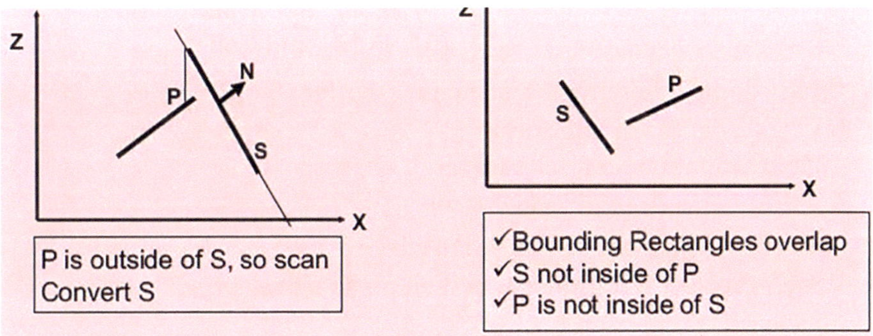

Figure 9.18: Tests of Inside and Outside Surface fails

Test 4. For Depth-Overlapping

Check for overlap for actual projections in x-y plane since may have bounding rectangles overlap but not actual overlap. For example: Look at projection of two polygons in the x-y plane X Z.

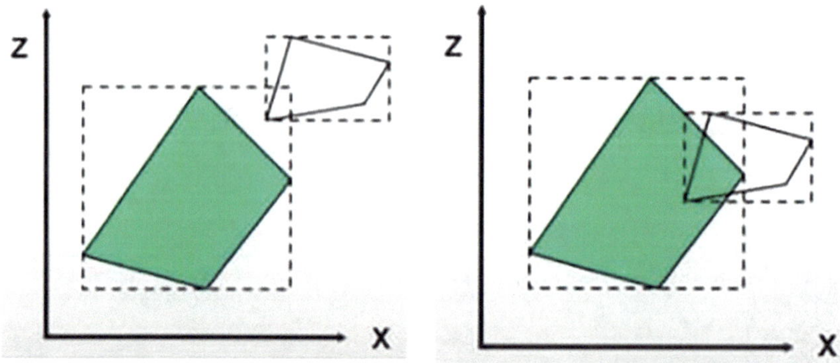

Figure 9.19: Overlap for Actual Projections in X-Y Plane

- Bounding Rectangle Overlap, But Projection Don't
- Use Line eq. and test for Intersection
- No intersection, scan convert S

Ordering S and S′ if all previous tests fail, interchange S and S′ in the list x-z.

OBJECTIVE QUESTIONS

1. Which of the following is not a hidden surface removal algorithm?
   (a) Z-buffering (b) Binary space partitioning
   (c) Warnock algorithm (d) Sutherland Cohen
2. Which of the following is true about z-buffer algorithm?
   (a) It is a depth sort algorithm
   (b) No limitation on total number of objects
   (c) Comparisons of objects is done
   (d) Z-buffer is initialized to background colour at start of algorithm
3. Which surface algorithm is based on perspective depth?
   (a) Depth comparison
   (b) Z-buffer or depth-buffer algorithm
   (c) Subdivision method
   (d) Back-face removal
4. The types of hidden surface removal algorithm are
   (a) Depth comparison, Z-buffer, back-face removal
   (b) Scan line algorithm, priority algorithm
   (c) BSP method, area subdivision method
   (d) All of these

5. In the depth buffer method which buffer is/are used?
   (a) Depth buffer (b) Refresh buffer
   (c) Frame buffer (d) Both (a) and (b)
6. The painter algorithm are also called
   (a) Depth sort algorithm (b) Priority algorithm
   (c) Both (a) and (b) (d) None of these
7. The painter algorithm are based on the property of
   (a) Polygon (b) Frame buffer
   (c) Depth buffer (d) None of these
8. All the hidden surface algorithms employer image space approach except
   (a) Back face removal (b) Depth buffer method
   (c) Scan line method (d) Depth sort method
9. The method which is based on the principle of comparing objects and parts of objects to each other to find which are visible and which are hidden are called
   (a) Object-space method (b) Image-space method
   (c) Both (a) and (b) (d) None of these
10. The problems of hidden surface are
    (a) Removal of hidden surface (b) Identification of hidden surface
    (c) Both (a) and (b) (d) None of these
11. Why we need removal of hidden surface
    (a) For displaying realistic view
    (b) For determining the closest visible surface
    (c) Both (a) and (b)
    (d) None of these
12. Which is true for back-face detection?
    (a) The back-face detection algorithm is always working well for all polyhedron
    (b) The back-face detection algorithm always works for a concave polyhedron
    (c) The back-face detection algorithm always works for a convex polyhedron
    (d) All of these
13. In which type of visible-surface detection Algorithms visibility is decided point by point at each pixel position on the projection plane?
    (a) Object-Space methods (b) Image-Space methods
    (c) Both (a) and (b) (d) None of these

14. In the back-face detection algorithm, If V is along the positive Z direction than polygon is back face if ______. (V = vector in viewing direction from eye, C = Plane constant)
    (a) $C \geq 0$ (b) $C \leq 0$
    (c) $C \geq 1$ (d) $C \leq 1$

15. How much memory is required to implement z-buffer algorithm for a $512 \times 512 \times 24$ bit-plane image?
    (a) 768 KB (b) 1 MB
    (c) 1.5 MB (d) MB

ANSWERS

1. (d)	4. (d)	7. (c)	10. (c)	13. (b)
2. (b)	5. (d)	8. (b)	11. (c)	14. (a)
3. (b)	6. (b)	9. (a)	12. (c)	15. (c)

EXERCISES

1. Write a short note on Visible Surface Detection or Hidden Surface Elimination.
2. Differentiate between the Object Space and Image Space method for the hidden surface removal of an image.
3. Give the classification of the Visible Surface Detection algorithm. Explain any one with example.
4. Discuss Back-Face Detection method also write Back-Face Detection algorithm of hidden lines.
5. Explain the Back Face Detection algorithm for hidden surface removal.
6. Write Depth-buffer method algorithm of hidden lines.
7. Describe in detail the Depth Buffer visible surface detection technique. Derive the equation to find the depth values for a surface position (x, y).
8. If polygon Q has the same depth value as polygon P, which polygon has priority, that is, which is painted first, and why?
9. Discuss A-buffer method.
10. In case of an A-buffer algorithm, what information is stored in a linked list?
11. Explain the Difference between Depth-Buffer and A-Buffer.
12. List the advantage and disadvantage of Back-Face Detection and A-buffer method.

13. Describe about the Depth-Sorting method to display the visible surfaces of any given object with plane faces. Also explain the tests to identify overlapping surfaces.
14. Explain Z-buffer visible surface determination algorithm Explain in detail the scan line algorithm for visible surface detection by pointing out the data structures used in this algorithm.
15. How would the Z-buffer algorithm be altered to allow figures to be superimposed on a surface?
16. List out the differences between Z-buffer method and A-buffer method for determining the visible surfaces.
17. What happens when two polygons have the same z value and the Z-buffer algorithm is used?
18. Given points P1 (1, 2, 0), P2 (3, 6, 20), and P3 (2, 4, 6) and a viewpoint C (0, 0, -10), determine which points obscure the others when viewed from C.
19. What is the underlying concept of the Painter's or the Priority Algorithm?
20. What difficulties are encountered in implementing the Painter's Algorithm?
21. Discuss the Scan-Line Algorithm for the removal of hidden lines from a scene of 3D graphics display.
22. How does the basic Scan-Line method determine which surfaces are hidden?
23. Explain the Scan–Line method used in visible surface detection with an example.

10

Illumination Model

Generating transformations, applying perceptive projection to objects, and adding lighting effects onto visible surfaces are all crucial in creating realistic scenes. Illumination models, which are also known as lighting or shading models, are utilized to calculate the intensity of light that we see at a given point on the surface of an object. This chapter focuses on shading 3-D objects and their models, discussing light, various color models, and how colors can be applied in graphics applications. Studying shading models helps to determine how an object's surface appears under different lighting conditions. This chapter also touches upon the Phong model and interpolative shading model. Additionally, color can be used to convey more information in visual messages or pictures. It is important to examine and define the role of color in various applications to utilize it properly in the visualization of ideas, information, or concepts. Mathematical models can be used to determine shading, and each shading model helps to establish the relationship between the surface and the light source. Identifying this relationship helps to create a specific shading effect.

10.1 INTRODUCTION OF ILLUMINATION

Light sources are called light-emitting sources, for example, the sun and reflective surfaces such as the walls of a room are called light-reflecting sources. A luminous object, in general, can be both a light source and a light reflector. The simplest model for a light emitter is a point source. When light is incident on an opaque surface, some part of it is reflected and part is absorbed. The amount of incident light reflected by a surface depends on the type of material. Shiny materials reflect the incident light more while dull surfaces absorb the incident light more. For an illuminated transparent surface, some of the incident light will be reflected and some will be transmitted through the material.

The surface which is rough or grainy, scatters the reflected light in all directions, such scattered light is called diffused reflection.

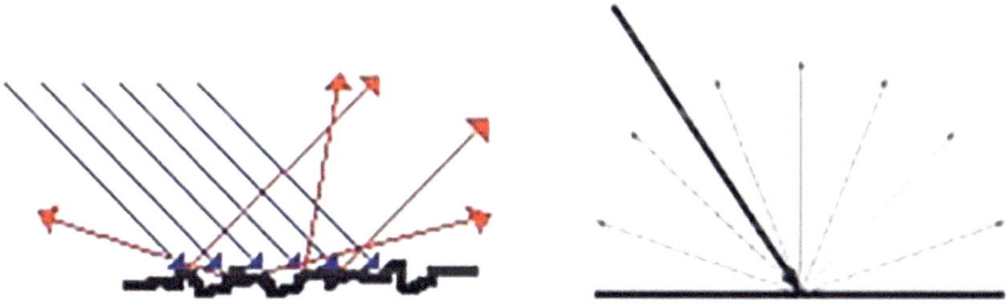

Figure 10.1: Diffused Reflections

In addition to diffuse reflection, light sources create highlights or bright spots, which are called specular reflections.

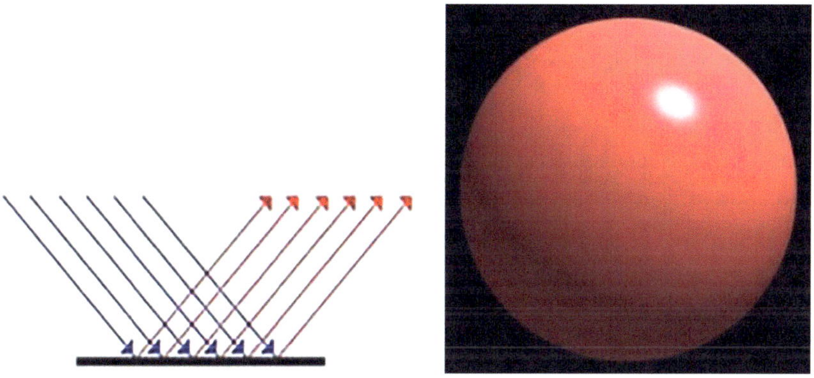

Figure 10.2: Specular Reflections

This highlighting effect is more pronounced on glossy surfaces than on dull ones. Illumination models determine the intensity of light that we should see at a given point on the surface of an object. Due to the relationship defined in the model between the surface of the object and the light affecting it, the illumination model is also called the shading model or the lighting model. The model for calculating light intensity at a single surface point is called the illumination model. Surface rendering is a procedure for applying a lighting model to obtain pixel intensities for all the projected surface positions in a scene.

Illumination Model Parameters: Lighting effects are described with models that consider the interaction of light sources with object surfaces. The factors determining the lighting effects are:

- The light source parameters:
  - Positions
  - Electromagnetic Spectrum
  - Shape

- The surface parameters
  - Position
  - Reflectance properties
  - Position of nearby surfaces
- The eye (camera) parameters
  - Position
  - Sensor spectrum sensitivities

10.2 TYPES OF ILLUMINATION

There are two types of illumination models one is local illumination and other is global illumination

10.2.1 Local illumination

These models are local in that they do not consider light from objects in the scene. Only light sources generate light. Light reflected from objects in the environment does not affect other objects. This type of illumination model expresses light from a single-light, a single-surface interaction. If the light arrives straight from the light source then it is known as a direct illumination. In local illumination algorithms, only direct lights are taken into account.

10.2.2 Global Illumination

In global illumination model express light from multiple sources that is from direct light source as well as light reflected from object in the environment. If light arrives after interacting with the rest of the scene is known as indirect illumination. The global illumination model is equal to direct illumination + indirect illumination. In global illumination algorithms, both kinds of sources are considered.

10.3 AMBIENT LIGHT/DIFFUSION ILLUMINATION MODEL

A surface that is not directly exposed to a light source may be visible even when nearby objects are illuminated. In our basic illumination model, we can set a normal level of brightness for the scene. This is a simple way to model the combination of light reflections from different surfaces to produce a uniform illumination called ambient light or background light.

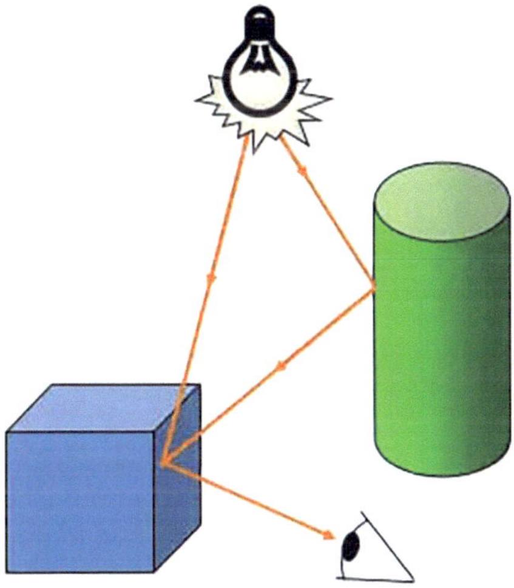

Figure 10.3: Specular Reflections

So, the product of multiple reflections of light from several reflecting surfaces in the environment is called ambient light. However, the amount of ambient light incident on each object is a constant for all surfaces and overall direction. Ambient Illumination is the one where the source of light is indirect. The intensity of ambient reflected light is proportional to ambient intensity. If the reflected intensity of any point on the surface is Iambi then:

$$I_{ambi} = K_a I_a$$

Where I_a is intensity of ambient light.

K_a is the coefficient of reflection which range from 0 to 1.

Ambient light has no spatial or directional characteristics. The amount of ambient light incident on each object is constant for all surfaces and in all directions. Ambient light is independent of surface orientation and viewer location.

10.4 DIFFUSE REFLECTION MODEL

Diffuse reflection occurs on surfaces that are rough or grainy. Objects illuminated by only ambient light have equal intensity everywhere. If there is a light source then different objects should have different intensities based on distance and orientation with respect to light source and viewer position. A point on a diffuse surface appears equally bright from all viewing positions because it scattered (reflects) light equally in all directions, that is, intensity is independent of viewer position. The intensity of a point on a diffuser depends on the orientation (direction) of the surface with respect to the light source and the distance to the light source. The diffuse reflections model follows Lamberts cosine rule.

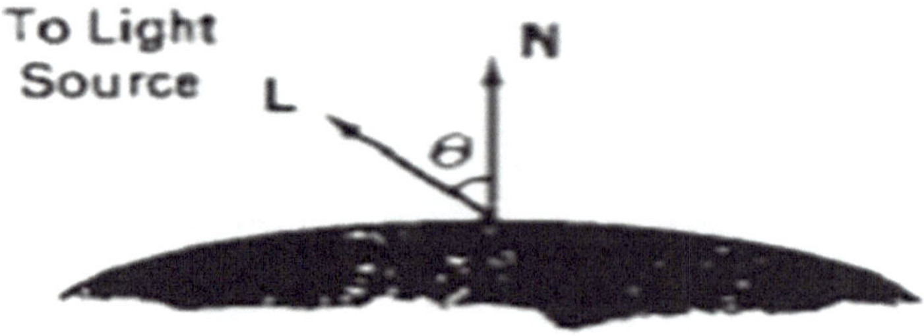

Figure 10.4: Angle of incidence θ between the unit light-source direction vector L and the unit surface normal N

Where N_a Unit normal vector to a surface

L_a Unit direction vector to the point light source from a position on the surface

This law states that when light falls obliquely on a surface, the illumination of the surface is directly proportional to the cosine of the angle θ between the direction of the incident light and the surface normal N. If I_i is the intensity of the point light source, then the diffuse reflection equation for a point on the surface can be written as

$$I_{diff} = K_d I_i \cos\theta$$

Since

$$NL = |N|.|L| \cos\theta$$

$$NL = 1.1 \cos\theta$$

$$NL = \cos\theta$$

So diffuse reflection equation for single point source illumination is

$$I_{diff} = K_d I_i (N.L)$$

If the light source is at an infinite distance from the object then L will be the same for all points on the object, the light source becomes a directional light source. So diffuse reflection is a combination of ambient and point source intensity

$$I_{diff} = K_a I_a + K_d\ I_i (N.L) \quad K_a, K_d \in [0.1]$$

10.5 SPECULAR REFLECTION MODEL

When light falls on any shiny or glossy surface most of it is reflected back, such reflection is known as Specular Reflection. Whenever a light surface produces highlights or bright spots, then the light effect is known as specular reflection. Reflection intensity changes with to reflection angle. An ideal specular surface is a mirror which reflects light exclusively in one direction R. Specular reflection is the result of total or near total reflection of the incident light in a concentrated region around the specular reflection angle.

$$I_{sp} = I_i \; K_d \, cos^n \, \theta$$

Where n → specific Intensity

$$\cos \phi = R \cdot V$$

$$\& \; R = (2N.L) \; N - L$$

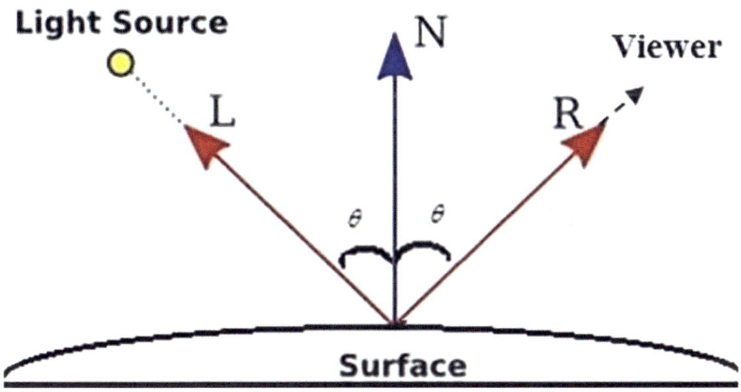

Figure 10.5: Specular Reflections

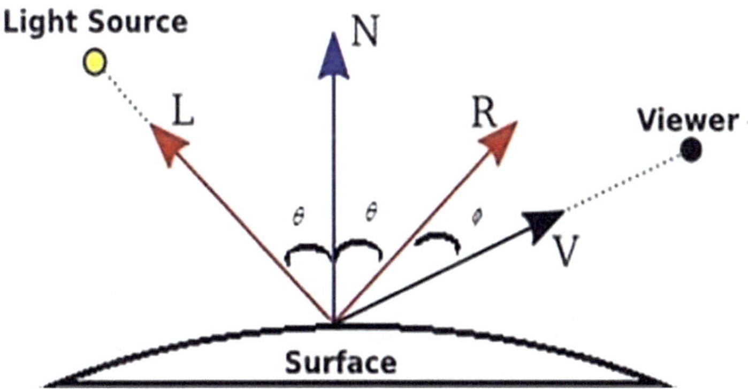

Figure 10.6: Specular Reflections

Where

R → Unit vector in the direction of ideal specular reflection

L → Unit vector direction towards the point light source

V → Unit vector pointing to the viewer from surface position

θ → Viewing angle relative to specular reflection direction R

Table 10.1: Differences between Diffuse and Specular Reflection

S. No.	*Diffuse Reflection*	*Specular Reflection*
1.	It generates scattered light in all directions.	It produces highlights or bright spots of light.
2.	It has a rough or grainy surface.	It is shiny or dull surface
3.	Diffused reflection remains constant on every surface.	highlights or bright spots in certain viewing direction
4.	The reflected reflections from this surface are independent of the viewing directions.	The reflection by this surface depends on the viewing directions.

10.6 SHADING MODEL

Different illumination models (ambient illumination, diffuse reflection and specular reflection) were discussed to calculate the intensity of light at given points on the surface of an object. Now we have to discuss different models to calculate intensity in a given polygon for a surface defined by the polygon.

10.7 TYPES OF SHADING MODEL

The shading model defines how to color the entire object. Some of them are constant intensity shading, Gouraud shading and Phong shading.

10.7.1 Flat Shading

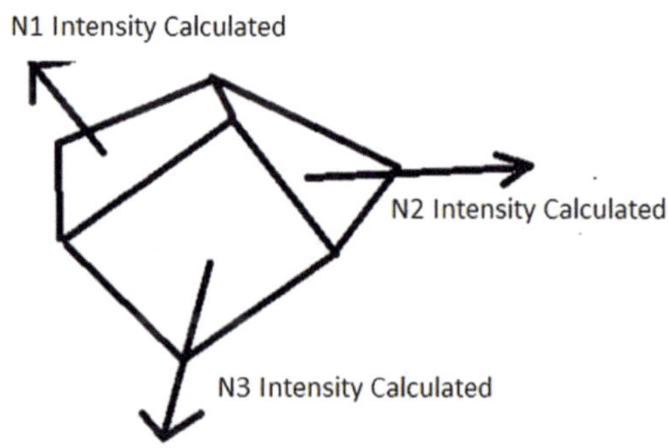

Figure 10.7: Flat shading

It is also known as Constant Intensity Shading. This is the most simple and very fast method to specify color for an object. Flat shading of a polygon assumes that each polygon is strictly planar and all the points on the polygon have exactly the same kind of lighting treatment. In this method, the illumination model is applied only once for each polygon to determine a single intensity value. The entire polygon is then displayed with the single intensity value. It defines a single color for the face implementation, it may vary, but the main idea is that we use only one surface normal per polygon.

Advantages of Flat Shading

- Constant shading can be useful for quickly displaying the general appearance of a curved surface.

Disadvantage of Flat Shading

- One of the disadvantages of constant-intensity shading is a very poor display of polygon-mesh approximations to curved surfaces.
- *Discontinuity:* Discontinuity of colors can be observed in different faces of the polygon.
- *Realistic image:* It does not produce a realistic image.
- *Match bending:* Brightness perceived by the eye tends to exceed the boundary of the region of constant intensity.

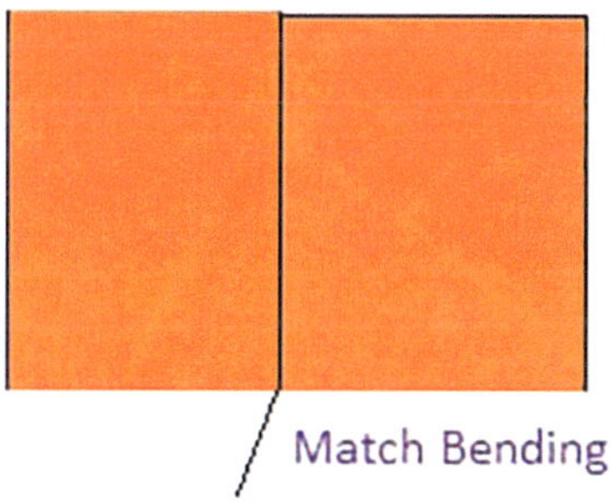

Figure 10.8: Match Bending

10.7.2 Gouraud Shading Model

It is a form of intensity-interpolation shading. This was invented as an improvement to allow for more smooth transitions of color on round objects. Intensity levels are calculated at each vertex and interpolated across the surface. This intensity interpolation scheme renders the polygon surface by linearly interpolating intensity values across the surface. Intensity values for each polygon are matched with the values of adjacent polygons along the common edges.

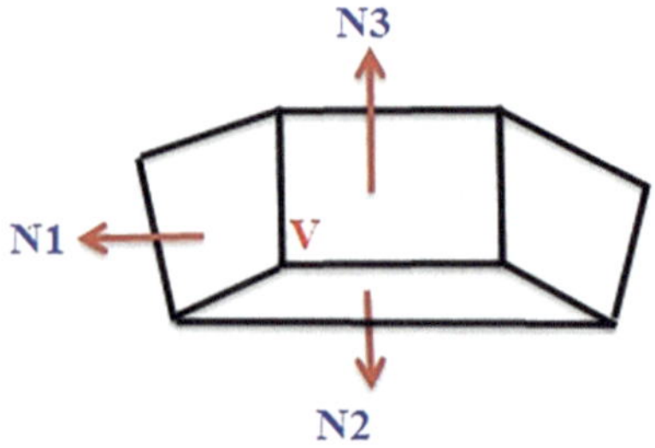

Figure 10.9: Gouraud Shading

Thus it eliminates the intensity discontinuity that occurs in flat shading. This technique uses the concept of intensity interpolation, hence it is also known as intensity interpolation or color interpolation shading. Each polygon surface is rendered with Gouraud shading by performing the following calculations:

A. Determine the average unit normal vector at each polygon vertex.

At each polygon vertex, we obtain a normal vector by averaging the surface normal of all polygons starting that vertex, as given in Figure 10.10.

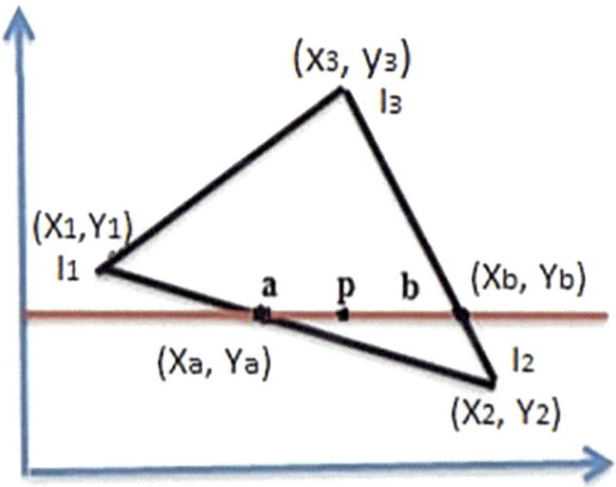

Figure 10.10: Average Unit Normal Vector at each polygon vertex

Thus, for any vertex position V, we obtain the unit vertex normal with the calculation

$$N_v = \frac{N_1 + N_2 + N_3}{|N_1 + N_2 + N_3|} = \frac{\sum_{i=1}^{n} N_i}{\left|\sum_{i=1}^{n} N_i\right|}$$

Where, n is the number of surfaces of polygon sharing that vertex

B. Apply an illumination model to each vertex to calculate the vertex intensity.

Output is I1, I2 and I3 in our example.

C. Linearly interpolate the vertex intensities over the surface of the polygon.

The intensity at point *a* is linearly interpolated from the intensities at vertices (x1, y1) and (x2, y2). The intensity at point *b* is linearly interpolated from intensities at vertices (x3, y3) and (x2, y2). An interior point *p* is then assigned an intensity value that is linearly interpolated from intensities at positions *a*, and *b*.

Intensity of I_a $$I_a = \frac{y_a - y_2}{y_1 - y_2} I_1 + \frac{y_1 - y_a}{y_1 - y_2} I_2$$

Intensity of I_a $$I_b = \frac{y_b - y_2}{y_3 - y_2} I_3 + \frac{y_3 - y_b}{y_3 - y_2} I_2$$

Then intensity at point p is given by I_p $$I_p = \frac{x_b - x_p}{x_b - x_a} I_a + \frac{x_p - x_a}{x_b - x_a} I_b$$

Advantages of Gouraud Shading

- Gouraud shading removes the intensity discontinuities associated with the constant-shading model
- Gouraud shading can be combined with a hidden-surface algorithm to fill in the visible polygons along each scan line.

Disadvantages of Gouraud Shading Model

- The sharp drop of intensity values on the polygon surface cannot be displayed.
- Highlights on the surface are sometimes displayed with anomalous shapes.
- Linear intensity interpolation can cause bright or dark intensity streaks to appear on the surface. These bright or dark intensity streaks are called Mach bands.
- These effects can be reduced by dividing the surface into a greater number of polygonal faces, or by using other methods such as Phong shading that require more calculations.

10.7.3 Phong Shading Model

A more accurate interpolation-based approach for rendering a polygon was developed by Phong Bui Tuong. Phong shading improves upon Gouraud shading and provides a better approximation of the shading of a smooth surface. It interpolates unit normal vectors instead of intensity values. It displays more realistic highlights on a surface and greatly reduces the Mach-band effect.

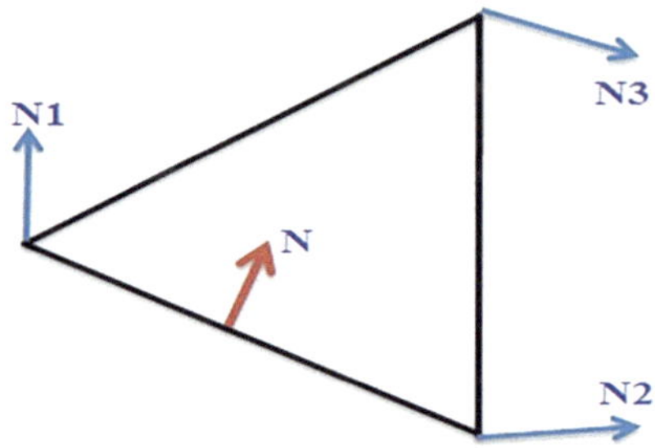

Figure 10.11: Phong shading

A polygon surface is rendered using Phong shading by carrying out the following steps:

A. Determine the average unit normal vector at each polygon vertex.

$$N_v = \frac{N_1 + N_2 + N_3}{|N_1 + N_2 + N_3|} = \frac{\sum_{i=1}^{n} N_i}{\left|\sum_{i=1}^{n} N_i\right|}$$

Where, n is the number of surfaces of polygon sharing that vertex.

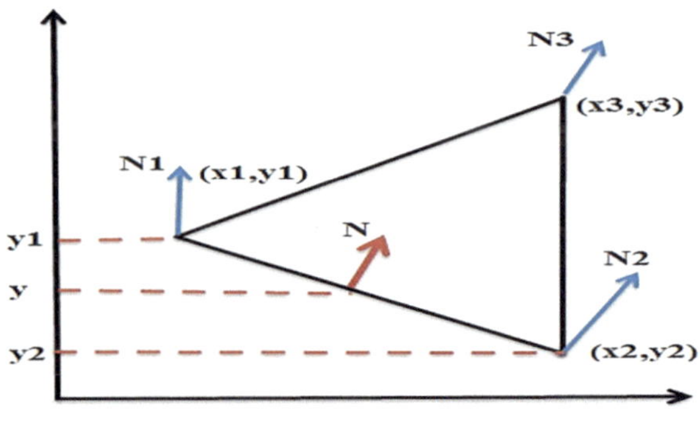

Figure 10.12: Average unit normal vector at each polygon vertex

B. Linearly interpolate the vertex normals over the surface of the polygon.

$$N = \frac{y - y_2}{y_1 - y_2} N_1 + \frac{y_1 - y}{y_1 - y_2} N_2$$

C. Apply the illumination model along each scan line to calculate projected pixel intensities for the surface points.

The interpolation of surface normals along a polygon edge between two vertices is illustrated in Figure 10.11. The normal vector N for the scan-line intersection point along the edge between vertices (x1, y1) and (x2, y2) can be obtained by vertically interpolating between edge endpoint normal:

Advantages of Phong shading

- Linear intensity interpolation causes bright or dark intensity streak bands to appear on the surface, called Mach bands. This method reduces the mach band effect and displays more realistic highlights.
- It is more accurate than Gouraud shading.

Disadvantages of Phong Shading

- It is slower than Gouraud shading.
- It requires more calculation, hence greatly increasing the cost of shading at each successive step.

Table 10.2: Differences between Gouraud Shading and Phong shading

S. No.	*Gouraud Shading*	*Phong Shading*
1.	Gouraud shading is named after Henri Gouraud.	The Phong shading model is named after Bul Tuong Phong.
2.	Calculates and interpolates illumination on boundary vertices.	Illumination at each point of the polygon surface.
3.	Interpolate the colors along the edges and scan line.	Interpolates the normal instead of the color.
4.	Not that expensive.	More expensive than Gouraud shading.
5.	Requires moderate processing and time.	Requires complex processing and is slow.
6.	The lighting equation is used for each vertex.	Lighting equalization is applied to each pixel.

Contd.

Table 10.2: Differences between Gouraud Shading and Phong shading

S. No.	*Gouraud Shading*	*Phong Shading*
7.	Gouraud shading is in between the two: like Phong shading, each polygon has one normal vector per vertex, but instead of interpolating the vectors, the color of each vertex is computed and then interpolated across the surface of the polygon.	Each rendered polygon has one normal vector per vertex; Shading is performed by interpolating vectors across the surface and computing a color for each point of interest.
8.	Smooth surfaces.	Smooth and shiny surfaces.

OBJECTIVE QUESTIONS

1. Concerning phong shading and Gouraud shading in a 3D scene, which of the following statements are true?
   I. Gouraud shading requires more computation than phong shading.
   II. Gouraud shading linearly interpolates the color of an interior pixel from the color at the vertices
   III. Phong shading interpolates over the normal vectors specified at the vertices. Choose the correct answer from the options given below:
   (a) (I) and (II) only (b) (I) and (III) only
   (c) (II) and (III) only (d) (I), (II) and (III)
2. Which is the correct equation of specular reflection?
   (a) $I_{spec} = K_s I_i (V + R)^{-ns}$ (b) $I_{spec} = K_s I_i (V \times R)^{-ns}$
   (c) $I_{spec} = K_s I_i (V \times R)^{ns}$ (d) $I_{spec} = K_s I_i (V \cdot R)^{ns}$
3. The intensity of specular reflection depends on the:
   (b) Material properties of the surface
   (c) Angle of incidence
   (d) Specular reflection coefficient
   (e) All of these
4. In phong model, for dull surface assigned _______ to specular reflection parameter.
   (a) Large value nearly 100 (b) Small value nearly 1
   (c) Medium value nearly 50 (d) None of these
5. The shiny surface has _____.
   (a) Narrow specular reflection range
   (b) Wide specular reflection range

(c) Medium specular reflection range
(d) None of these

6. When we look at an illuminated shiny surface, such as polished metal we see a highlight, or bright spot, at certain viewing directions. This phenomenon is called:
(a) Directional reflection (b) Diffuse reflection
(c) Specular reflection (d) Both (A) and (C)

7. Which is the correct equation of diffuse reflection?
(a) $I_{diff} = K_a I_a + K_d I_i (N \times L)$ (b) $I_{diff} = K_a I_a + K_d I_i (N.L)$
(c) $I_{diff} = K_a I_a - K_d I_i (N.L)$ (d) $I_{diff} = K_a I_a - K_d I_i (N \times L)$

8. Diffuse reflection from a source are scattered with equal intensity in all directions, independent of the viewing direction such a surface are called:
(a) Ideal diffuse reflector (b) Specular reflector
(c) Lambertian reflector (d) Both (A) and (C)

9. Amount of reflected light depends on the parameter ________, which is depending on reflecting property of the surface.
(a) Diffuse reflection coefficient
(b) Diffuse reflectivity
(c) Both (A) and (B)
(d) None of these

10. When some intensity of light is falling on the object surface and that surface reflects light in all the direction in equal amount then the resulting reflection is called:
(a) Directional reflection
(b) Diffuse reflection
(c) Specular reflection
(d) Both (A) and (C)

11. A simple way to model the combination of light reflection from various surfaces to produce a uniform illumination is called:
(a) Ambient light (b) Reflected light
(c) Background light (d) Both (A) and (C)

12. Find the odd man out.
(a) Basic illumination models (b) Shading model
(c) Colour model (d) Lighting model

13. An object is illuminated when:
(a) Directly exposed to a light source
(b) Light is completely absent

(c) Not directly exposed to light may also visible if a nearby object is illuminated
(d) Both (A) and (C)

14. Tube light in a room can be considered as:
(a) Point light source
(b) Distributed light source
(c) Line light source
(d) Symmetric light source

15. The term Phong associated with
(a) Ray tracing
(b) Shading
(c) Hidden line removal
(d) A game

ANSWERS

1. (c)	4. (b)	7. (b)	10. (b)	13. (d)
2. (d)	5. (a)	8. (d)	11. (d)	14. (b)
3. (d)	6. (c)	9. (c)	12. (c)	15. (b)

EXERCISES

1. What is Illumination? What are the various types of Illumination?
2. Explain the basic Illumination model.
3. Derive simple illumination model. Include the contribution of Diffuse, Ambient and Specular Reflection. What are the various logical graphics input primitives?
4. Explain Specular Reflection and Phong model.
5. Explain the difference Illuminations methods and Rendering methods in detail. Write its advantage and disadvantage.
6. Explain Phong and Warn model for illumination.
7. What do you mean by Intensity Attenuation?
8. List the problems with Interpolated Shading methods.
9. Compare and contrast between Flat and Smooth Shading models with necessary examples.
10. Explain the classification of Shading Models.
11. Discuss how the Mach-band effects are eliminated in Phong shading.
12. Write the characteristics of the following illumination parameters.
    a. Diffuse refection
    b. Specular reflection
    c. Refraction
13. Explain the following two types of smooth shading?

   a. Gouraud shading
   b. Phong shading
14. Discuss relative advantages and disadvantages of Gouraud Shading and Phong Shading
15. Discuss Specular Reflection and Phong Model.
16. Explain Gouraud shading model. Also state the difference between phong and gouraud shading models.
17. Discuss in detail various shading models
18. What steps are required to shade an object using Phong shading method of polygon rendering? How it overcomes the drawbacks of Gouraud Shading Method?

11

Colour Model

In computer graphics, colors play an important role in enhancing images by making it easier to spot information and features that are not as clear in black-and-white pictures. The visual spectrum consists of red, orange, yellow, green, blue, and violet colors. When light shines on objects, certain wavelengths are absorbed while the rest are reflected to the viewer as color. To ensure that colors in computer graphics are compatible with the hardware used and user-friendly, it is important to meet both hardware and user-oriented requirements. However, it is difficult to find a model that meets both requirements. The basic colors, red, green, and blue, represent long, medium, and short wavelengths, respectively, and are based on the principle of tri-chromic, where the human vision is three-dimensional and the spectrum of light is encoded into three values that correspond to the amount of light absorbed by each type of cone. This chapter provides an overview of the RGB color model and the CMYK color model, and explains how to set the color attributes of pixels.

11.1 INTRODUCTION OF COLOUR MODEL

Light is a form of electromagnetic wave. It has two main properties Frequency (f) and Wavelength. Frequency is defined as the number of cycles per second and is measured in hertz and Wavelength is the distance between the crests (peaks) of the wave or the width of a period is the wavelength of light and is inversely proportional to the frequency.

Light can be characterized by different terms. Luminance (Brightness) measures the total energy in the light. Higher the luminance, the brighter the light to be observes. Hue (Dominant) distinguishes white light from red light or green light. It is also known as the dominant wavelength or color of light. When white light is incident on an object, some part of it gets reflected. It is the combination of the frequency of the reflected light that is responsible for the color of an object called hue. Saturation (Purity) refers to how far a colour is from white color. It is defined as the percentage of luminance allocated to the pure colour component that is

$$\text{Saturation} = \frac{\text{Pure Colour}}{\text{Pure Colour} + \text{White Colour}}$$

When adding a black pigment to the original color to create a darker version of the colour is known as shades. Maroon is a shade of red. When adding a white pigment to the original color we get a lighter version of the color known as Tints. An example of a tint is pink. Pink is a tint created by adding white to red. When adding both black and white color pigments is known as Tone.

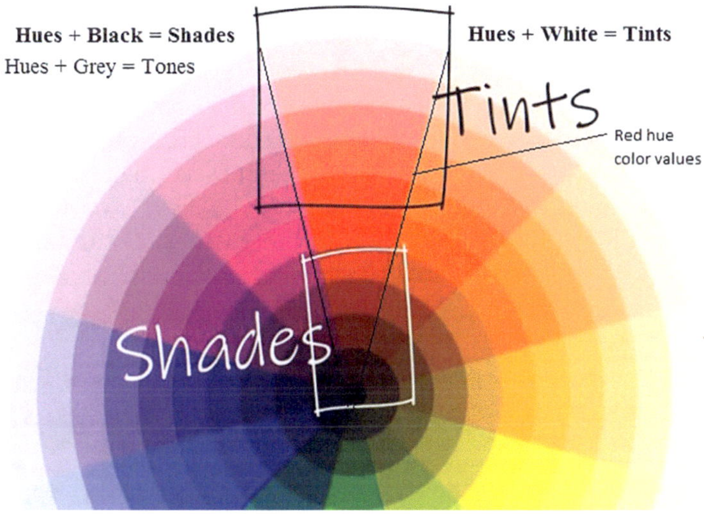

Figure 11.1: Pigment of the color

11.2 TYPES OF COLOR MODELS

Color is a sense produced by the human eye and nervous system. It is useful to represent a color by a set of exactly three numbers. A color model is an orderly system for creating a whole range of colors from a small set of primary colors. There are two types of color models, those that are subtractive and those that are additive. Additive color models use light to display color while subtractive models use printing inks. Colors perceived in additive models are the result of transmitted light for example RGB. Colors perceived in subtractive models are the result of reflected light for example CMY. There are many types of color models, some of them are RGB, CMY, and HSV Color Models.

11.2.1 RGB Color Model

The RGB model is usually represented by a unit cube with one corner located at the origin of a 3D color coordinate system, the axes being labeled R, G, B, and having a range of values [0, 1]. The origin (0, 0, 0) is considered black and the diagonally opposite corner (1, 1, 1) is called white. The line joining black to white represents a grayscale and has equal components of R, G, B. Vertices of the cube on the axis represent the primary colors, i.e. red, green, blue and the remaining vertices represent the complementary colour for each of the primary colors. White light is created when all color of the EM spectrum (electromagnetic spectrum) converge in full intensity. It is also called an additive colour model as we add three colour components together to form any colour. The working of the RGB colour model is the same as that of the human eye. The RGB colour model describes a colour by using three variables (R, G, and B). These variables can be compared to the strength of the signal from the three types of colour receptors in the nerves. The primary colors can be added to produce the secondary colors of light-Magenta (Red + Blue), Cyan (Green + Blue), and Yellow (Red + Green). The combination of Red, Green and Blue at full intensities makes white.

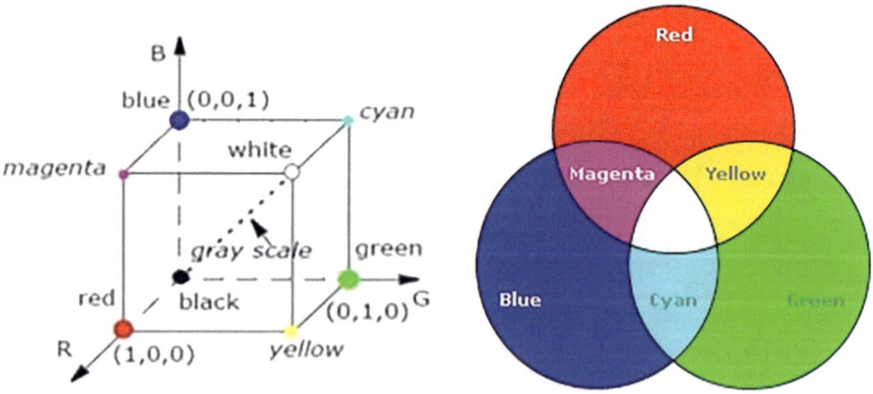

Figure 11.2: RGB Model

Each color point within the unit cube can be represented as a weighted vector sum of the primary colors, using unit vectors R, G and B.

$$C(\lambda) = (R, G, B) = RR + GG + BB$$

Where R, G, and B are assigned values in the range from 0 to 1, for example, the magenta vertex is obtained by adding the maximum red and blue values to produce: (1, 0, 1). The total number of bits used to represent each pixel in an RGB image is called pixel depth. For example, in an RGB image, if each of the red, green, and blue images is an 8-bit image, the pixel depth of the RGB image is 24-bit.

Application of RGB Color Model

- The RGB model is widely used in the representation and display of images in electronic systems like computers and televisions.
- It is also used in conventional photography.
- Image scanner which scans images and converts them to a digital image mostly supports RGB color.
- It is used in web graphics.

11.2.2 CMY Color Model

The CMY color model is a subset of the RGB model and is primarily used in color print production. CMY is an acronym for cyan, magenta, and yellow. In the CMY model, we begin with white and take away the appropriate primary components to yield the desired color. Cyan, Magenta, and yellow are the secondary colors concerning the primary colors of red green, and blue. However, in this, subtraction model, they are the primary colors and red, green and blue are the secondary. It is a subtractive color model i.e. as we know; cyan can be formed by adding green and blue light. Thus, when white light is reflected from cyan-colored ink, the reflected light must have no red component, that is, red light is absorbed or subtracted by the ink. Similarly, magenta ink subtracts the green component from incident light and yellow subtracts the blue component. A unit cube representation of a CMY model is shown in the following Figure 11.3.

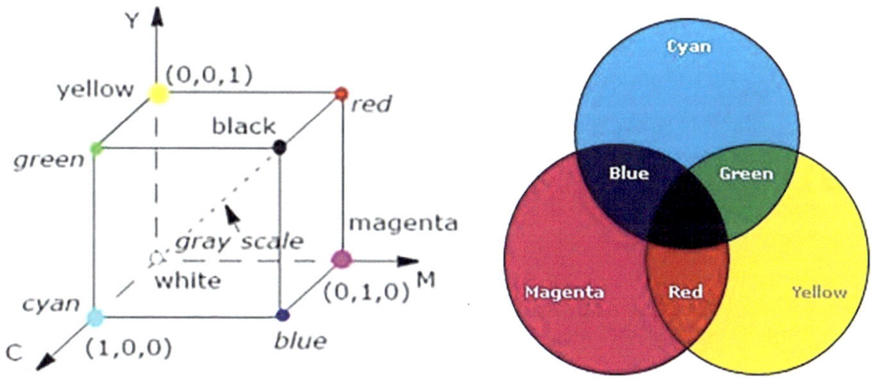

Figure 11.3: CMY Model

In the CMY model, point (1, 1, 1) represents black because all components of the incident light are subtracted. The origin represents white light (0 0, 0). Equal amounts of each of the primary colors produce grays along the main diagonal of the cube. In the printing process combining equal amounts of cyan, magenta and yellow produces muddy-looking black. In order to produce true black, a fourth color black is added, giving to the CMYK color model.

Applications of CMY Color Model

- The CMY color model is used in color printers.
- It is created by the subtractive mode.
- Used in most commercial color printing (Books, Magazines, etc.).
- Good hands feel because of using less color on the ground.
- CMY can be used for different items of print because of the common color way.

We can express the conversion from an RGB representation to a CMY representation with the matrix transformation.

$$\begin{bmatrix} C \\ M \\ Y \end{bmatrix} = \begin{bmatrix} 1 \\ 1 \\ 1 \end{bmatrix} - \begin{bmatrix} R \\ G \\ B \end{bmatrix}$$

Where white is represented as a unit column vector in the RGB system, similarly, we convert from a CMY color representation to an RGB representation with the matrix transformation.

$$\begin{bmatrix} R \\ G \\ B \end{bmatrix} = \begin{bmatrix} 1 \\ 1 \\ 1 \end{bmatrix} - \begin{bmatrix} C \\ M \\ Y \end{bmatrix}$$

Where, black is represented in the CMY system as the unit column vector.

Table 11.1: Differences between RGB color and CM color model

S. No.	*RGB Color Model*	*CMY Color Model*
1.	It is obtained by **adding together lights** of different colors.	It is obtained by subtracting lights of different colors.
2.	It is used for computer displays	It is used for printed material
3.	Uses light to display color	Uses ink to display color
4.	Colors result from transmitted light	Colors result from reflected light
5.	RGB Scheme has a wider range of colors than CMYK	CMYK has a lesser range of colors than RGB.
6.	Red + Green +Blue = White	Cyan + Magenta +Yellow = Black
7.	file formats:- JPEG, PNG, GIF, etc.	file formats:- PDF, EPS, etc

Table 11.1: Differences between RGB color and CM color model

S. No.	*RGB Color Model*	*CMY Color Model*
8.	The **absence** of all colors is **black**, and the **presence** of all colors is **white**.	The **absence** of all colors is **white**, and the **presence** of all colors is **black**.
9.	It is used for online logos, online ads, digital graphics, photographs for websites, social media, apps, etc.	Basically it is used for business cards, stationery, stickers, posters, brochures, etc.

11.2.3 HSV Color Model

In the HSV color model, a color is defined by its hue (H), its saturation (S), and it's Value (V) so; it looks like the human color perception more than the additive and the subtractive color models. If we look at the RGB cube along the gray diagonal we can see a hexagon that is the HSV hexagon.

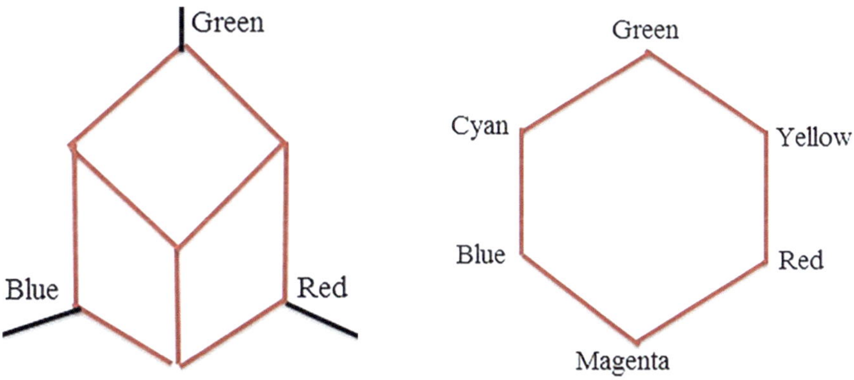

Figure 11.4: RGB cube along the gray diagonal

The boundary of the hexagon represents the top of HSV hexacone.

In the hexagon (Figure 11.5), the saturation (S) is measured along the horizontal axis. The value (V) is measured along the vertical axis through centre of the hexagon. The Hue (H) is represented as an angle about the vertical axis from 0° at red through 360 °. The top surface is a regular hexagon, showing the change in hue in the vertical axis, from 0° to 360° is the entire spectrum of visible light. The six corners of the hexagon represent the positions of the six colors red, yellow, green, cyan, blue, and magenta, each of which is 60° apart. The value of saturation S varies from 0 to 1. It gives the purity of the color. The saturation of colors increases as you move closer to the hexagonal boundary. The color of the hexagonal boundary is the most saturated, that is S = 1 (max. pure); the color saturation at the

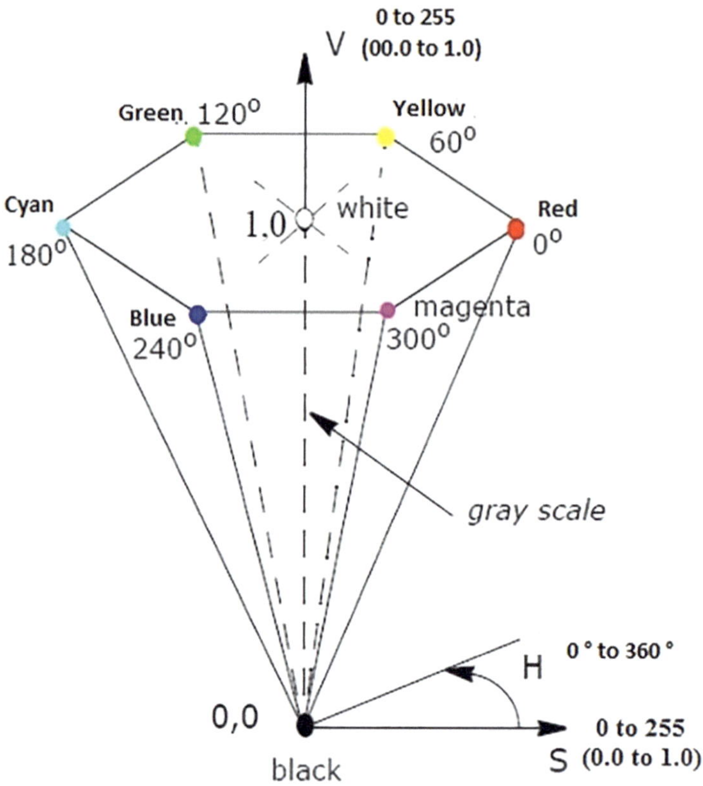

Figure 11.5: Hexagon structure of HSV color model

center of the hexagon is 0, that is S = 0 (we have a gray scale). The height of the hexagonal pyramid represents a black-to-white gradation from bottom to top. The bottom of V is black, V = 0; the top of V is white, V = 1. For almost all users, this model is very intuitive. We can describe the desired color by adding white or black, starting with a selection for a pure color.

So to choose the color we do the following:

- Select your hue (specifies H and sets S=V=1).
- To add black decrease V
- To add white decrease S
- To add black and white decrease V and S.

For example

- Pure blue H=240, S=V=1.
- Dark blue H=240, S=1, V=0.40.
- Light blue H=240, S=0.3, V=1.0.

The human eye can distinguish about 128 different hues, 130 different tints (saturation level), and 23 shades. So we can distinguish about 128 *130*23 =380, 000 colors.

Applications of HSV

- The HSV color space is widely used to generate high quality computer graphics.
- In simple terms, it is used to select various, different colors needed for a particular picture.
- It gives the color according to human perception.

Advantages of HSV

- The HSV color space is quite similar to the way in which humans perceive color.
- The colors used in HSV can be clearly defined by human perception, which is not always the case with RGB or CMYK.

11.2.4 YIQ Model

YIQ model is used for US commercial color television broadcasting. This model was designed to separate chrominance (I and Q) from luminance (Y). This was a requirement in the early days of color television when black-and-white sets were still originally expected to take and display color pictures. The Y-channel contains luminance information (sufficient for black-and-white television sets) while I and Q channels carry the color information in short YIQ (Luminance, In-phase, Quadrature). A color television set would take these three channels, Y, I, and Q, and map the information back to R, G, and B levels for display on a screen. The advantage of this model is that more bandwidth can be assigned to the Y-component (luminance) because the human visual system is more sensitive to changes in luminance than to changes in hue or saturation.

Convert From YIQ to RGB

$$\begin{bmatrix} R \\ G \\ B \end{bmatrix} = \begin{bmatrix} 1 & 0.956 & 0.619 \\ 1 & -0.272 & -0.647 \\ 1 & -1.106 & 1.703 \end{bmatrix} \begin{bmatrix} Y \\ I \\ Q \end{bmatrix}$$

Convert From RGB to YIQ

$$\begin{bmatrix} Y \\ I \\ Q \end{bmatrix} = \begin{bmatrix} 0.299 & 0.587 & 0.144 \\ 0.596 & -0.275 & -0.321 \\ 0.212 & -0.523 & 0.311 \end{bmatrix} \begin{bmatrix} R \\ G \\ B \end{bmatrix}$$

Advantages of HSV Color Model

- The advantage of this model is that more width can be assigned to the Y-component (Luminance) because the human visual system is more sensitive to changes in luminance than to changes in hue or saturation.
- For display on a screen, color television sets map these channels Y, I, and Q to R, G, and B.

Disadvantage of HSV Color Model

- Due to the high implementation costs for true I and Q decoding, few television sets do it.
- To accommodate the bandwidth variances between I and Q, each of I and Q needs a distinct filter.
- Due to different bandwidths, the "I" filter has a time delay to match the "Q" filter's long delay.
- In black-and-white TV only Y can be noticed

OBJECTIVE QUESTIONS

1. What are the RGB co-ordinates of a color at (0.25, 0.65, 0) in CMY space?
   (a) (0.75, 0.35, 1) (b) (0.65, 0.25, 0)
   (c) (0.75, 0.25, 1) (d) (0.85, 0.25, 0)
2. Which among the below set of colors are generally known as the primary colors of light?
   (a) White, Yellow, Blue (b) Red, Green, Blue
   (c) Red, Green, Black (d) Black, White, Red
3. Which colour has the shortest wavelength?
   (a) Yellow (b) Violet
   (c) Green (d) Red
4. Images with colors depths of sixteen bits have 65356 colors and it is known as ______.
   (a) High color Images (b) True color images
   (c) Palette images (d) Monochrome images

5. Below given table represent the eight color codes for a three-bit per pixel frame buffer.

Code	RED	GREEN	BLUE	Displayed Color
6	1	1	0	

What will be the displayed color?
(a) Magenta (b) Cyan
(c) Yellow (d) Pink

6. In YIQ color model Y represented as :
(a) Luminance (b) Hue
(c) Purity (d) Saturation

7. Which color model is generally used in television?
(a) XYZ color model (b) YIQ color model
(c) RGB color model (d) CMY color model

8. Which color model is generally used in hardcopy devices?
(a) XYZ color model (b) YIQ color model
(c) RGB color model (d) CMY color model

9. Which color model is generally used in websites?
(a) XYZ color model (b) YIQ color model
(c) RGB color model (d) CMY color model

10. Typical color models that are used to describe the combination of light in terms of dominant frequency use three colors to obtain reasonable wide range of colors, called:
(a) Dominant wavelength (b) Chromaticity
(c) Color gamut (d) Saturation triangle

11. If two color sources combined to produce white light they are called:
(a) Supplementary colors (b) Complementary colors
(c) Primary colors (d) None of these

12. ________ both collectively refers as chromaticity.
(a) Dominant frequency and purity
(b) Purity and saturation
(c) Brightness and purity
(d) Brightness and hue

13. ________ of the light describes how washed out or how "pure" the color of the light appears.
(a) Purity (b) Saturation
(c) Both (A) and (B) (d) Dominant frequency

14. _______ is the radiant energy emitted per unit time, per unit solid angle and per unit projected area of the source.
    (a) Dominant frequency (b) Intensity
    (c) Hue (d) Purity
15. Frequency reflected back from surface is deciding the color we see and this frequency is called as:
    (a) Dominant frequency (b) Color frequency
    (c) Hue (d) Both (A) and (C)

ANSWERS

1. (a)	4. (a)	7. (b)	10. (c)	13. (c)
2. (b)	5. (c)	8. (d)	11. (b)	14. (b)
3. (b)	6. (a)	9. (c)	12. (a)	15. (d)

EXERCISE

1. What is Color models compare and contrast between RGB and CMY systems?
2. Draw the RGB color model cube and explain how shades of Gray are represented.
3. Write short note on RGB Color Model.
4. Explain in detail YIQ color model.
5. Distinguish between CMY and HSV color models.
6. Write the procedure for converting HSV color values to RGB values.
7. How CMY and YIQ color models differ from RGB color model? Briefly explain?
8. Write short note on CMY Color Model.
9. Explain in detail about HSV color model.
10. Explain in detail about the conversion between HSV and RGB color models.

12

Multimedia

The rise of multimedia technology has led to a strong connection between multimedia and the web. Nowadays, multimedia has enabled us to combine education and entertainment, which is commonly known as "Edutainment". The integration of communication modes and information encoding, also known as media convergence, is a significant factor in the development of distributed multimedia applications. The latest trend in multimedia systems is the presentation of information in 3D. This chapter provides an overview of the fundamental tools required for developing a multimedia. These tools include text editing tools, presentation tools, painting and drawing tools, image editing tools, animation tools, sound editing tools, video editing, and plug-in multimedia authoring tools. Additionally, we will explore the two types of target users for authoring systems. Finally, we will look at ad hoc authoring, which involves authoring done at the user's desktop using common camera sounds and light.

12.1 INTRODUCTION OF MULTIMEDIA

The word multi and media are combined to form the word multimedia. The word "multi" signifies "many." Multimedia is a type of medium that allows information to be easily transferred from one location to another. Therefore multimedia is a form of communication that combines different content forms such as text, audio, images, animations, or video into a single interactive presentation, in contrast to traditional mass media which features little to no interaction from users, such as printed material or audio recordings. Popular examples of multimedia include video podcasts, audio slideshows, and Animated Videos. Multimedia can be recorded for playback on computers, laptops, Smartphone, and other electronic devices, either on-demand or in real-time (streaming). In the early years of multimedia, the term "rich media" was synonymous with interactive multimedia. Over time, hypermedia extensions brought multimedia to the World Wide Web.

Multimedia is the use of a computer to present and combine text, graphics, audio, and video with links and tools that allow the user to navigate, interact, create and communicate. A media application is an application that uses a collection of multiple media sources e.g., text, graphics, images, audio, animation and video. Some Multimedia applications are:

- World Wide Web
- Hypermedia courseware
- Video conferencing
- Video-on-demand
- Interactive TV
- Groupware
- Home shopping
- Games
- Virtual reality
- Digital video editing and production systems
- Multimedia Database systems

12.2 TYPES OF MULTIMEDIA

Multimedia is broadly divided into linear and non-linear multimedia.

12.2.1 Linear Multimedia

The end-user cannot control the content of the application. A linear multimedia application lacks all the features with the help of which, a user can interact with the application such as the ability to choose different options, click on icons, control the flow of the media, or change the pace at which the media is displayed. It works very well for providing information to a large group of people such as at training sessions, seminars, workplace meetings, etc.

12.2.2 Non-Linear Multimedia

The end-user is allowed the navigational control to rove through multimedia content at his own desire. The user can control the access of the application. Non-linear offers user interactivity to control the movement of data. For example computer games, websites self-paced computer-based training packages, etc.

12.3 COMPONENTS OF MULTIMEDIA

The components of multimedia are

- **Text:** These are the primary forms of multimedia elements. Different colors, fonts, styles, etc. are allowed here.
- **Graphics:** These are generally used with text to present the information in an attractive way

- **Audio:** It has its combination with animation. Audio includes sounds, music, speech, etc.
- **Video:** The moving images with sound effects are the main component of video.
- **Animation:** The sequence of still images present in a way that look likes moving images.

12.4 DIGITIZATION OF MULTIMEDIA CONTENT

Principles that may be used in the digitization of multimedia content include data compression, error correction, sampling, quantization and synchronization. Sampling and Quantization are two principles that are used in the digitization of multimedia content.

- **Data Compression:** Data Compression is used to reduce the size of multimedia files. Data compression is a reduction in the amount of bits required to represent data. Data compression can reduce network bandwidth and storage hardware expenses while accelerating file transfers and preserving store capacity.
- **Sampling:** Sampling is the process of converting an analog signal, such as an audio or video signal, into a digital signal. This involves taking periodic snapshots or samples of the analog signal at regular intervals, and converting each sample into a digital representation, typically using pulse code modulation (PCM).
- **Quantization:** Quantization is the process of representing the digital samples of the analog signal with a finite set of discrete values, rather than a continuous range of values. This process involves assigning a numerical value to each sample, based on the amplitude of the sample. The resolution of the quantization process is determined by the number of bits used to represent each sample, with more bits providing higher resolution and higher quality.

12.5 MULTIMEDIA FILE FORMAT STANDARDS

A bitmap describes a type of image. Pixels are the basic sources of information. BMP, GIF, JPEG, EXIF, PNG, and TIFF are bitmap file formats. Bitmap format is commonly used raster graphic format for saving image files. Raster graphics are independent of display devices which means a bitmap image file can be viewed without any graphics adaptor. The file can store a 2D digital image in both monochrome and colour format.

- **GIF:** GIF stands for Graphics Interchange Formats. The GIF format was created by CompuServe. It supports 256 colors. GIF format is the most popular on the Internet because of its compact size. It is ideal for small icons used for navigational purposes and simple diagrams. Thus GIF format is lossless only for the image with 256 colors or less. GIF files can be saved with a maximum of 256 colors. GIFs can be animated, which is another reason they became so successful. This provision allows the background colors of the web page to be shown through the image.

- **JPEG:** JPEG stands for Joint Photographic Experts Group. It is a method to compress graphics and pictures JPEG is a commonly used method of lossy compression for digital images, particularly for those images produced by digital photography. JPEG files are bitmapped images. It stores information in 24-bit color. Digital cameras save images in a JPEG format by default. It has become the main graphics file format for the World Wide Web and any browser can support it without plug-ins. JPEG images work much better than GIFs. Though JPEG can be interlaced, still this format lacks many of the other special abilities of GIFs, like animations and transparency, but they are only for photos.
- **PNG:** PNG (Portable Network Graphics) is the only lossless format that web browsers support. PNG supports 8-bit, 24-bits, 32-bits, and 48-bits data types. One version of the format PNG-8 is similar to the GIF format. But PNG is superior to the GIF. PNG-24 is in no way a replacement format for JPEG because it is a lossless compression format. This means that file size can be rather big against a comparable JPEG. Also, PNG supports up to 48 bits of color information.
- **TIFF:** TIFF (Tagged Image File Format) file format is a widely used bitmapped file format. TIFF is capable of storing a wide variety of image types, such as 1-bit images, grayscale images, 8-bit color images, 24-bit RGB images, etc. TIFF files originally use lossless compression. Today TIFF files also use lossy compression according to the requirement. Therefore, it is a very flexible format. This file format is suitable when the output is printed. Multi-page documents can be stored as a single TIFF file and that is why this file format is so popular. The TIFF format is now used and controlled by Adobe.
- **BMP:** The bitmap file format (BMP) is a very basic format supported by most Windows applications. The BMP format has the capability to store various image types such as 1-bit images, grayscale images, 8-bit color images, 24-bit RGB images, etc. BMP files are uncompressed. Therefore, these are not suitable for the internet. BMP files can be compressed using lossless data compression algorithms.
- **MPEG:** The Moving Picture Experts Group (MPEG), a working group of authorities formed by ISO and IEC, is responsible for establishing standards for audio and video compression and transmission. The term also refers to the family of digital video compression standards and file formats developed by the group. MPEG involves both spatial compression and temporal compression. The spatial compression is similar to JPEG and temporal compression removes redundant frames.

MPEG compression stores the differences between successive frames. MPEG compression doesn't store the compression values of each frame.

12.6 MULTIMEDIA HARDWARE

Most computers today come equipped with the necessary hardware components to develop or view multimedia applications. Following are the various categories in which we can define the different types of hardware required for multimedia applications.

- **Processor:** The heart of any multimedia computer is its processor. Today core 15 or higher processor is recommended for a multimedia computer.
- **RAM:** A minimum of 8 MB is required, although 332 MB is recommended for smoother playback.
- **Hard disk:** Requires a huge amount of disk space around 10 GB with 40 GB recommended.
- **VDU:** SVGA standard and should be able to support 800 x 600 display mode with true color (16.7 million colors). VRAM amount should be at least 4MB with 8MB recommended.
- **CD-ROM:** PC should be equipped with a CD-ROM drive having a speed of at least 4x but higher speeds like 36x, 48x, or 52x are also recommended. This may be replaced by a DVD drive. In addition, the PC should have a CD writer.
- **Sound card:** The PC should have a sound card with attached speakers to hear sounds. In addition, for recording sounds such as human speech or environmental sounds, one or more microphones are required.
- **Input device:** Standard 101-keys or 102-keys keyboard and two-button mouse should be presented. Additional input devices required are a scanner, and video capture card for converting analog signal to digital signal.

12.7 MULTIMEDIA SOFTWARE

Multimedia software tells the hardware to display the color blue, play the sound of cymbals crashing, etc. There are various software's available in the market such as Paint Brush, Photoshop, Animator, Corel Draw, and Picture Publisher to produce these media elements (movies, sound, text, animation, graphics, etc.). Following are the various categories of multimedia software.

- **Device Driver Software**: This software are used to install and configure the multimedia peripherals such as media players.
- **Graphic and Image Editing Software**: These software are used to image editing such as Corel Photo-Paint.
- **Audio and Sound Editing Software**: Today, the most popular audio editing programs are Sony Sound Forge, Audacity, and Adobe Audition.

Sony Sound Forge is digital audio editing software for professional as well as amateur or nonprofessional users.

- **Video Editing Software**: With video editing software, we can create our own original and unique movies for our personal or business purposes. For example Avid's Media Composer, and Xpress Pro.
- **Animation Authoring Software**: As more and more Flash movies are created, delivered, and viewed by millions of Internet users. We can use Flash to create simple animations, advertisements, or even online banners for our personal homepage or weblog (blog). We can even embed or integrate flash video into our web pages.

12.8 ANIMATION

A key frame (or keyframe) in animation and filmmaking is a drawing or shot that defines the starting and ending points of any smooth transition. These are called frames because their position in time is measured in frames on a strip of film or on a digital video editing timeline. A symbol is a graphic, button, or movie clip that you create once in the animate authoring environment or by using the SimpleButton (AS 3.0) and MovieClip classes. You can then reuse the symbol throughout your document or in other documents. A scene is a single event or conversation between characters, occurring during one period of time and in one single place, that moves the story forward toward a climax and resolution. A keyframe is a frame where a new symbol instance appears in the timeline. You can also add a blank keyframe to the timeline as a placeholder for symbols you plan to add later or explicitly leave the frame blank.

12.9 MORPHING

Morphing is an animation that changes one image to another through seamless transition. It is mostly used to change one face to another face. Some points are identified after and before the objects to do the morphing. Then pixels of one image are slowly changed into the pixels of another image by the creation of in between frames. This is widely used in movies, games, and education purposes. It is done by coupling image warping with colour interpolation. Two ways of morphing are mesh-based methods and feature-based methods. In the mesh-based method, features of the image are specified by nonuniform mesh. In the feature-based method, the features of image are specified as a set of points.

12.10 MULTIMEDIA AUTHORING TOOL

Multimedia authoring is a process of assembling different types of media content like text, audio, image, animations, and video as a single stream of information with the help of various software tools available in the market. Classification of Multimedia authoring tools:

- Card or Page based authoring tools
- Icon based or Event-driven authoring tools
- Time-based authoring tools
- Object-Oriented authoring tools

OBJECTIVE QUESTIONS

1. ______ audio/video refers to on-demand requests for compressed audio/video files.
   (a) Streaming stored (b) Streaming live
   (c) Interactive (d) Mixing
2. What is the extension of MPEG Audio file?
   (a) .mov (b) .mp4
   (c) .mpeg (d) .mp3
3. What is used to set the starting and ending points of an animation?
   (a) Key frames (b) Graphic symbols
   (c) Scenes (d) Blank frames
4. Which principles are used in digitization of multimedia content?

   I. Sampling

   II. Quantization

   (a) Only II (b) Only I
   (c) Neither I nor II (d) Both I and II
5. ______ is used to reduce the size of multimedia files
   (a) Data handling (b) Data coupling
   (c) Data compression (d) Data dependency
6. MPEG involves both spatial compression and temporal compression. The spatial compression is similar to JPEG and temporal compression removes_________ Frames
   (a) Temporal (b) Spatial
   (c) Voice (d) Redundant

7. Which of the following is a special effect in motion pictures and animation that changes one image/picture into another through a seamless transition?
   (a) Modeling (b) Morphing
   (c) Animating (d) Wrapping
8. ______ is NOT a common bitmap-based file type extension.
   (a) .odt (b) .tiff
   (c) .png (d) .pcx
9. Which of the following is/are FALSE about MPEG compression?
   (b) MPEG compression stores the compression values of each frame.
   (c) MPEG compression stores the differences between successive frames.
   (d) Spatial compression of MPEG is similar to JPEG.
   (e) Temporal compression of MPEG removes redundant frames.
10. Which of the following is NOT a type of multimedia authoring tool?
    (a) Time based (b) Card based
    (c) Sound based (d) Icon based
11. Which of the following are used for combing different kinds of media formats and deliver them as multimedia contents?
    (a) Multimedia authoring tools (b) Device drivers
    (c) Scanners (d) Media players
12. ________ is a special effect in motion pictures and animations that changes one image or shape in to another through a seamless transition.
    (a) Inverse Kinematics (b) Tweaking
    (c) Morphing (d) Twining
13. Video and audio are the examples of –
    (a) Temporal media (b) Non-temporal media
    (c) Media content (d) None of the above
14. The ratio of the size of the original data to the size of compressed data is called as
    (a) Hit-ratio (b) Compression ratio
    (c) Compression rate (d) None of the above
15. Multimedia contains?
    (a) Audio (b) Video
    (c) Both (A) and (B) (d) None of the above

ANSWERS

1. (a)	4. (d)	7. (b)	10. (c)	13. (a)
2. (d)	5. (c)	8. (a)	11. (a)	14. (b)
3. (a)	6. (d)	9. (a)	12. (c)	15. (c)

EXERCISES

1. What is multimedia?
2. Give some multimedia applications.
3. What are the multimedia file formats?
4. What are multimedia components? Explain.
5. Explain how to define an object for a multimedia system.
6. Explain the various issues and challenges in multimedia projects.
7. Discuss the steps in creating a multimedia project and also discuss the different types of software required for implementing multimedia production.
8. Discuss computer animation design and types of animation.
9. Discuss the different types of software and hardware required for multimedia.
10. What are the Different Types of Authoring Tools in Multimedia? Briefly discuss each.

Appendix I

LIST OF COMPUTER GRAPHICS AND MULTIMEDIA PRACTICAL ASSIGNMENTS

1. Program to draw a Pixel on computer screen.
2. Program to draw a line using direct method.
3. Program to draw a line using simple method
4. Program to draw a line using increment DDA method
5. Program to draw line using Bresenham's algorithm.
6. Program to draw circle using Midpoint algorithm
7. Program to draw circle using Bresenham's algorithm.
8. Program to fill polygon using Flood-fill algorithm.
9. Program to fill polygon using Boundary-fill algorithm.
10. Program to fill polygon using Scan line algorithm.
11. Program to implement 2D Translation of a triangle.
12. Program to implement 2D Scaling using matrix multiplication for triangle.
13. Program to implement 2D Rotation of triangle.
14. Program to implement 2D Shearing
15. Program to implement 2D Reflection
16. Program to implement composite transformation on Rotation about an arbitrary point.
17. Program to implement composite transformation on Scaling about a fixed point.
18. Program to implement Line Clipping algorithm using Cohen Sutherland algorithm.
19. Program to implement Line Clipping algorithm using Sutherland Hodgman algorithm.
20. Program to display a Moving Car.

Appendix-II

EXPERIMENTS IN COMPUTER GRAPHICS LAB

1. Program to draw a Pixel on computer screen.

```
#include<graphics.h>
#include<stdio.h>
#include<conio.h>
int main(void)
{
int gdriver=DETECT,gmode;
int x,y;
clrscr();
initgraph(&gdriver,&gmode,"c:\\tc\\bgi");
printf("Enter the value of x");
scanf("%d",&x);
printf("Enter the value of y");
scanf("%d",&y);
putpixel(x,y,1);
putpixel(x+10,y+10,2);
putpixel(x+20,y+20,3);
putpixel(x+30,y+30,4);
putpixel(x+40,y+40,5);
putpixel(x+50,y+50,6);
putpixel(x+60,y+60,7);
getch();
closegraph();
return 0;
}
```

2. Program to draw a line using direct method

```
include<graphics.h>
#include<stdio.h>
#include<conio.h>
#include<math.h>
```

```
int main(void)
{
int x,y,x1,y1,x2,y2,dx,dy,m,b;
int gdriver=DETECT,gmode;
clrscr();
initgraph(&gdriver,&gmode,"C:\\TC\\bgi");
printf("Enter point1 (x1,y1): ");
scanf("%d%d",&x1,&y1);
printf("\nEnter point2 (x2,y2): ");
scanf("%d %d",&x2,&y2);
dx=x2-x1;
dy=y2-y1;
m=dy/dx;
b=y1-(m*x1);
x=x1;
y=y1;
putpixel(x,y,1);
while(x<=x2 || y<=y2)
{
if(m<1)
{
x++;
y=(m*x)+b;
}//if ends
else
{
y++;
x=(y-b)/m;
}//else ends
putpixel((abs(x)),(abs(y)),1);
}//while loop ends
getch();
closegraph();
return 0;
}
```

3. Program to draw a line using simple method

```
#include<graphics.h>
#include<stdio.h>
#include<conio.h>
#include<math.h>
int main(void)
```

```
{
int x,y,x1,y1,x2,y2,dx,dy,m;
int gdriver = DETECT,gmode;
clrscr();
initgraph(&gdriver,&gmode,"C:\\tc:\\bgi");
printf("Enter point1 (x1,y1): ");
scanf("%d%d",&x1,&y1);
printf("Enter point2 (x2,y2): ");
scanf("%d%d", &x2,&y2);
dy=y2-y1;
dx=x2-x1;
m=dy/dx;
x=x1;
y=y1;
putpixel(x,y,1);
while(x<=x2||y<=y2)
{
if(m<1)
{
x++;
y=y+m;
}
else
{
y++;
x=x+(1/m);
}
putpixel(x,y,1);
}
getch();
closegraph();
return 0;
}
```

4. Program to draw a line using increment DDA method

```
#include<graphics.h>
#include<stdio.h>
#include<conio.h>
int main(void)
{
int x,y,i,x1,y1,x2,y2,dx,dy,m,xin,yin,steps;
int gdriver=DETECT,gmode;
```

```
clrscr();
initgraph(&gdriver,&gmode,"C:\\TC\\bgi");
printf("Line Drawing Using Increment Method..\n");
printf("Enter point1 (x1,y1): ");
scanf("%d%d",&x1,&y1);
printf("Enter point2 (x2,y2): ");
scanf("%d %d",&x2,&y2);
dx=x2-x1;
dy=y2-y1;
m=dy/dx;
if(m<=1)
{
steps=dx;
}
else
{
steps=dy;
}
xin=dx/steps;
yin=dy/steps;
x=x1;
y=y1;
i=1;
putpixel(x,y,1);
while(i<=steps)
{
x=x+xin; y=y+yin; i=i+1;
putpixel(x,y,1);
}
getch();
closegraph();
return 0;
}
```

5. Program to draw line using Bresenham's algorithm.

```
#include<graphics.h>
#include<stdio.h>
#include<conio.h>
#include<math.h>
int main(void)
{
int x,y,x1,y1,x2,y2,m,dx,dy,p;
```

```
int gdriver=DETECT,gmode;
clrscr();
initgraph(&gdriver,&gmode,"C:\\TC\\bgi");
printf("Line Drawing Using Bresenham's Algorithm..\n");
printf("Enter point1 (x1,y1): ");
scanf("%d%d",&x1,&y1);
printf("Enter point2 (x2,y2): ");
scanf("%d %d",&x2,&y2);
dx=x2-x1;
dy=y2-y1;
m=dy/dx;
p=(2*dy)-dx;
x=x1;
y=y1;
putpixel(x,y,1);
while(x!=x2 || y!=y2)
{
if(m<=1)
{
if(p<0)
{
x=x+1;
y=y;
p=p+(2*dy);
}
else
{
x=x+1;
y=y+1;
p=p+(2*dy)-(2*dx);
}
}//outer if ends
else
{
if(p<0)
{
y=y+1;
x=x;
p=p+(2*dx);
}
else
{
```

```
x=x+1;
y=y+1;
p=p+(2*dx)-(2*dy);
}
}//outer else ends
putpixel(x,y,1);
}//whileends
getch();
closegraph();
return 0;
}
```

6. Program to draw circle using Midpoint algorithm

```
#include<graphics.h>
#include<stdio.h>
#include<conio.h>
#include<math.h>
int main(void)
{
int xc,yc,r,x,y,p;
int gdriver=DETECT,gmode;
clrscr();
initgraph(&gdriver,&gmode,"c:\\tc\\bgi");
printf("Circle Drawing Using MidPoint Algorithm..\n");
printf("Enter centre point (xc,yc) and radius(r): ");
scanf("%d%d%d",&xc,&yc,&r);
x=0;
y=r;
p=1-r;
while(x<=y)
{
putpixel(x+xc,y+yc,1);
putpixel(y+xc,x+yc,1);
putpixel(-y+xc,x+yc,1);
putpixel(x+xc,-y+yc,1);
putpixel(-x+xc,-y+yc,1);
putpixel(-y+xc,-x+yc,1);
putpixel(y+xc,-x+yc,1);
putpixel(-x+xc,y+yc,1);
if(p<0)
{
x=x+1;
```

```
y=y;
p=p+(2*x)+1;
}
else
{
x=x+1;
y=y-1;
p=p+(2*x)+1-(2*y);
}
}
getch();
closegraph();
return 0;
}
```

7. Program to draw circle using Bresenham's algorithm.

```
#include<graphics.h>
#include<stdio.h>
#include<conio.h>
#include<math.h>
int main(void)
{
int xc,yc,r,x,y,p;
int gdriver=DETECT,gmode;
clrscr();
initgraph(&gdriver,&gmode,"c:\\tc\\bgi");
printf("Circle Drawing Using Bresenham's Algorithm..\n");
printf("Enter centre point (xc,yc) and radius(r): ");
scanf("%d%d%d",&xc,&yc,&r);
x=0;
y=r;
p=3-(2*r);
while(x<=y)
{
putpixel(xc+x,yc+y,1);
putpixel(xc+y,yc+x,1);
putpixel(xc-y,yc+x,1);
putpixel(xc+x,yc-y,1);
putpixel(xc-x,yc-y,1);
putpixel(xc-y,yc-x,1);
putpixel(xc+y,yc-x,1);
putpixel(xc-x,yc+y,1);
```

```
if(p<=0)
{
x=x+1;
y=y;
p=p+(4*x)+6;
}
else
{
x=x+1;
y=y-1;
p=p+(4*(x-y))+10;
}
}
getch();
closegraph();
return 0;
}
```

8. Program to fill polygon using Flood-fill algorithm.

```
#include<stdio.h>
#include<conio.h>
#include<graphics.h>
void flood(int,int,int,int);
int main()
{
int gdriver=DETECT,gmode;
initgraph(&gdriver,&gmode,"C:\\TC\\BGI");
rectangle(50,50,100,100);
flood(55,55,7,0);    //10 =>gray 0=>black is default color
getch(); closegraph();
return 0;
}
void flood(int x, int y, int fillColor, int defaultColor)
{
if(getpixel(x,y)==defaultColor)
{
putpixel(x,y,fillColor);
flood(x+1,y,fillColor,defaultColor);
flood(x-1,y,fillColor,defaultColor);
flood(x,y+1,fillColor,defaultColor);
flood(x,y-1,fillColor,defaultColor);
flood(x+1,y+1,fillColor,defaultColor);
```

```
flood(x-1,y-1,fillColor,defaultColor);
flood(x+1,y-1,fillColor,defaultColor);
flood(x-1,y+1,fillColor,defaultColor);
}//if
}//flood
```

9. Program to fill polygon using Boundary-fill algorithm.

```
#include<stdio.h>
#include<conio.h>
#include<graphics.h>
void boundary(int,int,int,int);
int main()
{
int gdriver=DETECT,gmode;
initgraph(&gdriver,&gmode,"C:\\TC\\BGI");
rectangle(50,50,100,100);
boundary(55,55,7,15);
getch(); closegraph();
return 0;
}
void boundary(int x, int y, int fillColor, int defaultColor)
{
if(getpixel(x,y)!=defaultColor && getpixel(x,y)!=fillColor)
{ //delay(50);
putpixel(x,y,fillColor);
boundary(x+1,y,fillColor,defaultColor);
boundary(x-1,y,fillColor,defaultColor);
boundary(x,y+1,fillColor,defaultColor);
boundary(x,y-1,fillColor,defaultColor);
boundary(x+1,y+1,fillColor,defaultColor);
boundary(x-1,y-1,fillColor,defaultColor);
boundary(x+1,y-1,fillColor,defaultColor);
boundary(x-1,y+1,fillColor,defaultColor);
}//if
}//flood
```

10. Program to fill polygon using Scan line algorithm.

```
#include<stdio.h>
#include<conio.h>
#include<graphics.h>
int main()
```

```
{
int n,i,j,k,gdriver,gmode,dy,dx;
int x,y,temp;
int a[20][2],xi[20];   //a two dimensional array
float slope[20];
clrscr();
printf("\nEnter number of edges of polygon:");
scanf("%d",&n);
printf("\nEnter the coordinates of polygon:\n ");
for(i=0;i<n;i++){
printf("X%d Y%d:",i,i);
scanf("%d%d",&a[i][0],&a[i][1]);}
a[n][0]=a[0][0];  //last coordinate value =first coordinate value for closed
polygon
a[n][1]=a[0][1];
detectgraph(&gdriver,&gmode);
initgraph(&gdriver,&gmode,"C:\\TC\\BGI");
for(i=0;i<n;i++){
line(a[i][0],a[i][1],a[i+1][0],a[i+1][1]);}//draw polygon
getch();
for(i=0;i<n;i++){
dy=a[i+1][1]-a[i][1];    //find slope  difference between y values & x values
dx=a[i+1][0]-a[i][0];
if(dy==0) slope[i]=1.0;
if(dx==0) slope[i]=0.0;
if(dy!=0 && dx!=0){
slope[i]=(float)dx/dy;} }
for(y=0;y<480;y++){ //find intersection point //assume 480 lines in y-direction
//different scan line
k=0;
for(i=0;i<n;i++){    //different edges
if(((a[i][1]<=y)&&(a[i+1][1]>y))||((a[i][1]>y)&&(a[i+1][1]<=y))){  //check if y
values is whether greater or lesser than scan line                 //check if
y values greater or lesser than previous one
xi[k]=(int)(a[i][0]+slope[i]*(y-a[i][1])); //calculate x for each scan line
k++;} }
              //convert into int for pixel as slope in float
for(j=0;j<k-1;j++)
for(i=0;i<k-1;i++) {
if(xi[i]>xi[i+1]){
temp=xi[i];      //interchange x values
xi[i]=xi[i+1];  //sorting for smaller and greater value of x
```

```
xi[i+1]=temp; } }
setcolor(7);
for(i=0;i<k;i+=2) {
line(xi[i],y,xi[i+1]+1,y);    //draw intersection point lines
getch(); } }
return 0;
}
```

11. Program to implement Translation of a triangle.

```
#include<stdio.h>
#include<conio.h>
#include<graphics.h>
#include<math.h>
int x1,y1,x2,y2,x3,y3;
void draw();
void tri();
int main(void)
{
int gdriver = DETECT, gmode;
clrscr();
initgraph(&gdriver,&gmode,"C:\\tc\\bgi");
printf("Enter (x1,y1): ");
scanf("%d%d",&x1,&y1);
printf("Enter (x2,y2): ");
scanf("%d%d",&x2,&y2);
printf("Enter (x3,y3): ");
scanf("%d%d",&x3,&y3);
draw();
tri();
getch();
closegraph();
return 0;
}
void draw()
{
line(x1,y1,x2,y2);
line(x2,y2,x3,y3);
line(x3,y3,x1,y1);
}
void tri()
{
int tx,ty,a1,a2,a3,b1,b2,b3;
```

```
printf("Enter translation coordinates(tx,ty): ");
scanf("%d%d",&tx,&ty);
a1=x1+tx;
b1=y1+ty;
a2=x2+tx;
b2=y2+ty;
a3=x3+tx;
b3=y3+ty;
line(a1,b1,a2,b2);
line(a2,b2,a3,b3);
line(a3,b3,a1,b1);
}
```

12. Program to implement Scaling of triangle

```
#include<stdio.h>
#include<conio.h>
#include<graphics.h>
#include<math.h>
int i,j,k,n,x[10],y[10];
int old[10][10],scale[10][10],newm[10][10];
void getOld(int old[][10]){ //FUNCTION getOld
for(i=0;i<3;++i){
for(j=0;j<3;++j){
if(j==0||j==1){
printf("Enter elements (a%d%d): ",i+1,j+1);
scanf("%d",&old[i][j]); }
else{
old[i][j]=1;
printf("\n");}} }
line(old[0][0],old[0][1],old[1][0],old[1][1]);
line(old[1][0],old[1][1],old[2][0],old[2][1]);
line(old[2][0],old[2][1],old[0][0],old[0][1]);
} //ENDS getOld
void getScale(int scale[][10]){ //FUNCTION getScale
for(i=0;i<3;++i){
for(j=0;j<3;++j){
if((i==j) && (j!=2)){
printf("Enter scaling vector elements s%d%d: ",i+1,j+1);
scanf("%d",&scale[i][j]);}
else if(i==j && j==2){
scale[i][j]=1;}
}}} //ENDS getScale
```

```
void mul(int old[][10], int scale[][10],int newm[][10]){ //FUNCTION mul
for(i=0;i<3 && i<3;++i){
for(j=0;j<3;j++){
newm[i][j]=0;}}
for(i=0;i<3;++i){
for(j=0;j<3;++j){
for(k=0;k<3;++k){
newm[i][j]+=old[i][k]*scale[k][j];}
}}} //ENDS mul
void display(int result[][10]){//FUNCTION  display
printf("\nOutput Matrix: \n");
for(i=0;i<3;++i){
for(j=0;j<3;++j){
printf("%d ",result[i][j]);
if(j==2)
printf("\n");}}
line(result[0][0],result[0][1],result[1][0],result[1][1]);
line(result[1][0],result[1][1],result[2][0],result[2][1]);
line(result[2][0],result[2][1],result[0][0],result[0][1]);
}//ENDS display
int main(){//FUNCTION main()
int gdriver = DETECT, gmode;
clrscr();
initgraph(&gdriver,&gmode,"C:\\tc\\bgi");
getOld(old); //get elements of the old_matrix
getch();
cleardevice();
getScale(scale);  //get elements of the scale_matrix
mul(old,scale,newm);  //multiply two matrices
display(newm);   //display the new_matrix
getch();
closegraph();
return 0;
}
```

13. Program to implement Rotation of triangle

```
#include<stdio.h>
#include<conio.h>
#include<graphics.h>
#include<math.h>
int main()
{
```

```
int gdriver=DETECT,gmode;
int x1,y1,x2,y2,x3,y3;
double s,c,A;
clrscr();
printf("Enter the co-ordinates: (x1,y1) " );
scanf("%d%d",&x1,&y1);
printf("Enter the co-ordinates: (x2,y2) " );
scanf("%d%d",&x2,&y2);
printf("Enter the co-ordinates: (x3,y3) " );
scanf("%d%d",&x3,&y3);
initgraph(&gdriver,&gmode,"c:\\tc\\bgi");
line(x1,y1,x2,y2);
line(x2,y2,x3,y3);
line(x3,y3,x1,y1);
printf("Enter the angle of rotation: ");
scanf("%lf",&A);
c=cos(A*3.14f/180);
s=sin(A*3.14f/180);
x1=floor(x1*c+y1*s);
y1=floor(-x1*s+y1*c);
x2=floor(x2*c+y2*s);
y2=floor(-x2*s+y2*c);
x3=floor(x3*c+y3*s);
y3=floor(-x3*s+y3*c);
printf("(x1,y1,x2,y2,x3,y3) : %d,%d,%d,%d,%d,%d \n",x1,y1,x2,y2,x3,y3);
line(x1,y1,x2,y2);
line(x2,y2,x3,y3);
line(x3,y3,x1,y1);
getch();
closegraph();
return 0;
}
```

14. Program to implement 2D Shearing

```
#include<stdio.h>
#include<conio.h>
#include<graphics.h>
int x1,y1,x2,y2,x3,y3,shear_fx,shear_fy;
void shearX();
void shearY();
void shearXY();
void draw();
```

```
void before();
int main()
{
int gdriver=DETECT,gmode,n;
char ch;
initgraph(&gdriver,&gmode,"C:\\TC\\BGI");
do
{
printf("Enter choice:\n1.'X'for X-diection \n");
printf("2.'Y'for Y-direction\n3.'Z'for both XY -direction\n");
scanf("%c",&ch);
switch(ch)
{
case 'x':
case 'X':
{
before();
printf("Enter shearing factor: x ");
scanf("%d",&shear_fx);
printf("After shearing..in X-direction..\n");
shearX();
draw();
getch();
cleardevice();
break;
}
case 'y':
case 'Y':
{
before();
printf("Enter shearing factor: y ");
scanf("%d",&shear_fy);
printf("After shearing..in Y-direction..\n");
shearY();
draw();
getch();
cleardevice();
break;
}
case 'z':
case 'Z':
{
```

```
before();
printf("Enter shearing factor: x ");
scanf("%d",&shear_fx);
printf("Enter shearing factor: y ");
scanf("%d",&shear_fy);
printf("After shearing..in XY-direction..\n");
shearXY();
draw();
getch();
cleardevice();
break;
}
default:
printf("Wrong choice..\n");
}
printf("To quit press 0..\n");
scanf("%d",&n);
}while(n!=0);
closegraph();
return 0;
}
void before()
{
printf("Before shearing..\n");
printf("Enter coordinates: (x1,y1) ");
scanf("%d%d",&x1,&y1);
printf("Enter coordinates: (x2,y2) ");
scanf("%d%d",&x2,&y2);
printf("Enter coordinates: (x3,y3) ");
scanf("%d%d",&x3,&y3);
cleardevice();
getch();
draw();
}
void draw()
{
line(x1,y1,x2,y2);
line(x2,y2,x3,y3);
line(x3,y3,x1,y1);
}
void shearX()
{
```

```
x1=x1+y1*shear_fx;     //100+100*2=300
x2=x2+y2*shear_fx;     //200+100*2=400
x3=x3+y3*shear_fx;     //100+200*2=500
y1=y1;            //100
y2=y2;            //100
y3=y3;            //200
}
void shearY()
{
y1=y1+x1*shear_fy;    //100+100*2=300
y2=y2+x2*shear_fy;    //150+100*2=350
y3=y3+x3*shear_fy;    //150+150*2=450
x1=x1;           //100
x2=x2;           //100
x3=x3;           //150
}
void shearXY()
{
x1=x1+y1*shear_fx;   //100+120*2=340
x2=x2+y2*shear_fx;   //120+100*2=320
x3=x3+y3*shear_fx;   //100+100*2=300
y1=y1+x1*shear_fy;   //120+340*1=460
y2=y2+x2*shear_fy;   //100+320*1=420
y3=y3+x3*shear_fy;   //100+300*1=400
}
```

15. Program to implement 2D Reflection

```
#include<stdio.h>
#include<conio.h>
#include<graphics.h>
#include<math.h>
int main()
{
int gdriver=DETECT,gmode;
int x1,x2,x3,y1,y2,y3;
initgraph(&gdriver,&gmode,"C:\\tc\\bgi");
cleardevice();
line(getmaxx()/2,0,getmaxx()/2,getmaxy());
line(0,getmaxy()/2,getmaxx(),getmaxy()/2);
printf("Enter the coordinates:(x1,y1) ");
scanf("%d%d",&x1,&y1);
printf("Enter the coordinates:(x2,y2) ");
```

```
scanf("%d%d",&x2,&y2);
printf("Enter the coordinates:(x3,y3) ");
scanf("%d%d",&x3,&y3);
line(x1,y1,x2,y2);
line(x2,y2,x3,y3);
line(x3,y3,x1,y1);
getch();
printf("After Reflection..along origin..\n");
line(getmaxx()-x1,getmaxy()-y1,getmaxx()-x2,getmaxy()-y2);
line(getmaxx()-x2,getmaxy()-y2,getmaxx()-x3,getmaxy()-y3);
line(getmaxx()-x3,getmaxy()-y3,getmaxx()-x1,getmaxy()-y1);
getch();
printf("After Reflection..along x-axis..\n");
line(getmaxx()-x1,y1,getmaxx()-x2,y2);
line(getmaxx()-x2,y2,getmaxx()-x3,y3);
line(getmaxx()-x3,y3,getmaxx()-x1,y1);
getch();
printf("After Reflection..along y-axis..\n");
line(x1,getmaxy()-y1,x2,getmaxy()-y2);
line(x2,getmaxy()-y2,x3,getmaxy()-y3);
line(x3,getmaxy()-y3,x1,getmaxy()-y1);
getch();
closegraph();
return 0;
}
```

16. Program to implement composite transformation on Rotation about an arbitrary point.

```
//w100,150,200,250,300,300;30;400,300
#include<stdio.h>
#include<conio.h>
#include<graphics.h>
#include<math.h>
int main(){
int gdriver=DETECT,gmode,x1,y1,x2,y2,x3,y3,xr,yr;
double s,c,A;//clrscr();
printf("Enter the co-ordinates: " );
scanf("%d%d%d%d%d%d",&x1,&y1,&x2,&y2,&x3,&y3);
initgraph(&gdriver,&gmode,"c:\\tc\\bgi");
line(x1,y1,x2,y2);
line(x2,y2,x3,y3);
line(x3,y3,x1,y1);
```

```
printf("Enter the angle of rotation: ");
scanf("%lf",&A);
printf("Enter the arbitary point coordinates: ");
scanf("%d%d",&xr,&yr);
c=cos(A*3.14f/180); s=sin(A*3.14f/180);
x1=floor(xr+(x1-xr)*c-(y1-yr)*s);
x2=floor(xr+(x2-xr)*c-(y2-yr)*s);
x3=floor(xr+(x3-xr)*c-(y3-yr)*s);
y1=floor(yr+(x1-xr)*s+(y1-yr)*c);
y2=floor(yr+(x2-xr)*s+(y2-yr)*c);
y3=floor(yr+(x3-xr)*s+(y3-yr)*c);
printf("(x1,y1,x2,y2,x3,y3: %d,%d,%d,%d,%d,%d",x1,y1,x2,y2,x3,y3);
line(x1,y1,x2,y2);
line(x2,y2,x3,y3);
line(x3,y3,x1,y1);
getch();
 closegraph();
return 0;
}
```

17. Program to implement composite transformation on Scaling about a fixed point.

```
#include<stdio.h>
#include<conio.h>
#include<graphics.h>
int i,j,k,n,x[10],y[10],tx,ty,old[10][10],scale[10][10],newm[10][10];  //100,150
,120,150,200,200;20,20;2,2
void getOld(int old[][10]){  //FUNCTION getOld                          //ouput
180,280;220,280;380,380
for(i=0;i<3;++i){ for(j=0;j<3;++j){
if(j==0||j==1){
printf("Enter elements (a%d%d): ",i+1,j+1);
scanf("%d",&old[i][j]); }
else{
old[i][j]=1;
printf("\n");}} }
line(old[0][0],old[0][1],old[1][0],old[1][1]);
line(old[1][0],old[1][1],old[2][0],old[2][1]);
line(old[2][0],old[2][1],old[0][0],old[0][1]);}  //ENDS getOld
void getScale(int scale[][10]){ //FUNCTION getScale
printf("Enter translation vector (tx,ty)");
scanf("%d%d",&tx,&ty);
```

```
for(i=0;i<3;++i){for(j=0;j<3;j++){
if((i==j) && (j!=2)){
printf("Enter scaling vector elements s%d%d: ",i+1,j+1);
scanf("%d",&scale[i][j]);}
else if(j==0 && i==2){
scale[i][j]=tx*(1-scale[0][0]);}
else if(j==1 && i==2){
scale[i][j]=ty*(1-scale[1][1]);}
else if(i==2 && j==2){
scale[i][j]=1;}
else
scale[i][j]=0;}}} //ENDS getScale
void mul(int old[][10], int scale[][10],int newm[][10]){ //FUNCTION mul
for(i=0;i<3 && i<3;++i){
for(j=0;j<3;j++){
newm[i][j]=0;}}
for(i=0;i<3;++i){
for(j=0;j<3;++j){
for(k=0;k<3;++k){
newm[i][j]+=old[i][k]*scale[k][j];} }}} //ENDS mul
void display(int result[][10]){//FUNCTION  display
printf("\nOutput Matrix: \n");
for(i=0;i<3;++i){
for(j=0;j<3;++j){
printf("%d ",result[i][j]);
if(j==2)
printf("\n");}}
line(result[0][0],result[0][1],result[1][0],result[1][1]);
line(result[1][0],result[1][1],result[2][0],result[2][1]);
line(result[2][0],result[2][1],result[0][0],result[0][1]); }//ENDS display
int main(){//FUNCTION main()
int gdriver = DETECT, gmode; //clrscr();
initgraph(&gdriver,&gmode,"C:\\tc\\bgi");
getOld(old); //get elements of the old_matrix
getch();cleardevice();
getScale(scale);  //get elements of the scale_matrix
mul(old,scale,newm);  //multiply two matrices
display(newm);   //display the new_matrix
getch();
closegraph();
return 0;
}
```

18. Program to implement Line Clipping algorithm using Cohen Sutherland algorithm.

```
//w 100,100,400,400; l 50 300 300 300
#include<stdio.h>
#include<conio.h>
#include<graphics.h>
static int LEFT=1,RIGHT=2,BOTTOM=4,TOP=8;
int xmin,ymin,xmax,ymax;
int getcode(int x,int y){
int code=0;
if(y>ymax) code=TOP;
if(y<ymin) code=BOTTOM;
if(x<xmin) code=LEFT;
if(x>xmax) code=RIGHT;
return code;}
int main(){ //main starts
int x1,y1,x2,y2,outcode1,outcode2,accept;
int gdriver=DETECT,gmode;
initgraph(&gdriver,&gmode,"C:\\TC\\BGI");
printf("Enter window minimum and maximum values: ");
scanf("%d%d%d%d",&xmin,&ymin,&xmax,&ymax);
rectangle(xmin,ymin,xmax,ymax);
printf("Enter endpoints of the line: ");
scanf("%d%d%d%d",&x1,&y1,&x2,&y2);
line(x1,y1,x2,y2); getch();
outcode1=getcode(x1,y1);
outcode2=getcode(x2,y2);
accept=0;
while(1){ //while starts
float m=(float)(y2-y1)/(x2-x1);   //calculate slope
if(outcode1==0 && outcode2==0){
accept=1; break;}//if
else if((outcode1 & outcode2)!=0){
break;}//else if
else{//else starts
int x,y,temp;
if(outcode1==0) {temp=outcode2;}
else {temp=outcode1;}
if(temp & TOP){    //bitwise & is true  find top boundary intersection
x=x1+(ymax-y1)/m; y=ymax;}
else if(temp & BOTTOM){
x=x1+(ymin-y1)/m; y=ymin;}
```

```
else if(temp & LEFT){
x=xmin;
y=y1+m*(xmin-x1);}
else if(temp & RIGHT){
x=xmax;
y=y1+m*(xmax-x1);}
if(temp==outcode1){//if ..
x1=x; y1=y;
outcode1=getcode(x1,y1);}//..
else{
x2=x; y2=y;
outcode2=getcode(x2,y2);} } }//while
printf("After cliping: ");
if(accept) { cleardevice(); }
rectangle(xmin,ymin,xmax,ymax);
line(x1,y1,x2,y2);
getch();
closegraph();
 return 0;
 }
```

19. Program to implement Line Clipping algorithm using Sutherland Hodgman algorithm.

```
#include<stdio.h>  //w 100,100,400,400; l 50 300 300 300
#include<conio.h>
#include<graphics.h>
int main()
{
int gdriver=DETECT,gmode,n,*x,i,k=0;
int w[]={100,100,400,100,400,400,100,400,100,100};
initgraph(&gdriver,&gmode,"C:\\TC\\BGI");//initalizing graphics
setcolor(RED);
drawpoly(5,w);//window drawn
printf("Enter the number of vertices of polygon: ");
scanf("%d",&n);
x=malloc(n*2+1);
printf("Enter the coordinates of points:\n");
k=0;
for(i=0;i<n*2;i+=2)
 { //reading vertices of polygon
 printf("(x%d,y%d):",k,k);
 scanf("%d%d",&x[i],&x[i+1]);
```

```
k++;
}
x[n*2]=x[0];//assigning the coordrinates of first vertex to last additional
vertex for drawpoly method
x[n*2+1]=x[1];
setcolor(WHITE);
drawpoly(n+1,x);
printf("Press a key to clip a polygon..");
getch();
setcolor(RED);
drawpoly(5,w);
setfillstyle(SOLID_FILL,BLACK);
floodfill(2,2,RED);
gotoxy(1,1);//bringing cursor at starting position
printf("This is the clipped polygon...");
getch();
closegraph();
return 0;
}
```

20. Program to display a Moving Car.

```
#include<stdio.h>
#include<conio.h>
#include<graphics.h>
int main()
{
int gdriver=DETECT,gmode,x;
initgraph(&gdriver,&gmode,"C:\\TC\\BGI");
for(x=0;x<=420;x+=10)
{
cleardevice();
rectangle(50+x,100,150+x,200);
rectangle(150+x,150,200+x,200);
circle(75+x,210,10);
circle(175+x,210,10);
line(50,220,600,220);
delay(100);
}
getch();
closegraph();
return 0;
}
```

Appendix-III

Bibliography

1. Computer Graphics, Principles and Practice, Second Edition, by James D. Foley, Andries van Dam, Steven K. Feiner, John F. Hughes, Addison-Wesley2.
2. Computer Graphics, Third Edition, by Pradeep K. Bhatia, I.K .International Publisher.
3. High Resolution Computer Graphics using Pascal/C, by Ian O. Angell and Gareth Griffith, John Wiley & Sons4.
4. Computer Graphics (C Version), by Donald Hearn and M. Pauline Baker, Prentice Hall, 5.
5. Advanced Animation and Rendering Techniques, Theory and Practice, by Alan Watt and Mark Watt, ACM Press/Addison-Wesley6.
6. Graphics gems by Glassner, Andrew S., ed.. Elsevier, 2013.
7. Overview of Computer Graphics by Taneja, Abhishek. 2005.
8. Principles of Interactive Computer Graphics, by Newman, William M., and Robert F. Sproull, eds. McGraw-Hill, Inc., 1979.
9. Computer Graphics C Version by Hearn, Donald, and M. Pauline Baker. Pearson Education, 2015.
10. Computer Graphics by Xiang, Zhigang, and Roy A. Plastock McGraw hill Education.
11. Computer graphics, by Rajiv Chopra,. S. Chand Publishing, 2010.
12. Pachghare, V.K., "Computer Graphics", Second Edition, Laxmi Publications, 2007.
13. Baluja GS., "Computer Graphics and Multimedia", Dhanpat Rai & Co. Reprint 2004.
14. Sinha, N. Amarendra and Udai D Arun, "Computer Graphics". First Reprint 2008, Tata McGraw Hill (T MH), 2008.
15. Goel Rohit and Goel Mukta, "Multimedia Technology", Dhanpat Rai and Co. First Edition 2010.

Index

Printed in the United States
by Baker & Taylor Publisher Services